AN AU   E X T

INTELLE   Hamlet

EXTRACTS FROM THE S

E S

※ A NORTON CRITICAL EDITION ≪

WILLIAM SHAKESPEARE

HAMLET

AN AUTHORITATIVE TEXT
INTELLECTUAL BACKGROUNDS
EXTRACTS FROM THE SOURCES
ESSAYS IN CRITICISM

※≪

Edited by

CYRUS HOY
UNIVERSITY OF ROCHESTER

W · W · NORTON & COMPANY · INC · *New York*

Library of Congress Catalog Card No. 63-8029

Title page of *The Tragicall Historie of Hamlet*, London, 1604, reproduced by permission of The Huntington Library, San Marino, California (HM 69305).

ISBN   0   393   09591   6

0

Contents

Preface

Everything about *The Tragedy of Hamlet, Prince of Denmark* is problematic. Critical uncertainty concerning the character of the Prince, his attitudes, and the tragic quality of his highly dramatic situation is matched by a corresponding diversity of scholarly opinion regarding such matters as the date of the play, its precise relation to its sources, and its textual authority. An editor approaches his task with a proper awe which is the more profound from his steady realization that he is, after all, dealing with the most celebrated work in English literature.

The present edition includes a text of the play in modern spelling, with explanatory and textual notes; extracts from the only two pre-Shakespearean treatments of the Hamlet story that are extant; a selection of late sixteenth-century opinion on four subjects—melancholy, demonology, the nature of man, and death—which, in one way or another, bear directly, and crucially, on the play's meaning; and a selection of critical commentary on the play, ranging in time from the early eighteenth century to the present.

The text of the present edition of *Hamlet* is based on that of the second quarto, published in 1604–5. Since there is good reason to suppose that the second quarto was printed from Shakespeare's own manuscript, its authority is very high, and I have adhered to it closely, but not slavishly. The second quarto of *Hamlet* is, unfortunately, a very carelessly printed book. It exhibits a number of obvious misreadings, and it is riddled with omissions of all sorts, from single letters to whole lines. In such cases, an editor must turn to other textual authority, usually to the text of the play printed in the 1623 folio collection of Shakespeare's complete works. The folio must be consulted as well for some 80 lines, scattered throughout the play, which are omitted from the second quarto. My editorial practices will be evident from the textual notes, printed after the play, where a complete list of all substantive departures from the text of the second quarto is given. The editorial problem which the play poses is summarized, together with an account of the principles which have governed the preparation of the present edition, in the Textual Commentary section.

The relevant portions of the Hamlet story as it is recorded in the *Historia Danica* of Saxo Grammaticus and the *Histoires tra-*

giques of Belleforest are presented under the section dealing with Shakespeare's sources. In estimating the relevance of these to Shakespeare's tragedy, it is necessary to avoid either exaggerating or underestimating their importance. Since they provide us with the only pre-Shakespearean accounts of the story that are extant, their relevance to any serious study of the play is obvious. But they are sources of Shakespeare's tragedy only in an indirect sense. It is by no means certain that he knew either of them. Saxo's *Danish History*, written at the end of the twelfth century, was first printed in 1514, and had gone through a number of Continental editions by the end of the sixteenth century; but no edition is known to have been printed in England before or during Shakespeare's lifetime. Belleforest's *Tragical Histories* present a roughly similar case. His account of Hamlet's story is contained in Volume V of the *Histoires tragiques*, and this was widely printed on the Continent after its first edition in 1576, but there is no known English edition prior to Shakespeare's play. *The Historie of Hamblet*, an English translation of Belleforest, was published in 1608, five years after the appearance of the first edition of Shakespeare's *Hamlet*. This, far from influencing Shakespeare's treatment of the story, has in fact been influenced by it, as the anonymous translator's departures from his French text (to which attention is drawn in the note on page 136) make clear. The immediate source of Shakespeare's tragedy was an earlier *Hamlet* play, presumably the work of the dramatist Thomas Kyd, which is now lost, but which we know from contemporary references to it—in Nashe's preface to Greene's *Menaphon* (1589), in Lodge's *Wit's Miserie* (1596), in Henslow's Diary (June 9, 1594)—was being acted on the London stage in the late 1580's and early 1590's. There has been much speculation concerning the nature of this lost play, and necessarily so. Between the Hamlet of Saxo and Belleforest, and the Hamlet of Shakespeare, a number of vast changes have been wrought, and the effort of critics to define the dramatist's intentions in this, the most ambiguous of all his tragedies, could proceed on very much surer ground if it were possible to know which of the changes were Shakespeare's own innovation, and which had already been introduced into the earlier dramatization of the Hamlet story. It is possible to conjecture something of the general features of the lost *Hamlet* play from the example of such other Elizabethan revenge plays as Kyd's *Spanish Tragedy* and Marston's *Antonio's Revenge*; from *Der Bestrafte Brudermord* (*Fratricide Punished*), a badly debased German version of what would appear to be Shakespeare's play but with traces of the *Ur-Hamlet*, carried to the Continent presumably by a touring company of English actors; and from certain elements in the remarkably garbled text of the first quarto (printed in 1603) of Shakespeare's *Hamlet*. But no amount of conjecture—clever and elaborate though much of it has been—can conceal the fact that the lost play is lost, and in the absence of it one must necessarily turn to Saxo and Belleforest in order to assess Shakespeare's source material. Turning to them can be a salutary experience for the student of the play, if for no other reason than to witness just what an energetic fellow the Hamlet of the original saga is, by comparison with the highly introspective figure of the Prince which Shakespeare, or Shakespeare's critics, have made of him. It is only for the student to keep in mind the fact that, between the Hamlet story as it is narrated in Saxo and Belleforest, and as it is dramatized in Shakespeare's tragedy, there is a missing link, and that the action of the old saga had already been adapted to the conditions of the Elizabethan stage, and refashioned in accordance with the conventions of Elizabethan revenge tragedy, before Shakespeare took it in hand.

The selection of critical commentary contained in the present volume is designed to put before the reader at least the more significant of the multifarious opinions and attitudes to which the *Tragedy of Hamlet* has given rise over the past two and a half centuries. The play has never ceased to elicit and sustain critical attention, which is surely one measure of its greatness. A lesser work would have been exhausted long ago. For the early eighteenth century, the play posed no problem. The severest stricture that Dennis, writing in 1712, could level at it was its failure—which it shared with all Shakespeare's tragedies—to observe the law of poetic justice. For the anonymous author of *Some Remarks on the Tragedy of Hamlet* (1736), the famous question of why the Prince delayed in avenging his father's murder, the answer was simple; if he had not delayed, there would have been no play. For the critics of the Romantic period, the play distinctly posed a problem; they isolated it in Hamlet's delay to action; and they found the explanation for his delay in the particular make-up of his nature. On these issues, critical discussion of the play has turned ever since, though the best recent criticism has stressed the need to look beyond the character of the Prince and to view the play in its totality.

Modern criticism of Shakespeare's plays has also drawn attention to the need to see them in the context of the moral and intellectual assumptions and attitudes that were current when they were composed. The selections from the writings of such figures as Lavater, Primaudaye, and Montaigne, included in the present volume, are designed to suggest something at least of the climate of late-Renaissance opinion as this would appear to have affected the conception

of Shakespeare's treatment of the Hamlet story. The four subjects
—melancholy, demonology, the nature of man, and death—on
which I have focused attention here were, in their several ways, of
absorbing interest to the late Renaissance, and each, in varying degrees, impinges on important issues raised by *The Tragedy of
Hamlet*. The statements of Shakespeare's contemporaries on these
matters warrant the attention of any serious student of the play.
While it may be doubted whether or not knowledge of late sixteenth-century attitudes toward ghosts, or the physiological theory
of the four humors, will provide the key to the play's profoundest
meanings, there is no doubt at all that the failure to understand
the opinions of Shakespeare's age concerning such matters as these
(and one might include the subject of revenge as well) can seriously
impede the effort to deal with the play on its own terms. The unquiet spirit which haunts the play is, after all, the agent which sets
the action in motion; and Hamlet's melancholy is both the cause
and the effect of a pervasive sense of evil which is the very ambiance
of the tragedy.

Questions concerning the nature of man, and the nature of death,
carry us to the heart of the play. About the nature of man, the
Renaissance was of two minds, as the late Professor Theodore
Spencer tells us in an essay reprinted below. The divergent views
are recorded, among other places, in Primaudaye's *French Academy*
and Montaigne's *Apology of Raymond Sebond*, selections from
which are also reprinted below. They have come together, in Shakespeare, in such a passage as Hamlet's speech beginning "What a
piece of work is a man" (II.ii.292ff.). Whether Shakespeare had
read Montaigne when he wrote *Hamlet* has been much debated
(Florio's translation appeared in the same year—1603—as the first
edition of the play, but Shakespeare could have seen it in manuscript). The parallels of thought and language between *Hamlet* and
Florio's rendition of the *Essais* are very striking, but positive proof
of a direct influence at this point in Shakespeare's career is lacking.
It does not finally matter. The identity of feeling and thought evident again and again in the essays and the tragedy is the important
thing, however one accounts for it. The great passage on death,
time, and change, at the end of the *Apology of Raymond Sebond*,
might be spoken at any number of points in *Hamlet*. In effect, it is.
"And nothing remaineth or ever continueth in one state," says
Montaigne. "And nothing is at a like goodness still," says Claudius
at one of the most impressive moments in the play (IV.vii.116).
"If we should ever continue one and the same, how is it then that
now we rejoice at one thing, and now at another?" asks Montaigne.
"How comes it to pass we love things contrary, or we hate

them * * * ?" This is as much as to ask what Hamlet is ago-
nizingly asking himself from the beginning of the play: how his
mother could so readily transfer her affections from her Hyperion-
like first husband to his satyrlike brother—a question which he
puts to her directly in the course of the scene in her chamber
("Could you on this fair mountain leave to feed, / And batten on
this moor?" [III.iv.66–67]). This is but a single demonstration,
in a play which abounds with like examples, of the contradictory
nature of reality as Montaigne defines it. He does so in terms of
its most profound metaphysical implications—implications which
take the form of a series of bewildering paradoxes.

How is it that we have different affections, holding no more the
same sense in the same thought? For it is not likely that without
alteration we should take other passions, and *what admitteth alterations, continueth not the same;* and if it be not one selfsame, then
is it not; but rather with being all one, the simple being doth also
change, ever becoming other from other. And by consequence,
nature's senses are deceived and lie falsely; taking what appeareth
for what is; for want of truly knowing what it is that is.

The paradoxes are present in *Hamlet,* where they have been raised
to the power of so many tragic truths: tragic because they point
directly to as many appalling contradictions in the nature of things.
Appearance contradicts reality, words contradict deeds, behavior
contradicts purpose; nothing is what it appears to be, and nothing
endures, least of all the high dedication of a passionate moment.

> What to ourselves in passion we purpose,
> The passion ending, doth the purpose lose.   (III.ii.206–7)

Thus the Player King to the Player Queen, in answer to her loud
protestations of eternal fidelity. If, in the context, the words reflect
most immediately upon Gertrude, they reflect as well upon her son,
who has also proposed something to himself in a fit of passion,
just after his first encounter with the ghost. Ironically enough, it
is the other King, the one of shreds and patches, who has the final
comment on this matter, which involves nothing less than the need,
so urgently felt by the tragic protagonist throughout the play, for
suiting the action to the word, the word to the action.

> That we would do,
> We should do when we would, for this "would" changes,
> And hath abatements and delays as many
> As there are tongues, are hands, are accidents;
> And then this "should" is like a spendthrift sigh,
> That hurts by easing.   (IV.vii.118–123)

Any modern editor of a Shakespearean play is heavily indebted to the work that has been done in the field of textual bibliography over the past half century. My own indebtedness to the work of the late W. W. Greg will be evident to anyone familiar with the problems of Elizabethan textual criticism. I have also laid under heavy contribution studies of the second quarto of *Hamlet* by F. T. Bowers and J. R. Brown, and of the folio text by Charlton Hinman and Harold Jenkins. Professor Jenkins's account of actors' interpolations in the folio text, to which reference is made in the notes and Textual Commentary, has been a source of continual enlightenment to me throughout the preparation of this edition. To him and it, I have a special obligation which I gratefully record. To the staffs of the Folger Shakespeare Library, Washington, D.C., where work on this edition was begun, and the Bodleian Library, Oxford, where it was completed, I wish to acknowledge my appreciation for many courtesies.

CYRUS HOY

October, 1962

The Text of
Hamlet

THE Tragicall Historie of HAMLET,

Prince of Denmarke.

By William Shakespeare.

Newly imprinted and enlarged to almost as much againe as it was, according to the true and perfect Coppie.

AT LONDON,
Printed by I. R. for N. L. and are to be sold at his shoppe vnder Saint Dunstons Church in Fleetstreet. 1604.

[Dramatis Personae

CLAUDIUS, *King of Denmark.*
HAMLET, *son to the former and nephew to the present King.*
POLONIUS, *Lord Chamberlain.*
HORATIO, *friend to Hamlet.*
LAERTES, *son to Polonius.*

VOLTEMAND,
CORNELIUS,
ROSENCRANTZ,
GUILDENSTERN,   } *courtiers.*
OSRIC,
A GENTLEMAN,

A PRIEST.
MARCELLUS,
BERNARDO,   } *officers.*
FRANCISCO, *a soldier.*
REYNALDO, *servant to Polonius.*
PLAYERS.
TWO CLOWNS, *grave-diggers.*
FORTINBRAS, *Prince of Norway.*
A NORWEGIAN CAPTAIN.

ENGLISH AMBASSADORS.
GERTRUDE, *Queen of Denmark, and mother of Hamlet.*
OPHELIA, *daughter to Polonius.*

GHOST OF HAMLET'S FATHER.

LORDS, LADIES, OFFICERS, SOLDIERS, SAILORS, MESSENGERS, *and*
ATTENDANTS.

SCENE: *Denmark.*]

Hamlet

[I.i]

Enter BERNARDO *and* FRANCISCO, *two sentinels.*

BER. Who's there?

FRAN. Nay, answer me. Stand and unfold yourself.

BER. Long live the king!

FRAN. Bernardo?

BER. He.   5

FRAN. You come most carefully upon your hour.

BER. 'Tis now struck twelve. Get thee to bed, Francisco.

FRAN. For this relief much thanks. 'Tis bitter cold,
    And I am sick at heart.

BER. Have you had quiet guard?

FRAN.   Not a mouse stirring.   10

BER. Well, good night.
    If you do meet Horatio and Marcellus,
    The rivals of my watch, bid them make haste.

Enter HORATIO *and* MARCELLUS.

FRAN. I think I hear them. Stand, ho! Who is there?

HOR. Friends to this ground.

MAR.   And liegemen to the Dane.   15

FRAN. Give you good night.

MAR.   O, farewell, honest soldier!
    Who hath relieved you?

FRAN.   Bernardo hath my place.
    Give you good night.   *Exit* FRANCISCO.

MAR.   Holla, Bernardo!

BER.   Say—
    What, is Horatio there?

HOR.   A piece of him.

BER. Welcome, Horatio. Welcome, good Marcellus.   20

HOR. What, has this thing appeared again to-night?

BER. I have seen nothing.

MAR. Horatio says 'tis but our fantasy,
    And will not let belief take hold of him
    Touching this dreaded sight twice seen of us.   25
    Therefore I have entreated him along
    With us to watch the minutes of this night,
    That if again this apparition come,

[I.i] 13. *rivals* partners.   15. *Dane* King of Denmark.

He may approve our eyes and speak to it.

HOR. Tush, tush, 'twill not appear.

BER.   Sit down awhile,   30
And let us once again assail your ears,
That are so fortified against our story,
What we have two nights seen.

HOR.   Well, sit we down,
And let us hear Bernardo speak of this.

BER. Last night of all,   35
When yond same star that's westward from the pole
Had made his course t' illume that part of heaven
Where now it burns, Marcellus and myself,
The bell then beating one—

Enter GHOST.

MAR. Peace, break thee off. Look where it comes again.   40

BER. In the same figure like the king that's dead.

MAR. Thou art a scholar; speak to it, Horatio.

BER. Looks 'a not like the king? Mark it, Horatio.

HOR. Most like. It harrows me with fear and wonder.

BER. It would be spoke to.

MAR.   Question it, Horatio.   45

HOR. What art thou that usurp'st this time of night
Together with that fair and warlike form
In which the majesty of buried Denmark
Did sometimes march? By heaven I charge thee, speak.

MAR. It is offended.

BER.   See, it stalks away.

HOR. Stay. Speak, speak. I charge thee, speak.   *Exit* GHOST.   50

MAR. 'Tis gone and will not answer.

BER. How now, Horatio! You tremble and look pale.
Is not this something more than fantasy?
What think you on't?   55

HOR. Before my God, I might not this believe
Without the sensible and true avouch
Of mine own eyes.

MAR.   Is it not like the king?

HOR. As thou art to thyself.
Such was the very armor he had on   60
When he the ambitious Norway combated.
So frowned he once when, in an angry parle,
He smote the sledded Polacks on the ice.
'Tis strange.

29. *approve* confirm.
36. *pole* polestar.
44. *harrows* afflicts, distresses.
48. *buried Denmark* the buried King of Denmark.
49. *sometimes* formerly.

57. *sensible* confirmed by one of the senses.
61. *Norway* King of Norway.
62. *parle* parley.
63. *sledded Polacks* the Poles mounted on sleds or sledges.

MAR. Thus twice before, and jump at this dead hour,   65
  With martial stalk hath he gone by our watch.
HOR. In what particular thought to work I know not,
  But in the gross and scope of mine opinion,
  This bodes some strange eruption to our state.
MAR. Good now, sit down, and tell me he that knows,   70
  Why this same strict and most observant watch
  So nightly toils the subject of the land,
  And why such daily cast of brazen cannon
  And foreign mart for implements of war;
  Why such impress of shipwrights, whose sore task   75
  Does not divide the Sunday from the week.
  What might be toward that this sweaty haste
  Doth make the night joint-laborer with the day?
  Who is't that can inform me?
HOR.   That can I.
  At least, the whisper goes so. Our last king,   80
  Whose image even but now appeared to us,
  Was as you know by Fortinbras of Norway,
  Thereto pricked on by a most emulate pride,
  Dared to the combat; in which our valiant Hamlet
  (For so this side of our known world esteemed him)   85
  Did slay this Fortinbras; who by a sealed compact
  Well ratified by law and heraldry,
  Did forfeit, with his life, all those his lands
  Which he stood seized of, to the conqueror;
  Against the which a moiety competent   90
  Was gagéd by our king; which had returned
  To the inheritance of Fortinbras,
  Had he been vanquisher; as, by the same comart
  And carriage of the article designed,
  His fell to Hamlet. Now, sir, young Fortinbras,   95
  Of unimprovéd mettle hot and full,
  Hath in the skirts of Norway here and there
  Sharked up a list of lawless resolutes
  For food and diet to some enterprise
  That hath a stomach in't; which is no other,   100
  As it doth well appear unto our state,
  But to recover of us by strong hand
  And terms compulsatory, those foresaid lands
  So by his father lost; and this, I take it,

65. *jump* just, exactly.
68. *gross and scope* general drift.
72. *toils* causes to toil; *subject* people.
74. *mart* traffic, bargaining.
75. *impress* conscription.
77. *toward* imminent, impending.
83. *emulate* ambitious
87. *heraldry* the law of arms, regulating tournaments and state combats.
89. *seized* possessed.
90. *moiety competent* sufficient portion.
91. *gaged* pledged.
93. *comart* joint bargain.
94. *carriage* import.
96. *unimproved* unused.
98. *Sharked up* picked up indiscriminately.
100. *stomach* spice of adventure.

Is the main motive of our preparations, 105
The source of this our watch, and the chief head
Of this post-haste and romage in the land.
BER. I think it be no other but e'en so.
Well may it sort that this portentous figure
Comes arméd through our watch so like the king 110
That was and is the question of these wars.
HOR. A mote it is to trouble the mind's eye.
In the most high and palmy state of Rome,
A little ere the mightiest Julius fell,
The graves stood tenantless, and the sheeted dead 115
Did squeak and gibber in the Roman streets;
As stars with trains of fire, and dews of blood,
Disasters in the sun; and the moist star,
Upon whose influence Neptune's empire stands,
Was sick almost to doomsday with eclipse. 120
And even the like precurse of feared events,
As harbingers preceding still the fates
And prologue to the omen coming on,
Have heaven and earth together demonstrated
Unto our climatures and countrymen. 125

Enter GHOST.
But soft, behold, lo where it comes again!
I'll cross it though it blast me.—Stay, illusion.
[GHOST] *spreads his arms.*
If thou hast any sound or use of voice,
Speak to me.
If there be any good thing to be done, 130
That may to thee do ease, and grace to me,
Speak to me.
If thou art privy to thy country's fate,
Which happily foreknowing may avoid,
O, speak! 135
Or if thou hast uphoarded in thy life
Extorted treasure in the womb of earth,
For which, they say, you spirits oft walk in death,
The cock crows.
Speak of it. Stay, and speak. Stop it, Marcellus.
MAR. Shall I strike at it with my partisan? 140
HOR. Do, if it will not stand.
BER. 'Tis here.

106. *head* fountainhead.
107. *romage* turmoil.
109. *sort* suit, be in accordance.
112. *mote* particle of dust.
113. *palmy* flourishing.
115. *sheeted* in shrouds.
118. *Disasters* ominous signs; *moist star* the moon.
121. *precurse* heralding, foreshadowing.
122. *harbingers* forerunners; *still* ever.
123. *omen* ominous event.
125. *climatures* regions.
127. *cross it* cross its path.
134. *happily* haply, perchance.
140. *partisan* pike.

HOR.   'Tis here.
MAR. 'Tis gone.   [*Exit* GHOST.]
   We do it wrong, being so majestical,
   To offer it the show of violence;
   For it is as the air, invulnerable,   145
   And our vain blows malicious mockery.
BER. It was about to speak when the cock crew.
HOR. And then it started like a guilty thing
   Upon a fearful summons. I have heard
   The cock, that is the trumpet to the morn,   150
   Doth with his lofty and shrill-sounding throat
   Awake the god of day, and at his warning,
   Whether in sea or fire, in earth or air,
   Th' extravagant and erring spirit hies
   To his confine; and of the truth herein   155
   This present object made probation.
MAR. It faded on the crowing of the cock.
   Some say that ever 'gainst that season comes
   Wherein our Savior's birth is celebrated,
   This bird of dawning singeth all night long,   160
   And then, they say, no spirit dare stir abroad,
   The nights are wholesome, then no planets strike,
   No fairy takes, nor witch hath power to charm,
   So hallowed and so gracious is that time.
HOR. So have I heard and do in part believe it.   165
   But look, the morn in russet mantle clad
   Walks o'er the dew of yon high eastward hill.
   Break we our watch up, and by my advice
   Let us impart what we have seen tonight
   Unto young Hamlet, for upon my life   170
   This spirit, dumb to us, will speak to him.
   Do you consent we shall acquaint him with it,
   As needful in our loves, fitting our duty?
MAR. Let's do't, I pray, and I this morning know
   Where we shall find him most convenient.   *Exeunt.* 175

[I.ii]

   Flourish. Enter CLAUDIUS KING OF DENMARK, GERTRUDE THE
   QUEEN, COUNCILLORS [*including*] POLONIUS, *and his son*
   LAERTES, HAMLET, *cum aliis* [*including* VOLTEMAND
   and CORNELIUS].
KING. Though yet of Hamlet our dear brother's death
   The memory be green, and that it us befitted
   To bear our hearts in grief, and our whole kingdom
   To be contracted in one brow of woe,

154. *extravagant* straying, vagrant; *er-*   influence.
ring wandering.   163. *takes* bewitches.
156. *probation* proof.
158. *'gainst* just before.   [I.ii] S.D. *cum aliis* with others.
162. *strike* blast, destroy by malign

Yet so far hath discretion fought with nature   5
That we with wisest sorrow think on him,
Together with remembrance of ourselves.
Therefore our sometime sister, now our queen,
Th' imperial jointress to this warlike state,
Have we, as 'twere with a defeated joy,   10
With an auspicious and a dropping eye,
With mirth in funeral, and with dirge in marriage,
In equal scale weighing delight and dole,
Taken to wife; nor have we herein barred
Your better wisdoms, which have freely gone   15
With this affair along. For all, our thanks.
Now follows that you know young Fortinbras,
Holding a weak supposal of our worth,
Or thinking by our late dear brother's death
Our state to be disjoint and out of frame,   20
Colleaguéd with this dream of his advantage,
He hath not failed to pester us with message
Importing the surrender of those lands
Lost by his father, with all bands of law,
To our most valiant brother. So much for him.   25
Now for ourself, and for this time of meeting,
Thus much the business is: we have here writ
To Norway, uncle of young Fortinbras—
Who, impotent and bedrid, scarcely hears
Of this his nephew's purpose—to suppress   30
His further gait herein, in that the levies,
The lists, and full proportions are all made
Out of his subject; and we here dispatch
You, good Cornelius, and you, Voltemand,
For bearers of this greeting to old Norway,   35
Giving to you no further personal power
To business with the king, more than the scope
Of these delated articles allow.
Farewell, and let your haste commend your duty.

COR.⎫
VOL.⎬ In that, and all things will we show our duty.   40

KING. We doubt it nothing, heartily farewell.
                    [*Exeunt* VOLTEMAND *and* CORNELIUS.]
And now, Laertes, what's the news with you?
You told us of some suit. What is't, Laertes?
You cannot speak of reason to the Dane
And lose your voice. What wouldst thou beg, Laertes,   45

9. *jointress* a widow who holds a jointure or life interest in an estate.
14. *barred* excluded.
21. *colleagued* united.
31. *gait* proceeding.
32. *proportions* forces or supplies for war.
38. *delated* expressly stated.
44. *Dane* King of Denmark.
45. *lose your voice* speak in vain.

That shall not be my offer, not thy asking?
The head is not more native to the heart,
The hand more instrumental to the mouth,
Than is the throne of Denmark to thy father.
What wouldst thou have, Laertes?
LAER.   My dread lord,   50
    Your leave and favor to return to France,
    From whence, though willingly, I came to Denmark
    To show my duty in your coronation,
    Yet now I must confess, that duty done,
    My thoughts and wishes bend again toward France,   55
    And bow them to your gracious leave and pardon.
KING. Have you your father's leave? What says Polonius?
POL. He hath, my lord, wrung from me my slow leave
    By laborsome petition, and at last
    Upon his will I sealed my hard consent.   60
    I do beseech you give him leave to go.
KING. Take thy fair hour, Laertes. Time be thine,
    And thy best graces spend it at thy will.
    But now, my cousin Hamlet, and my son—
HAM. [*Aside.*] A little more than kin, and less than kind.   65
KING. How is it that the clouds still hang on you?
HAM. Not so, my lord. I am too much in the sun.
QUEEN. Good Hamlet, cast thy nighted color off,
    And let thine eye look like a friend on Denmark.
    Do not for ever with thy vailéd lids   70
    Seek for thy noble father in the dust.
    Thou know'st 'tis common—all that lives must die,
    Passing through nature to eternity.
HAM. Ay, madam, it is common.
QUEEN.   If it be,
    Why seems it so particular with thee?   75
HAM. Seems, madam? Nay, it is. I know not 'seems'.
    'Tis not alone my inky cloak, good mother,
    Nor customary suits of solemn black,
    Nor windy suspiration of forced breath,
    No, nor the fruitful river in the eye,   80
    Nor the dejected haviour of the visage,
    Together with all forms, moods, shapes of grief,
    That can denote me truly. These indeed seem,
    For they are actions that a man might play,
    But I have that within which passes show—   85
    These but the trappings and the suits of woe.
KING. 'Tis sweet and commendable in your nature, Hamlet,

47. *native* joined by nature.
48. *instrumental* serviceable.
60. *hard* reluctant.
64. *cousin* kinsman of any kind except parent, child, brother or sister.

65. *kin* related as nephew; *kind* (1) affectionate (2) natural, lawful.
70. *vailed* lowered.
75. *particular* personal, individual.

To give these mourning duties to your father,
But you must know your father lost a father,
That father lost, lost his, and the survivor bound   90
In filial obligation for some term
To do obsequious sorrow. But to persevere
In obstinate condolement is a course
Of impious stubbornness. 'Tis unmanly grief.
It shows a will most incorrect to heaven,   95
A heart unfortified, a mind impatient,
An understanding simple and unschooled.
For what we know must be, and is as common
As any the most vulgar thing to sense,
Why should we in our peevish opposition   100
Take it to heart? Fie, 'tis a fault to heaven,
A fault against the dead, a fault to nature,
To reason most absurd, whose common theme
Is death of fathers, and who still hath cried,
From the first corse till he that died to-day,   105
'This must be so'. We pray you throw to earth
This unprevailing woe, and think of us
As of a father, for let the world take note
You are the most immediate to our throne,
And with no less nobility of love   110
Than that which dearest father bears his son
Do I impart toward you. For your intent
In going back to school in Wittenberg,
It is most retrograde to our desire,
And we beseech you, bend you to remain   115
Here in the cheer and comfort of our eye,
Our chiefest courtier, cousin, and our son.
QUEEN. Let not thy mother lose her prayers, Hamlet.
I pray thee stay with us, go not to Wittenberg.
HAM. I shall in all my best obey you, madam.   120
KING. Why, 'tis a loving and a fair reply.
Be as ourself in Denmark. Madam, come.
This gentle and unforced accord of Hamlet
Sits smiling to my heart, in grace whereof,
No jocund health that Denmark drinks to-day   125
But the great cannon to the clouds shall tell,
And the king's rouse the heaven shall bruit again,
Respeaking earthly thunder. Come away.
                    Flourish. Exeunt all but HAMLET.
HAM. O, that this too too sallied flesh would melt,

92. *obsequious* dutiful in performing funeral obsequies or manifesting regard for the dead; *persever* persevere.
105. *corse* corpse.
114. *retrograde* contrary.
127. *rouse* full draught of liquor; *bruit*
echo.
129. *sallied* sullied. "Sallied" is the reading of *Q2* (and *Q1*). *F* reads "solid." Since Hamlet's primary concern is with the fact of the flesh's impurity, not with its corporeality, the

Thaw, and resolve itself into a dew,   130
Or that the Everlasting had not fixed
His canon 'gainst self-slaughter. O God, God,
How weary, stale, flat, and unprofitable
Seem to me all the uses of this world!
Fie on't, ah, fie, 'tis an unweeded garden   135
That grows to seed. Things rank and gross in nature
Possess it merely. That it should come to this,
But two months dead, nay, not so much, not two.
So excellent a king, that was to this
Hyperion to a satyr, so loving to my mother,   140
That he might not beteem the winds of heaven
Visit her face too roughly. Heaven and earth,
Must I remember? Why, she would hang on him
As if increase of appetite had grown
By what it fed on, and yet, within a month—   145
Let me not think on't. Frailty, thy name is woman—
A little month, or ere those shoes were old
With which she followed my poor father's body
Like Niobe, all tears, why she, even she—
O God, a beast that wants discourse of reason   150
Would have mourned longer—married with my uncle,
My father's brother, but no more like my father
Than I to Hercules. Within a month,
Ere yet the salt of most unrighteous tears
Had left the flushing in her gallèd eyes,   155
She married. O, most wicked speed, to post
With such dexterity to incestuous sheets!
It is not, nor it cannot come to good.
But break my heart, for I must hold my tongue.

    Enter HORATIO, MARCELLUS, *and* BERNARDO.
HOR. Hail to your lordship!
HAM.   I am glad to see you well.   160
   Horatio—or I do forget myself.
HOR. The same, my lord, and your poor servant ever.
HAM. Sir, my good friend, I'll change that name with you.
   And what make you from Wittenberg, Horatio?

choice as between *Q* and *F* clearly lies with *Q*. "Sally" is a legitimate sixteenth-century form of "sully"; it occurs in Dekker's *Patient Grissil* (I.i.12), printed in 1603, as F. T. Bowers has pointed out (in "Hamlet's 'Sullied' or 'Solid' Flesh. A Bibliographical Case-History," *Shakespeare Survey 9* [1956], p. 44); and it occurs as a noun at II.i.39 of *Hamlet*.
132. *canon* law.
137. *merely* entirely.
140. *Hyperion* the sun god.
141. *beteem* allow.

149. *Niobe* wife of Amphion, King of Thebes, she boasted of having more children than Leto and was punished when her seven sons and seven daughters were slain by Apollo and Artemis, children of Leto; in her grief she was changed by Zeus into a stone, which continually dropped tears.
150. *wants* lacks; *discourse of reason* the reasoning faculty.
155. *galled* sore from rubbing or chafing.
163. *change* exchange.
164. *make* do.

Marcellus?   165
MAR. My good lord!
HAM. I am very glad to see you. [*To* BERNARDO.] Good even, sir.—
But what, in faith, make you from Wittenberg?
HOR. A truant disposition, good my lord.
HAM. I would not hear your enemy say so,   170
Nor shall you do my ear that violence
To make it truster of your own report
Against yourself. I know you are no truant.
But what is your affair in Elsinore?
We'll teach you to drink deep ere you depart.   175
HOR. My lord, I came to see your father's funeral.
HAM. I prithee do not mock me, fellow-student,
I think it was to see my mother's wedding.
HOR. Indeed, my lord, it followed hard upon.
HAM. Thrift, thrift, Horatio. The funeral baked-meats   180
Did coldly furnish forth the marriage tables.
Would I had met my dearest foe in heaven
Or ever I had seen that day, Horatio!
My father—methinks I see my father.
HOR. Where, my lord?
HAM.   In my mind's eye, Horatio.   185
HOR. I saw him once, 'a was a goodly king.
HAM. 'A was a man, take him for all in all,
I shall not look upon his like again.
HOR. My lord, I think I saw him yesternight.
HAM. Saw who?   190
HOR. My lord, the king your father.
HAM.   The king my father?
HOR. Season your admiration for a while
With an attent ear till I may deliver
Upon the witness of these gentlemen
This marvel to you.
HAM.   For God's love, let me hear!   195
HOR. Two nights together had these gentlemen,
Marcellus and Bernardo, on their watch
In the dead waste and middle of the night
Been thus encountered. A figure like your father,
Armed at point exactly, cap-a-pe,   200
Appears before them, and with solemn march
Goes slow and stately by them. Thrice he walked
By their oppressed and fear-surprisèd eyes
Within his truncheon's length, whilst they, distilled
Almost to jelly with the act of fear,   205
Stand dumb and speak not to him. This to me

182. *dearest* direst.
192. *Season* temper, moderate; *admira-*
tion wonder, astonishment.

200. *at point exactly* in every particular; *cap-a-pe* from head to foot.
204. *truncheon* military leader's baton.

In dreadful secrecy impart they did,
And I with them the third night kept the watch,
Where, as they had delivered, both in time,
Form of the thing, each word made true and good,   210
The apparition comes. I knew your father.
These hands are not more like.
HAM.   But where was this?
MAR. My lord, upon the platform where we watch.
HAM. Did you not speak to it?
HOR.   My lord, I did,
But answer made it none. Yet once methought   215
It lifted up it head and did address
Itself to motion, like as it would speak;
But even then the morning cock crew loud,
And at the sound it shrunk in haste away
And vanished from our sight.
HAM.   'Tis very strange.   220
HOR. As I do live, my honored lord, 'tis true,
And we did think it writ down in our duty
To let you know of it.
HAM.   Indeed, sirs, but
This troubles me. Hold you the watch to-night?
ALL. We do, my lord.
HAM.   Armed, say you?
ALL.   Armed, my lord.   225
HAM. From top to toe?
ALL.   My lord, from head to foot.
HAM. Then saw you not his face.
HOR. O yes, my lord, he wore his beaver up.
HAM. What, looked he frowningly?
HOR. A countenance more in sorrow than in anger.   230
HAM. Pale or red?
HOR. Nay, very pale.
HAM.   And fixed his eyes upon you?
HOR. Most constantly.
HAM.   I would I had been there.
HOR. It would have much amazed you.
HAM.   Very like.
Stayed it long?
HOR.   While one with moderate haste might tell a hundred. 235
BOTH. Longer, longer.
HOR.   Not when I saw't.
HAM. His beard was grizzled, no?
HOR. It was as I have seen it in his life,
A sable silvered.

216. *it* its.
228. *beaver* the part of the helmet that
was drawn down to cover the face.
235. *tell* count.

237. *grizzled* grayish.
239. *sable silvered* black mixed with
white.

HAM.   I will watch to-night.
   Perchance 'twill walk again.
HOR.   I warr'nt it will.   240
HAM. If it assume my noble father's person,
   I'll speak to it though hell itself should gape
   And bid me hold my peace. I pray you all,
   If you have hitherto concealed this sight,
   Let it be tenable in your silence still,   245
   And whatsomever else shall hap to-night,
   Give it an understanding but no tongue.
   I will requite your loves. So fare you well.
   Upon the platform 'twixt eleven and twelve
   I'll visit you.
ALL.   Our duty to your honor.   250
HAM. Your loves, as mine to you. Farewell.
                              Exeunt [all but HAMLET].
   My father's spirit in arms? All is not well.
   I doubt some foul play. Would the night were come!
   Till then sit still, my soul. Foul deeds will rise,
   Though all the earth o'erwhelm them, to men's eyes.   *Exit.* 255

[I.iii]

          Enter LAERTES *and* OPHELIA *his sister.*
LAER. My necessaries are embarked. Farewell.
   And, sister, as the winds give benefit
   And convoy is assistant, do not sleep,
   But let me hear from you.
OPH.   Do you doubt that?
LAER. For Hamlet, and the trifling of his favor,   5
   Hold it a fashion and a toy in blood,
   A violet in the youth of primy nature,
   Forward, not permanent, sweet, not lasting,
   The perfume and suppliance of a minute,
   No more.
OPH.   No more but so?
LAER.   Think it no more.   10
   For nature crescent does not grow alone
   In thews and bulk, but as this temple waxes
   The inward service of the mind and soul
   Grows wide withal. Perhaps he loves you now,
   And now no soil nor cautel doth besmirch   15
   The virtue of his will, but you must fear,

---

245. *tenable* retained.
246. *whatsomever* whatsoever.
253. *doubt* suspect.

[I.iii] 6. *fashion* the creation of a season only; *toy in blood* passing fancy.

7. *primy* of the springtime.
11. *crescent* growing.
12. *thews* sinews, strength; *this temple*
the body.
15. *cautel* deceit.
16. *will* desire.

His greatness weighed, his will is not his own,
For he himself is subject to his birth.
He may not, as unvalued persons do,
Carve for himself, for on his choice depends   20
The safety and health of this whole state,
And therefore must his choice be circumscribed
Unto the voice and yielding of that body
Whereof he is the head. Then if he says he loves you,
It fits your wisdom so far to believe it   25
As he in his particular act and place
May give his saying deed, which is no further
Than the main voice of Denmark goes withal.
Then weigh what loss your honor may sustain
If with too credent ear you list his songs,   30
Or lose your heart, or your chaste treasure open
To his unmastered importunity.
Fear it, Ophelia, fear it, my dear sister,
And keep you in the rear of your affection,
Out of the shot and danger of desire.   35
The chariest maid is prodigal enough
If she unmask her beauty to the moon.
Virtue itself scapes not calumnious strokes.
The canker galls the infants of the spring
Too oft before their buttons be disclosed,   40
And in the morn and liquid dew of youth
Contagious blastments are most imminent.
Be wary then; best safety lies in fear.
Youth to itself rebels, though none else near.
OPH. I shall the effect of this good lesson keep   45
As watchman to my heart. But, good my brother,
Do not as some ungracious pastors do,
Show me the steep and thorny way to heaven,
Whiles like a puffed and reckless libertine
Himself the primrose path of dalliance treads   50
And recks not his own rede.
LAER.   O, fear me not.
   Enter POLONIUS.
I stay too long. But here my father comes.
A double blessing is a double grace;
Occasion smiles upon a second leave.
POL. Yet here, Laertes? Aboard, aboard, for shame!   55
The wind sits in the shoulder of your sail,

17. *greatness weighed* high position considered.
19. *unvalued persons* persons of no social importance.
20. *Carve for himself* act according to his own inclination.
23. *yielding* assent.
30. *credent* trusting.
34. *affection* feeling.
39. *canker* canker-worm (which feeds on roses); *galls* injures.
40. *buttons* buds.
42. *blastments* blights.
51. *recks* regards; *rede* counsel.

And you are stayed for. There—my blessing with thee,
And these few precepts in thy memory
Look thou character. Give thy thoughts no tongue,
Nor any unproportioned thought his act.   60
Be thou familiar, but by no means vulgar.
Those friends thou hast, and their adoption tried,
Grapple them unto thy soul with hoops of steel;
But do not dull thy palm with entertainment
Of each new-hatched, unfledged courage. Beware   65
Of entrance to a quarrel, but being in,
Bear't that th' opposéd may beware of thee.
Give every man thy ear, but few thy voice;
Take each man's censure, but reserve thy judgment.
Costly thy habit as thy purse can buy,   70
But not expressed in fancy; rich not gaudy,
For the apparel oft proclaims the man,
And they in France of the best rank and station
Are of a most select and generous chief in that.
Neither a borrower nor a lender be,   75
For loan oft loses both itself and friend,
And borrowing dulls th' edge of husbandry.
This above all, to thine own self be true,
And it must follow as the night the day
Thou canst not then be false to any man.   80
Farewell. My blessing season this in thee!
LAER. Most humbly do I take my leave, my lord.
POL. The time invites you. Go, your servants tend.
LAER. Farewell, Ophelia, and remember well
What I have said to you.
OPH.   'Tis in my memory locked,   85
And you yourself shall keep the key of it.
LAER. Farewell.   *Exit* LAERTES.
POL. What is't, Ophelia, he hath said to you?
OPH. So please you, something touching the Lord Hamlet.
POL. Marry, well bethought.   90
'Tis told me he hath very oft of late
Given private time to you, and you yourself
Have of your audience been most free and bounteous.
If it be so—as so 'tis put on me,
And that in way of caution—I must tell you,   95
You do not understand yourself so clearly
As it behoves my daughter and your honor.
What is between you? Give me up the truth.
OPH. He hath, my lord, of late made many tenders

59. *character* engrave.   77. *husbandry* thriftiness.
60. *unproportioned* inordinate.   81. *season* ripen.
61. *vulgar* common.   83. *tend* attend, wait.
65. *courage* young blood, man of spirit.   90. *Marry* by Mary.
74. *chief* eminence.   99. *tenders* offers.

Of his affection to me. 100
POL. Affection? Pooh! You speak like a green girl,
Unsifted in such perilous circumstance.
Do you believe his tenders, as you call them?
OPH. I do not know, my lord, what I should think.
POL. Marry, I will teach you. Think yourself a baby 105
That you have ta'en these tenders for true pay
Which are not sterling. Tender yourself more dearly,
Or (not to crack the wind of the poor phrase,
Running it thus) you'll tender me a fool.
OPH. My lord, he hath importuned me with love 110
In honorable fashion.
POL. Ay, fashion you may call it. Go to, go to.
OPH. And hath given countenance to his speech, my lord,
With almost all the holy vows of heaven.
POL. Ay, springes to catch woodcocks. I do know, 115
When the blood burns, how prodigal the soul
Lends the tongue vows. These blazes, daughter,
Giving more light than heat, extinct in both
Even in their promise, as it is a-making,
You must not take for fire. From this time 120
Be something scanter of your maiden presence.
Set your entreatments at a higher rate
Than a command to parle. For Lord Hamlet,
Believe so much in him that he is young,
And with a larger tether may he walk 125
Than may be given you. In few, Ophelia,
Do not believe his vows, for they are brokers,
Not of that dye which their investments show,
But mere implorators of unholy suits,
Breathing like sanctified and pious bawds, 130
The better to beguile. This is for all:
I would not, in plain terms, from this time forth
Have you so slander any moment leisure
As to give words or talk with the Lord Hamlet.
Look to't, I charge you. Come your ways. 135
OPH. I shall obey, my lord. *Exeunt.*

[I.iv]

    Enter HAMLET, HORATIO, *and* MARCELLUS.
HAM. The air bites shrewdly; it is very cold.
HOR. It is a nipping and an eager air.
HAM. What hour now?
HOR.   I think it lacks of twelve.

102. *Unsifted* untried.
115. *springes* snares.
122. *entreatments* military negotiations
for a surrender.
127. *brokers* go-betweens.

128. *investments* clothes.
129. *implorators* solicitors.

[I.iv] 2. *eager* sharp.

MAR. No, it is struck.

HOR. Indeed? I heard it not. It then draws near the season 5
 Wherein the spirit held his wont to walk.
     A flourish of trumpets, and two pieces go off.
 What does this mean, my lord?

HAM. The king doth wake to-night and takes his rouse,
 Keeps wassail, and the swagg'ring up-spring reels,
 And as he drains his draughts of Rhenish down, 10
 The kettledrum and trumpet thus bray out
 The triumph of his pledge.

HOR.   Is it a custom?

HAM. Ay, marry, is't,
 But to my mind, though I am native here
 And to the manner born, it is a custom 15
 More honored in the breach than the observance.
 This heavy-headed revel east and west
 Makes us traduced and taxed of other nations.
 They clepe us drunkards, and with swinish phrase
 Soil our addition, and indeed it takes 20
 From our achievements, though performed at height,
 The pith and marrow of our attribute.
 So oft it chances in particular men,
 That for some vicious mole of nature in them,
 As in their birth, wherein they are not guilty 25
 (Since nature cannot choose his origin),
 By the o'ergrowth of some complexion,
 Oft breaking down the pales and forts of reason,
 Or by some habit that too much o'er-leavens
 The form of plausive manners—that these men, 30
 Carrying, I say, the stamp of one defect,
 Being nature's livery or fortune's star,
 His virtues else, be they as pure as grace,
 As infinite as man may undergo,
 Shall in the general censure take corruption 35
 From that particular fault. The dram of evil
 Doth all the noble substance often doubt
 To his own scandal.

   Enter GHOST.

HOR.   Look, my lord, it comes.

HAM. Angels and ministers of grace defend us!

9. *wassail* carousal; *up-spring* a German dance.
18. *taxed of* censured by.
19. *clepe* call.
20. *addition* title added to a man's name to denote his rank.
22. *attribute* reputation.
26. *his* its.
27. *complexion* one of the four temperaments (sanguine, melancholy, choleric and phlegmatic).
29. *o'er-leavens* works change throughout.
30. *plausive* pleasing.
32. *livery* badge; *star* a person's fortune, rank, or destiny, viewed as determined by the stars.
37. *doubt* put out, obliterate.
38. *his* its.

Be thou a spirit of health or goblin damned,   40
Bring with thee airs from heaven or blasts from hell,
Be thy intents wicked or charitable,
Thou com'st in such a questionable shape
That I will speak to thee. I'll call thee Hamlet,
King, father, royal Dane. O, answer me!   45
Let me not burst in ignorance, but tell
Why thy canonized bones, hearséd in death,
Have burst their cerements; why the sepulchre
Wherein we saw thee quietly interred
Hath oped his ponderous and marble jaws   50
To cast thee up again. What may this mean
That thou, dead corse, again in complete steel
Revisits thus the glimpses of the moon,
Making night hideous, and we fools of nature
So horridly to shake our disposition   55
With thoughts beyond the reaches of our souls?
Say, why is this? wherefore? What should we do?

                           [CHOST] *beckons.*

HOR. It beckons you to go away it,
  As if it some impartment did desire
  To you alone.
MAR.   Look with what courteous action   60
  It waves you to a more removéd ground.
  But do not go with it.
HOR.   No, by no means.
HAM. It will not speak; then I will follow it.
HOR. Do not, my lord.
HAM.   Why, what should be the fear?
  I do not set my life at a pin's fee,   65
  And for my soul, what can it do to that,
  Being a thing immortal as itself?
  It waves me forth again. I'll follow it.
HOR. What if it tempt you toward the flood, my lord,
  Or to the dreadful summit of the cliff   70
  That beetles o'er his base into the sea,
  And there assume some other horrible form,
  Which might deprive your sovereignty of reason
  And draw you into madness? Think of it.
  The very place puts toys of desperation,   75
  Without more motive, into every brain
  That looks so many fathoms to the sea
  And hears it roar beneath.
HAM.   It waves me still.

47. *canonized* buried according to the church's rule; *hearsed* coffined, buried.
59. *impartment* communication.
71. *beetles* juts out.

73. *sovereignty of reason* state of being ruled by reason.
75. *toys* fancies, impulses.

Go on. I'll follow thee.
MAR. You shall not go, my lord.
HAM.   Hold off your hands.   80
HOR. Be ruled. You shall not go.
HAM.   My fate cries out
And makes each petty artere in this body
As hardy as the Nemean lion's nerve.
Still am I called. Unhand me, gentlemen.
By heaven, I'll make a ghost of him that lets me.   85
I say, away! Go on. I'll follow thee.
                              [*Exeunt*] GHOST *and* HAMLET.
HOR. He waxes desperate with imagination.
MAR. Let's follow. 'Tis not fit thus to obey him.
HOR. Have after. To what issue will this come?
MAR. Something is rotten in the state of Denmark.   90
HOR. Heaven will direct it.
MAR.   Nay, let's follow him.   *Exeunt.*

[I.v]

          Enter GHOST *and* HAMLET.
HAM. Whither wilt thou lead me? Speak. I'll go no further.
GHOST. Mark me.
HAM.   I will.
GHOST.   My hour is almost come,
When I to sulph'rous and tormenting flames
Must render up myself.
HAM.   Alas, poor ghost!
GHOST. Pity me not, but lend thy serious hearing   5
To what I shall unfold.
HAM.   Speak. I am bound to hear.
GHOST. So art thou to revenge, when thou shalt hear.
HAM. What?
GHOST. I am thy father's spirit,
Doomed for a certain term to walk the night,   10
And for the day confined to fast in fires,
Till the foul crimes done in my days of nature
Are burnt and purged away. But that I am forbid
To tell the secrets of my prison house,
I could a tale unfold whose lightest word   15
Would harrow up thy soul, freeze thy young blood,
Make thy two eyes like stars start from their spheres,
Thy knotted and combinéd locks to part,
And each particular hair to stand an end,
Like quills upon the fretful porpentine.   20

82. *artere* artery.   85. *lets* hinders.
83. *Nemean lion* slain by Hercules in
the performance of one of his twelve   [I.v] 19. *an* on.
labors.   20. *porpentine* porcupine.

But this eternal blazon must not be
To ears of flesh and blood. List, list, O, list!
If thou didst ever thy dear father love—
HAM. O God!
GHOST. Revenge his foul and most unnatural murder.   25
HAM. Murder!
GHOST. Murder most foul, as in the best it is,
But this most foul, strange, and unnatural.
HAM. Haste me to know't, that I, with wings as swift
As meditation or the thoughts of love,   30
May sweep to my revenge.
GHOST.   I find thee apt,
And duller shouldst thou be than the fat weed
That rots itself in ease on Lethe wharf,
Wouldst thou not stir in this. Now, Hamlet, hear.
'Tis given out that, sleeping in my orchard,   35
A serpent stung me. So the whole ear of Denmark
Is by a forgéd process of my death
Rankly abused. But know, thou noble youth,
The serpent that did sting thy father's life
Now wears his crown.
HAM.   O my prophetic soul!   40
My uncle!
GHOST. Ay, that incestuous, that adulterate beast,
With witchcraft of his wits, with traitorous gifts—
O wicked wit and gifts that have the power
So to seduce!—won to his shameful lust   45
The will of my most seeming virtuous queen.
O Hamlet, what a falling off was there,
From me, whose love was of that dignity
That it went hand in hand even with the vow
I made to her in marriage, and to decline   50
Upon a wretch whose natural gifts were poor
To those of mine!
But virtue, as it never will be moved,
Though lewdness court it in a shape of heaven,
So lust, though to a radiant angel linked,   55
Will sate itself in a celestial bed
And prey on garbage.
But soft, methinks I scent the morning air.
Brief let me be. Sleeping within my orchard,
My custom always of the afternoon,   60
Upon my secure hour thy uncle stole,
With juice of cursed hebona in a vial,

21. *eternal blazon* proclamation of the secrets of eternity.
33. *Lethe* the river in Hades which brings forgetfulness.
37. *process* account.
61. *secure* free from suspicion.
62. *hebona* an imaginary poison, associated with henbane.

And in the porches of my ears did pour
The leperous distilment, whose effect
Holds such an enmity with blood of man   65
That swift as quicksilver it courses through
The natural gates and alleys of the body,
And with a sudden vigor it doth posset
And curd, like eager droppings into milk,
The thin and wholesome blood. So did it mine,   70
And a most instant tetter barked about
Most lazar-like with vile and loathsome crust
All my smooth body.
Thus was I sleeping by a brother's hand
Of life, of crown, of queen at once dispatched,   75
Cut off even in the blossoms of my sin,
Unhouseled, disappointed, unaneled,
No reck'ning made, but sent to my account
With all my imperfections on my head.
O, horrible! O, horrible! most horrible!   80
If thou hast nature in thee, bear it not.
Let not the royal bed of Denmark be
A couch for luxury and damnèd incest.
But howsomever thou pursues this act,
Taint not thy mind, nor let thy soul contrive   85
Against thy mother aught. Leave her to heaven,
And to those thorns that in her bosom lodge
To prick and sting her. Fare thee well at once.
The glowworm shows the matin to be near,
And gins to pale his uneffectual fire.   90
Adieu, adieu, adieu. Remember me.   [*Exit.*]
HAM. O all you host of heaven! O earth! What else?
And shall I couple hell? O, fie! Hold, hold, my heart,
And you, my sinews, grow not instant old,
But bear me stiffly up. Remember thee?   95
Ay, thou poor ghost, whiles memory holds a seat
In this distracted globe. Remember thee?
Yea, from the table of my memory
I'll wipe away all trivial fond records,
All saws of books, all forms, all pressures past   100
That youth and observation copied there,
And thy commandment all alone shall live
Within the book and volume of my brain,

68. *posset* curdle.
69. *eager* acid.
71. *tetter* a skin eruption; *barked* covered as with bark.
77. *Unhouseled* without having received the sacrament; *disappointed* unprepared; *unaneled* without extreme unction.
83. *luxury* lust.

89. *matin* morning.
97. *globe* head.
98. *table* writing tablet, memorandum book (as at line 107, below; here metaphorically of the mind).
99. *fond* foolish.
100. *saws* sayings; *forms* concepts; *pressures* impressions.

Unmixed with baser matter. Yes, by heaven!
O most pernicious woman!   105
O villain, villain, smiling, damnéd villain!
My tables—meet it is I set it down
That one may smile, and smile, and be a villain.
At least I am sure it may be so in Denmark.   [*Writing.*]
So, uncle, there you are. Now to my word: 110
It is 'Adieu, adieu. Remember me'.
I have sworn't.

        Enter HORATIO *and* MARCELLUS.
HOR. My lord, my lord!
MAR.   Lord Hamlet!
HOR.   Heavens secure him!
HAM. So be it!
MAR. Illo, ho, ho, my lord!   115
HAM. Hillo, ho, ho, boy! Come, bird, come.
MAR. How is't, my noble lord?
HOR.   What news, my lord?
HAM. O, wonderful!
HOR. Good my lord, tell it.
HAM.   No, you will reveal it.
HOR. Not I, my lord, by heaven.
MAR.   Nor I, my lord.   120
HAM. How say you then, would heart of man once think it?
  But you'll be secret?
BOTH.   Ay, by heaven, my lord.
HAM. There's never a villain dwelling in all Denmark
  But he's an arrant knave.
HOR. There needs no ghost, my lord, come from the grave   125
  To tell us this.
HAM.   Why, right, you are in the right,
  And so without more circumstance at all
  I hold it fit that we shake hands and part,
  You, as your business and desire shall point you,
  For every man hath business and desire   130
  Such as it is, and for my own poor part,
  I will go pray.
HOR. These are but wild and whirling words, my lord.
HAM. I am sorry they offend you, heartily;
  Yes, faith, heartily.
HOR.   There's no offence, my lord.   135
HAM. Yes, by Saint Patrick, but there is, Horatio,
  And much offence too. Touching this vision here,
  It is an honest ghost, that let me tell you.
  For your desire to know what is between us,

115. *Illo, ho, ho* cry of the falconer to summon his hawk.
136. *Saint Patrick* associated, in the late middle ages, with purgatory, whence the ghost has presumably come.

O'ermaster't as you may. And now, good friends,   140
As you are friends, scholars, and soldiers,
Give me one poor request.

HOR. What is't, my lord? We will.

HAM. Never make known what you have seen to-night.

BOTH. My lord, we will not.

HAM.   Nay, but swear't.

HOR.   In faith,   145
My lord, not I.

MAR.   Nor I, my lord, in faith.

HAM. Upon my sword.

MAR.   We have sworn, my lord, already.

HAM. Indeed, upon my sword, indeed.

                              Ghost cries under the stage.

GHOST.   Swear.

HAM. Ha, ha, boy, say'st thou so? Art thou there, truepenny?
Come on. You hear this fellow in the cellarage.   150
Consent to swear.

HOR.   Propose the oath, my lord.

HAM. Never to speak of this that you have seen,
Swear by my sword.

GHOST. [*Beneath.*] Swear.

HAM. Hic et ubique? Then we'll shift our ground.   155
Come hither, gentlemen,
And lay your hands again upon my sword.
Swear by my sword
Never to speak of this that you have heard.

GHOST. [*Beneath.*] Swear by his sword.   160

HAM. Well said, old mole! Canst work i' th' earth so fast?
A worthy pioneer! Once more remove, good friends.

HOR. O day and night, but this is wondrous strange!

HAM. And therefore as a stranger give it welcome.
There are more things in heaven and earth, Horatio,   165
Than are dreamt of in your philosophy.
But come.
Here as before, never, so help you mercy,
How strange or odd some'er I bear myself
(As I perchance hereafter shall think meet   170
To put an antic disposition on),
That you, at such times, seeing me, never shall,
With arms encumbered thus, or this head-shake,
Or by pronouncing of some doubtful phrase,
As 'Well, well, we know', or 'We could, and if we would'   175
Or 'If we list to speak', or 'There be, and if they might'
Or such ambiguous giving out, to note

149. *truepenny* honest fellow.   162. *pioneer* miner.
155. *Hic et ubique* here and every-   171. *antic* mad.
where.   173. *encumbered* folded.

That you know aught of me—this do swear,
So grace and mercy at your most need help you.
GHOST. [*Beneath.*] Swear.   180
HAM. Rest, rest, perturbéd spirit! So, gentlemen,
With all my love I do commend me to you,
And what so poor a man as Hamlet is
May do t'express his love and friending to you,
God willing, shall not lack. Let us go in together,   185
And still your fingers on your lips, I pray.
The time is out of joint. O curséd spite
That ever I was born to set it right!
Nay, come, let's go together.   *Exeunt.*

[II.i]
    Enter old POLONIUS, *with his man* [REYNALDO].
POL. Give him this money and these notes, Reynaldo.
REY. I will, my lord.
POL. You shall do marvell's wisely, good Reynaldo,
Before you visit him, to make inquire
Of his behavior.
REY.   My lord, I did intend it.   5
POL. Marry, well said, very well said. Look you, sir,
Enquire me first what Danskers are in Paris,
And how, and who, what means, and where they keep,
What company, at what expense; and finding
By this encompassment and drift of question   10
That they do know my son, come you more nearer
Than your particular demands will touch it.
Take you as 'twere some distant knowledge of him,
As thus, 'I know his father and his friends,
And in part him'. Do you mark this, Reynaldo?   15
REY. Ay, very well, my lord.
POL. 'And in part him, but,' you may say, 'not well,
But if't be he I mean, he's very wild,
Addicted so and so'. And there put on him
What forgeries you please; marry, none so rank   20
As many dishonour him. Take heed of that.
But, sir, such wanton, wild, and usual slips
As are companions noted and most known
To youth and liberty.
REY.   As gaming, my lord.
POL. Ay, or drinking, fencing, swearing, quarrelling,   25
Drabbing—you may go so far.
REY. My lord, that would dishonor him.
POL. Faith, no, as you may season it in the charge.

[II.i] 7. *Danskers* Danes.
8. *means* wealth.
10. *encompassment* talking round the matter.
20. *forgeries* invented **wrongdoings.**
24. *liberty* license.
26. *Drabbing* whoring.
28. *season* moderate.

You must not put another scandal on him,
That he is open to incontinency. 30
That's not my meaning. But breathe his faults so quaintly
That they may seem the taints of liberty,
The flash and outbreak of a fiery mind,
A savageness in unreclaiméd blood,
Of general assault.
REY.   But, my good lord— 35
POL. Wherefore should you do this?
REY.   Ay, my lord,
I would know that.
POL.   Marry, sir, here's my drift,
And I believe it is a fetch of warrant.
You laying these slight sallies on my son,
As 'twere a thing a little soiled i' th' working, 40
Mark you,
Your party in converse, him you would sound,
Having ever seen in the prenominatè crimes
The youth you breathe of guilty, be assured
He closes with you in this consequence, 45
'Good sir', or so, or 'friend', or 'gentleman',
According to the phrase or the addition
Of man and country.
REY.   Very good, my lord.
POL. And then, sir, does 'a this—'a does—What was I about to
    say? 50
By the mass, I was about to say something.
Where did I leave?
REY. At 'closes in the consequence'.
POL. At 'closes in the consequence'—ay, marry,
He closes thus: 'I know the gentleman. 55
I saw him yesterday, or th' other day,
Or then, or then, with such, or such, and as you say,
There was 'a gaming, there o'ertook in's rouse,
There falling out at tennis', or perchance
'I saw him enter such a house of sale', 60
Videlicet, a brothel, or so forth.
See you, now—
Your bait of falsehood takes this carp of truth,
And thus do we of wisdom and of reach,
With windlasses and with assays of bias, 65
By indirections find directions out;
So by my former lecture and advice

31. *quaintly* delicately.
34. *unreclaimed* untamed.
35. *Of general assault* assailing all.
38. *fetch of warrant* allowable device.
43. *prenominate* before-named.
45. *closes* agrees; *in this consequence* as follows.
47. *addition* title.
61. *Videlicet* namely.
64. *reach* ability.
65. *windlasses* roundabout approaches; *assays of bias* indirect attempts.

Shall you my son. You have me, have you not?
REY. My lord, I have.
POL.   God buy ye; fare ye well.
REY. Good my lord.   70
POL. Observe his inclination in yourself.
REY. I shall, my lord.
POL. And let him ply his music.
REY.   Well, my lord.
POL. Farewell.   *Exit* REYNALDO.

    Enter OPHELIA.
                How now, Ophelia, what's the matter?
OPH. O my lord, my lord, I have been so affrighted!   75
POL. With what, i' th' name of God?
OPH. My lord, as I was sewing in my closet,
    Lord Hamlet with his doublet all unbraced,
    No hat upon his head, his stockings fouled,
    Ungartered and down-gyvéd to his ankle,   80
    Pale as his shirt, his knees knocking each other,
    And with a look so piteous in purport
    As if he had been looséd out of hell
    To speak of horrors—he comes before me.
POL. Mad for thy love?
OPH.   My lord, I do not know,   85
    But truly I do fear it.
POL.   What said he?
OPH. He took me by the wrist, and held me hard,
    Then goes he to the length of all his arm,
    And with his other hand thus o'er his brow,
    He falls to such perusal of my face   90
    As 'a would draw it. Long stayed he so.
    At last, a little shaking of mine arm,
    And thrice his head thus waving up and down,
    He raised a sigh so piteous and profound
    As it did seem to shatter all his bulk,   95
    And end his being. That done, he lets me go,
    And with his head over his shoulder turned
    He seemed to find his way without his eyes,
    For out adoors he went without their helps,
    And to the last bended their light on me.   100
POL. Come, go with me. I will go seek the king.
    This is the very ecstasy of love,
    Whose violent property fordoes itself,
    And leads the will to desperate undertakings
    As oft as any passion under heaven   105

69. *God buy ye* God be with you.   gyves or fetters on a prisoner's ankles.
77. *closet* private room.   102. *ecstasy* madness.
78. *unbraced* unlaced.   103. *fordoes* destroys.
80. *down-gyved* hanging down, like

That does afflict our natures. I am sorry.
What, have you given him any hard words of late?
OPH. No, my good lord, but as you did command
 I did repel his letters, and denied
 His access to me.
POL.   That hath made him mad.   110
 I am sorry that with better heed and judgment
 I had not quoted him. I feared he did but trifle,
 And meant to wrack thee; but beshrew my jealousy.
 By heaven, it is as proper to our age
 To cast beyond ourselves in our opinions   115
 As it is common for the younger sort
 To lack discretion. Come, go we to the king.
 This must be known, which being kept close, might move
 More grief to hide than hate to utter love.
 Come.   *Exeunt.* 120

[II.ii]

  Flourish. Enter KING *and* QUEEN, ROSENCRANTZ *and* GUILD-
  ENSTERN [*and* ATTENDANTS].
KING. Welcome, dear Rosencrantz and Guildenstern.
 Moreover that we much did long to see you,
 The need we have to use you did provoke
 Our hasty sending. Something have you heard
 Of Hamlet's transformation—so call it,   5
 Sith nor th' exterior nor the inward man
 Resembles that it was. What it should be,
 More than his father's death, that thus hath put him
 So much from th' understanding of himself,
 I cannot deem of. I entreat you both   10
 That, being of so young days brought up with him,
 And sith so neighboured to his youth and havior,
 That you vouchsafe your rest here in our court
 Some little time, so by your companies
 To draw him on to pleasures, and to gather   15
 So much as from occasion you may glean,
 Whether aught to us unknown afflicts him thus,
 That opened lies within our remedy.
QUEEN. Good gentlemen, he hath much talked of you,
 And sure I am two men there is not living   20
 To whom he more adheres. If it will please you
 To show us so much gentry and good will
 As to expend your time with us awhile
 For the supply and profit of our hope,
 Your visitation shall receive such thanks   25

112. *quoted* observed.   [II.ii] 6. *Sith* since.
113. *wrack* ruin.   18. *opened* disclosed.
118. *close* secret; *move* cause.   22. *gentry* courtesy.

As fits a king's remembrance.
ROS.   Both your majesties
  Might, by the sovereign power you have of us,
  Put your dread pleasures more into command
  Than to entreaty.
GUIL.   But we both obey,
  And here give up ourselves in the full bent   30
  To lay our service freely at your feet,
  To be commanded.
KING. Thanks, Rosencrantz and gentle Guildenstern.
QUEEN. Thanks, Guildenstern and gentle Rosencrantz.
  And I beseech you instantly to visit   35
  My too much changed son. Go, some of you,
  And bring these gentlemen where Hamlet is.
GUIL. Heavens make our presence and our practices
  Pleasant and helpful to him!
QUEEN.   Ay, amen!
    Exeunt ROSENCRANTZ *and* GUILDENSTERN [*with some* AT-
    TENDANTS].

    Enter POLONIUS.
POL. Th' ambassadors from Norway, my good lord,   40
  Are joyfully returned.
KING. Thou still hast been the father of good news.
POL. Have I, my lord? I assure you, my good liege,
  I hold my duty as I hold my soul,
  Both to my God and to my gracious king;   45
  And I do think—or else this brain of mine
  Hunts not the trail of policy so sure
  As it hath used to do—that I have found
  The very cause of Hamlet's lunacy.
KING. O, speak of that, that do I long to hear.   50
POL. Give first admittance to th' ambassadors.
  My news shall be the fruit to that great feast.
KING. Thyself do grace to them, and bring them in.
                              [*Exit* POLONIUS.]
  He tells me, my dear Gertrude, he hath found
  The head and source of all your son's distemper.   55
QUEEN. I doubt it is no other but the main,
  His father's death and our o'erhasty marriage.
KING. Well, we shall sift him.

    Enter Ambassadors [(VOLTEMAND *and* CORNELIUS), *with*
    POLONIUS].
                    Welcome, my good friends,
  Say, Voltemand, what from our brother Norway?
VOLT. Most fair return of greetings and desires.   60
  Upon our first, he sent out to suppress

42. *still* ever.   56. *doubt* suspect.

His nephew's levies, which to him appeared
To be a preparation 'gainst the Polack,
But better looked into, he truly found
It was against your highness, whereat grieved, 65
That so his sickness, age, and impotence
Was falsely borne in hand, sends out arrests
On Fortinbras, which he in brief obeys,
Receives rebuke from Norway, and in fine,
Makes vow before his uncle never more 70
To give th' assay of arms against your majesty.
Whereon old Norway, overcome with joy,
Gives him threescore thousand crowns in annual fee,
And his commission to employ those soldiers,
So levied as before, against the Polack, 75
With an entreaty, herein further shown, [*Gives a paper.*]
That it might please you to give quiet pass
Through your dominions for this enterprise,
On such regards of safety and allowance
As therein are set down.
KING.   It like us well, 80
And at our more considered time we'll read,
Answer, and think upon this business.
Meantime we thank you for your well-took labor.
Go to your rest; at night we'll feast together.
Most welcome home!   *Exeunt* AMBASSADORS.
POL.   This business is well ended. 85
My liege and madam, to expostulate
What majesty should be, what duty is,
Why day is day, night night, and time is time,
Were nothing but to waste night, day, and time.
Therefore, since brevity is the soul of wit, 90
And tediousness the limbs and outward flourishes,
I will be brief. Your noble son is mad.
Mad call I it, for to define true madness,
What is't but to be nothing else but mad?
But let that go.
QUEEN.   More matter with less art. 95
POL. Madam, I swear I use no art at all.
That he is mad, 'tis true: 'tis true 'tis pity,
And pity 'tis 'tis true. A foolish figure,
But farewell it, for I will use no art.
Mad let us grant him, then, and now remains 100
That we find out the cause of this effect,
Or rather say the cause of this defect,

63. *the Polack* the Polish nation.
67. *borne in hand* deceived.
69. *in fine* in the end.
71. *assay* trial.

79. *regards* considerations.
90. *wit* understanding.
95. *matter* meaning, sense.

For this effect defective comes by cause.
Thus it remains, and the remainder thus.
Perpend.   105
I have a daughter—have while she is mine—
Who in her duty and obedience, mark,
Hath given me this. Now gather, and surmise.   [*Reads.*]
    'To the celestial, and my soul's idol, the most beautified
Ophelia.'—That's an ill phrase, a vile phrase, 'beautified' is a 110
vile phrase. But you shall hear. Thus: [*Reads.*]
    'In her excellent white bosom, these, etc.'
QUEEN. Came this from Hamlet to her?
POL. Good madam, stay awhile. I will be faithful.

                                        [*Reads Letter.*]

            'Doubt thou the stars are fire,   115
                Doubt that the sun doth move;
                Doubt truth to be a liar;
                But never doubt I love.

        O dear Ophelia, I am ill at these numbers.
I have not art to reckon my groans, but that I love thee best, O 120
most best, believe it. Adieu.
                        Thine evermore, most dear lady, whilst
                            this machine is to him, HAMLET.'
This in obedience hath my daughter shown me,
And more above, hath his solicitings,   125
As they fell out by time, by means, and place,
All given to mine ear.
KING.   But how hath she
Received his love?
POL.   What do you think of me?
KING. As of a man faithful and honorable.
POL. I would fain prove so. But what might you think,   130
When I had seen this hot love on the wing,
(As I perceived it, I must tell you that,
Before my daughter told me), what might you,
Or my dear majesty your queen here, think,
If I had played the desk or table-book,   135
Or given my heart a winking, mute and dumb,
Or looked upon this love with idle sight,
What might you think? No, I went round to work,
And my young mistress thus I did bespeak:
'Lord Hamlet is a prince out of thy star.   140
This must not be'. And then I prescripts gave her,
That she should lock herself from his resort,
Admit no messengers, receive no tokens.

105. *Perpend* consider.   103. *machine* body.
119. *numbers* verses.   138. *round* directly.

Which done, she took the fruits of my advice;
And he repelled, a short tale to make,   145
Fell into a sadness, then into a fast,
Thence to a watch, thence into a weakness,
Thence to a lightness, and by this declension,
Into the madness wherein now he raves,
And all we mourn for.
KING.   Do you think 'tis this?   150
QUEEN. It may be, very like.
POL. Hath there been such a time—I would fain know that—
    That I have positively said ' 'Tis so',
    When it proved otherwise?
KING.   Not that I know.
POL. [*Pointing to his head and shoulder.*] Take this from this, if
    this be otherwise.   155
    If circumstances lead me, I will find
    Where truth is hid, though it were hid indeed
    Within the centre.
KING.   How may we try it further?
POL. You know sometimes he walks four hours together
    Here in the lobby.
QUEEN.   So he does, indeed.   160
POL. At such a time I'll loose my daughter to him.
    Be you and I behind an arras then.
    Mark the encounter. If he love her not,
    And be not from his reason fall'n thereon,
    Let me be no assistant for a state,   165
    But keep a farm and carters.
KING.   We will try it.

            Enter HAMLET [*reading on a book*].
QUEEN. But look where sadly the poor wretch comes reading.
POL. Away, I do beseech you both away,
    I'll board him presently.
            [*Exeunt*] KING *and* QUEEN [*with* ATTENDANTS].
            O, give me leave.
    How does my good Lord Hamlet?   170
HAM. Well, God-a-mercy.
POL. Do you know me, my lord?
HAM. Excellent well, you are a fishmonger.
POL. Not I, my lord.
HAM. Then I would you were so honest a man.   175
POL. Honest, my lord?
HAM. Ay, sir, to be honest as this world goes, is to be one man
    picked out of ten thousand.
POL. That's very true, my lord.

147. *watch* sleeplessness.
148. *lightness* lightheadedness.
158. *centre* centre of the earth and of
the Ptolemaic universe.
169. *board* accost; *presently* immediately.

HAM. For if the sun breed maggots in a dead dog, being a god 180
kissing carrion—Have you a daughter?

POL. I have, my lord.

HAM. Let her not walk i' th' sun. Conception is a blessing, but as
your daughter may conceive—friend, look to't.

POL. How say you by that? [*Aside*.] Still harping on my daughter. 185
Yet he knew me not at first. 'A said I was a fishmonger. 'A is
far gone. And truly in my youth I suffered much extremity for
love. Very near this. I'll speak to him again.—What do you
read, my lord?

HAM. Words, words, words.   190

POL. What is the matter, my lord?

HAM. Between who?

POL. I mean the matter that you read, my lord.

HAM. Slanders, sir; for the satirical rogue says here that old men
have grey beards, that their faces are wrinkled, their eyes purg- 195
ing thick amber and plum-tree gum, and that they have a
plentiful lack of wit, together with most weak hams—all
which, sir, though I most powerfully and potently believe, yet
I hold it not honesty to have it thus set down, for yourself,
sir, shall grow old as I am, if like a crab you could go back- 200
ward.

POL. [*Aside*.] Though this be madness, yet there is method in't.
—Will you walk out of the air, my lord?

HAM. Into my grave?

POL. [*Aside*.] Indeed, that's out of the air. How pregnant some- 205
time his replies are! a happiness that often madness hits on,
which reason and sanity could not so prosperously be delivered
of. I will leave him, and suddenly contrive the means of meeting between him and my daughter.—My lord. I will take my
leave of you.   210

HAM. You cannot take from me anything that I will more willingly part withal—except my life, except my life, except my
life.

Enter GUILDENSTERN *and* ROSENCRANTZ.

POL. Fare you well, my lord.

HAM. These tedious old fools!   215

POL. You go to seek the Lord Hamlet. There he is.

ROS. [*To* POLONIUS.] God save you, sir!   [*Exit* POLONIUS.]

GUIL. My honored lord!

ROS. My most dear lord!

HAM. My excellent good friends! How dost thou, Guildenstern? 220
Ah, Rosencrantz! Good lads, how do you both?

ROS. As the indifferent children of the earth.

GUIL. Happy in that we are not over-happy;

205. *pregnant* full of meaning.   222. *indifferent* average.
206. *happiness* aptness.

On Fortune's cap we are not the very button.

HAM. Nor the soles of her shoe? 225

ROS. Neither, my lord.

HAM. Then you live about her waist, or in the middle of her favors.

GUIL. Faith, her privates we.

HAM. In the secret parts of Fortune? O, most true, she is a 230 strumpet. What news?

ROS. None, my lord, but that the world's grown honest.

HAM. Then is doomsday near. But your news is not true. Let me question more in particular. What have you, my good friends, deserved at the hands of Fortune, that she sends you to prison 235 hither?

GUIL. Prison, my lord?

HAM. Denmark's a prison.

ROS. Then is the world one.

HAM. A goodly one, in which there are many confines, wards, 240 and dungeons, Denmark being one o' th' worst.

ROS. We think not so, my lord.

HAM. Why then 'tis none to you; for there is nothing either good or bad, but thinking makes it so. To me it is a prison.

ROS. Why then your ambition makes it one. 'Tis too narrow for 245 your mind.

HAM. O God, I could be bounded in a nutshell and count myself a king of infinite space, were it not that I have bad dreams.

GUIL. Which dreams indeed are ambition; for the very substance of the ambitious is merely the shadow of a dream. 250

HAM. A dream itself is but a shadow.

ROS. Truly, and I hold ambition of so airy and light a quality that it is but a shadow's shadow.

HAM. Then are our beggars bodies, and our monarchs and outstretched heroes the beggars' shadows. Shall we to th' court? 255 for, by my fay, I cannot reason.

BOTH. We'll wait upon you.

HAM. No such matter. I will not sort you with the rest of my servants; for to speak to you like an honest man, I am most dreadfully attended. But in the beaten way of friendship, what 260 make you at Elsinore?

ROS. To visit you, my lord; no other occasion.

HAM. Beggar that I am, I am even poor in thanks, but I thank you; and sure, dear friends, my thanks are too dear a halfpenny. Were you not sent for? Is it your own inclining? Is it 265 a free visitation? Come, come, deal justly with me. Come, come, nay speak.

GUIL. What should we say, my lord?

HAM. Why anything but to th' purpose. You were sent for, and

224. *button* knob on the top of a cap.   258. *sort you with* put you in the same
256. *fay* faith.   class with.

there is a kind of confession in your looks, which your modes- 270
ties have not craft enough to color. I know the good king and
queen have sent for you.

ROS. To what end, my lord?

HAM. That you must teach me. But let me conjure you by the
rights of our fellowship, by the consonancy of our youth, by 275
the obligation of our ever-preserved love, and by what more
dear a better proposer can charge you withal, be even and direct with me whether you were sent for or no.

ROS. [*Aside to* GUILDENSTERN.] What say you?

HAM. [*Aside.*] Nay, then, I have an eye of you.—If you love me, 280
hold not off.

GUIL. My lord, we were sent for.

HAM. I will tell you why; so shall my anticipation prevent your
discovery, and your secrecy to the king and queen moult no
feather. I have of late—but wherefore I know not—lost all 285
my mirth, forgone all custom of exercises; and indeed it goes
so heavily with my disposition, that this goodly frame the
earth seems to me a sterile promontory, this most excellent
canopy the air, look you, this brave o'er-hanging firmament,
this majestical roof fretted with golden fire, why it appeareth 290
nothing to me but a foul and pestilent congregation of vapors.
What a piece of work is a man, how noble in reason, how infinite in faculties, in form and moving, how express and admirable in action, how like an angel in apprehension, how
like a god: the beauty of the world, the paragon of animals. 295
And yet to me, what is this quintessence of dust? Man delights not me, nor woman neither, though by your smiling you
seem to say so.

ROS. My lord, there was no such stuff in my thoughts.

HAM. Why did ye laugh, then, when I said 'Man delights not 300
me'?

ROS. To think, my lord, if you delight not in man, what lenten
entertainment the players shall receive from you. We coted
them on the way, and hither are they coming to offer you
service. 305

HAM. He that plays the king shall be welcome—his majesty shall
have tribute on me; the adventurous knight shall use his foil
and target; the lover shall not sigh gratis; the humorous man
shall end his part in peace; the clown shall make those laugh
whose lungs are tickle o' th' sere; and the lady shall say her 310
mind freely, or the blank verse shall halt for't. What players

283. *prevent* forestall.
284. *discovery* disclosure.
290. *fretted* decorated with fretwork.
302. *lenten* scanty.
303. *coted* passed.
307–8. *foil and target* spear and shield.
308. *humorous man* the actor who plays

the eccentric character dominated by
one of the four humors.
310. *tickle o' th' sere* easily set off
(*sere* is that part of a gunlock which
keeps the hammer at full or half cock).
311. *halt* limp.

are they?

ROS. Even those you were wont to take such delight in, the tragedians of the city.

HAM. How chances it they travel? Their residence, both in repu- ₃₁₅ tation and profit, was better both ways.

ROS. I think their inhibition comes by the means of the late innovation.

HAM. Do they hold the same estimation they did when I was in the city? Are they so followed? ₃₂₀

ROS. No, indeed, are they not.

HAM. How comes it? Do they grow rusty?

ROS. Nay, their endeavor keeps in the wonted pace; but there is, sir, an eyrie of children, little eyases, that cry out on the top of question, and are most tyrannically clapped for't. These are ₃₂₅ now the fashion, and so berattle the common stages (so they call them) that many wearing rapiers are afraid of goose quills and dare scarce come thither.

HAM. What, are they children? Who maintains 'em? How are they escoted? Will they pursue the quality no longer than they ₃₃₀ can sing? Will they not say afterwards, if they should grow themselves to common players (as it is most like, if their means are not better), their writers do them wrong to make them exclaim against their own succession?

ROS. Faith, there has been much to do on both sides; and the na- ₃₃₅ tion holds it no sin to tarre them to controversy. There was for a while no money bid for argument, unless the poet and the player went to cuffs in the question.

HAM. Is't possible?

GUIL. O, there has been much throwing about of brains. ₃₄₀

HAM. Do the boys carry it away?

ROS. Ay, that they do, my lord, Hercules and his load too.

HAM. It is not very strange, for my uncle is King of Denmark, and those that would make mouths at him while my father lived give twenty, forty, fifty, a hundred ducats apiece for his ₃₄₅

317. *inhibition* prohibition of plays by authority (possibly with reference to decree of the Privy Council of 22 June 1600, limiting the number of London theater companies to two, and stipulating that the two were to perform only twice a week); *innovation* meaning uncertain (generally taken to refer to the re-introduction, ca. 1600, on the London theatrical scene of companies of boy actors performing in private theaters; sometimes interpreted as "political upheaval," with special reference to Essex's rebellion, February, 1601).
324. *eyrie* nest; *eyases* nestling hawks (here, the boys in the children's companies training as actors).
324–25. *on the top of question* louder

than all others on matter of dispute.
326. *common stages* public theaters of the *common players* (below, line 332), organized in companies composed mainly of adult actors.
327. *goose quills* pens (of the satiric dramatists writing for the private theaters).
330. *escoted* maintained; *pursue the quality* continue in the profession of acting.
331. *sing* i.e., until their voices change.
336. *tarre* incite.
337. *argument* plot of a play.
342. *load* i.e., the world (the sign of the Globe Theatre represented Hercules bearing the world on his shoulders).
344. *mouths* grimaces.

picture in little. 'Sblood, there is something in this more than
natural, if philosophy could find it out.   *A flourish.*

GUIL. There are the players.

HAM. Gentlemen, you are welcome to Elsinore. Your hands.
Come then, th' appurtenance of welcome is fashion and cere- 350
mony. Let me comply with you in this garb, lest my extent
to the players, which I tell you must show fairly outwards,
should more appear like entertainment than yours. You are
welcome. But my uncle-father and aunt-mother are deceived.

GUIL. In what, my dear lord?   355

HAM. I am but mad north-north-west; when the wind is south-
erly I know a hawk from a handsaw.

        Enter POLONIUS.

POL. Well be with you, gentlemen.

HAM. Hark you, Guildenstern—and you too—at each ear a
hearer. That great baby you see there is not yet out of his 360
swaddling clouts.

ROS. Happily he is the second time come to them, for they say
an old man is twice a child.

HAM. I will prophesy he comes to tell me of the players. Mark it.
—You say right, sir, a Monday morning, 'twas then indeed. 365

POL. My lord, I have news to tell you.

HAM. My lord, I have news to tell you.
When Roscius was an actor in Rome—

POL. The actors are come hither, my lord.

HAM. Buzz, buzz.   370

POL. Upon my honor—

HAM. Then came each actor on his ass—

POL. The best actors in the world, either for tragedy, comedy,
history, pastoral, pastoral-comical, historical-pastoral, tragical-
historical, tragical-comical-historical-pastoral, scene individ- 375
able, or poem unlimited. Seneca cannot be too heavy nor
Plautus too light. For the law of writ and the liberty, these are
the only men.

HAM. O Jephthah, judge of Israel, what a treasure hadst thou!

POL. What a treasure had he, my lord?   380

HAM. Why—

346. *in little* in miniature.
350. *appurtenance* adjuncts.
351. *extent* welcome.
357. *hawk* mattock or pickaxe (also
called "hack," here used with a play
on *hawk* as a bird); *handsaw* a saw
managed with one hand (here used
with a play on some corrupt form of
kernshaw, "heron").
362. *Happily* perhaps.
368. *Roscius* the greatest of Roman
comic actors, though regarded by the
Elizabethans as a tragic one.

375–76. *scene individable* i.e., a play
which observes the unities of time and
place.
376. *poem unlimited* a play that does
not observe the unities; *Seneca* Roman
writer of tragedies.
377. *Plautus* Roman comic dramatist;
law of writ and the liberty i.e., plays
according to strict classical rules, and
those that ignored the unities of time
and place.
379. *Jephthah* was compelled to sacrifice a beloved daughter (Judges xi).

'One fair daughter, and no more,
The which he loved passing well'.

POL. [*Aside.*] Still on my daughter.
HAM. Am I not i' th' right, old Jephthah?   385
POL. If you call me Jephthah, my lord, I have a daughter that I
love passing well.
HAM. Nay, that follows not.
POL. What follows then, my lord?
HAM. Why—   390

'As by lot, God wot'

and then, you know,

'It came to pass, as most like it was'.

The first row of the pious chanson will show you more, for
look where my abridgement comes.   395

Enter the PLAYERS.
You are welcome, masters; welcome, all.—I am glad to see
thee well.—Welcome, good friends.—O, old friend! Why thy
face is valanced since I saw thee last. Com'st thou to beard
me in Denmark?—What, my young lady and mistress? By'r
lady, your ladyship is nearer to heaven than when I saw you   400
last by the altitude of a chopine. Pray God your voice, like a
piece of uncurrent gold, be not cracked within the ring.—
Masters, you are all welcome. We'll e'en to't like French fal-
coners, fly at anything we see. We'll have a speech straight.
Come give us a taste of your quality, come a passionate speech. 405
1 PLAY. What speech, my good lord?
HAM. I heard thee speak me a speech once, but it was never acted,
or if it was, not above once, for the play, I remember, pleased
not the million; 'twas caviary to the general. But it was—as I
received it, and others whose judgments in such matters cried   410
in the top of mine—an excellent play, well digested in the
scenes, set down with as much modesty as cunning. I remember one said there were no sallets in the lines to make the
matter savory, nor no matter in the phrase that might indict
the author of affectation, but called it an honest method, as   415
wholesome as sweet, and by very much more handsome than
fine. One speech in't I chiefly loved. 'Twas Æneas' tale to

394. *row* stanza.
398. *valanced* bearded.
399. *young lady* i.e., the boy who plays
female roles.
401. *chopine* a shoe with high cork heel
and sole.
402. *cracked within the ring* a coin
cracked within the circle surrounding
the head of the sovereign was no

longer legal tender and so *uncurrent*.
404. *straight* immediately.
409. *caviary* caviare; *general* multitude.
411. *digested* arranged.
413. *sallets* salads, highly seasoned
passages.
416–17. *more handsome than fine* admirable rather than appealing by mere
cleverness.

Dido, and thereabout of it especially where he speaks of
Priam's slaughter. If it live in your memory, begin at this
line—let me see, let me see: 420

'The rugged Pyrrhus, like th' Hyrcanian beast'—

'tis not so; it begins with Pyrrhus—

"The rugged Pyrrhus, he whose sable arms,
Black as his purpose, did the night resemble
When he lay couchéd in th' ominous horse,   425
Hath now this dread and black complexion smeared
With heraldry more dismal; head to foot
Now is he total gules, horridly tricked
With blood of fathers, mothers, daughters, sons,
Baked and impasted with the parching streets,   430
That lend a tyrannous and a damnéd light
To their lord's murder. Roasted in wrath and fire,
And thus o'er-sizéd with coagulate gore,
With eyes like carbuncles, the hellish Pyrrhus
Old grandsire Priam seeks.'   435

So proceed you.
POL. Fore God, my lord, well spoken, with good accent and
good discretion.
1 PLAY.   'Anon he finds him
Striking too short at Greeks. His antique sword,   440
Rebellious to his arm, lies where it falls,
Repugnant to command. Unequal matched,
Pyrrhus at Priam drives, in rage strikes wide.
But with the whiff and wind of his fell sword
Th' unnervéd father falls. Then senseless Ilium,   445
Seeming to feel this blow, with flaming top
Stoops to his base, and with a hideous crash
Takes prisoner Pyrrhus' ear. For, lo! his sword,
Which was declining on the milky head
Of reverend Priam, seemed i' th' air to stick.   450
So as a painted tyrant Pyrrhus stood,
And like a neutral to his will and matter,
Did nothing.
But as we often see, against some storm,
A silence in the heavens, the rack stand still,   455
The bold winds speechless, and the orb below
As hush as death, anon the dreadful thunder
Doth rend the region; so, after Pyrrhus' pause,

421. *Hyrcanian beast* tiger.
425. *horse* i.e., the Trojan horse.
428. *gules* heraldic term for red.
433. *o'er-sized* covered as with size;
coagulate clotted.

442. *Repugnant* refractory.
444. *fell* fierce, cruel.
454. *against* just before.
455. *rack* mass of cloud.
458. *region* air.

A roused vengeance sets him new awork,
And never did the Cyclops' hammers fall 460
On Mars's armor, forged for proof eterne,
With less remorse than Pyrrhus' bleeding sword
Now falls on Priam.
Out, out, thou strumpet, Fortune! All you gods,
In general synod take away her power, 465
Break all the spokes and fellies from her wheel,
And bowl the round nave down the hill of heaven
As low as to the fiends.'
POL. This is too long.
HAM. It shall to the barber's with your beard.—Prithee say on. 470
He's for a jig, or a tale of bawdry, or he sleeps. Say on; come
to Hecuba.
1 PLAY. 'But who, ah woe! had seen the mobled queen—'
HAM. 'The mobled queen'?
POL. That's good. 475
1 PLAY. 'Run barefoot up and down, threat'ning the flames
    With bisson rheum, a clout upon that head
    Where late the diadem stood, and for a robe,
    About her lank and all o'er-teeméd loins,
    A blanket, in the alarm of fear caught up— 480
    Who this had seen, with tongue in venom steeped,
    'Gainst Fortune's state would treason have pronounced.
    But if the gods themselves did see her then,
    When she saw Pyrrhus make malicious sport
    In mincing with his sword her husband's limbs, 485
    The instant burst of clamor that she made,
    Unless things mortal move them not at all,
    Would have made milch the burning eyes of heaven,
    And passion in the gods.'
POL. Look whe'r he has not turned his color, and has tears in's 490
eyes. Prithee no more.
HAM. 'Tis well. I'll have thee speak out the rest of this soon.—
Good my lord, will you see the players well bestowed? Do you
hear, let them be well used, for they are the abstract and brief
chronicles of the time; after your death you were better have 495
a bad epitaph than their ill report while you live.
POL. My lord, I will use them according to their desert.
HAM. God's bodkin, man, much better. Use every man after his
desert, and who shall 'scape whipping? Use them after your
own honor and dignity. The less they deserve, the more merit 500

460. *Cyclops* giant workmen who made armor in the smithy of Vulcan.
461. *proof eterne* to be forever impenetrable.
466. *fellies* the curved pieces forming the rim of a wheel.
467. *nave* hub of a wheel.
473. *mobled* muffled.
477. *bisson rheum* blinding tears.
479. *o'er-teemed* exhausted by many births.
482. *state* government.
488. *milch* moist, tearful (lit., milk-giving).
494. *abstract* summary account.
498. *God's bodkin* by God's dear body.

is in your bounty. Take them in.

POL. Come, sirs.

HAM. Follow him, friends. We'll hear a play to-morrow. [*Aside
to First Player.*] Dost thou hear me, old friend, can you play
'The Murder of Gonzago'?   505

1 PLAY. Ay, my lord.

HAM. We'll ha't to-morrow night. You could for a need study a
speech of some dozen or sixteen lines which I would set down
and insert in't, could you not?

1 PLAY. Ay, my lord.   510

HAM. Very well. Follow that lord, and look you mock him not.

                     Exeunt POLONIUS *and* PLAYERS.

My good friends, I'll leave you till night. You are welcome to
Elsinore.

ROS. Good my lord. *Exeunt* [ROSENCRANTZ *and* GUILDENSTERN].

HAM. Ay, so God buy to you. Now I am alone.   515

  O, what a rogue and peasant slave am I!

  Is it not monstrous that this player here,

  But in a fiction, in a dream of passion,

  Could force his soul so to his own conceit

  That from her working all his visage wanned;   .520

  Tears in his eyes, distraction in his aspect,

  A broken voice, and his whole function suiting

  With forms to his conceit? And all for nothing,

  For Hecuba!

  What's Hecuba to him or he to her,   525

  That he should weep for her? What would he do

  Had he the motive and the cue for passion

  That I have? He would drown the stage with tears,

  And cleave the general ear with horrid speech,

  Make mad the guilty, and appal the free,   530

  Confound the ignorant, and amaze indeed

  The very faculties of eyes and ears.

  Yet I,

  A dull and muddy-mettled rascal, peak

  Like John-a-dreams, unpregnant of my cause,   535

  And can say nothing; no, not for a king

  Upon whose property and most dear life

  A damned defeat was made. Am I a coward?

  Who calls me villain, breaks my pate across,

  Plucks off my beard and blows it in my face,   540

  Tweaks me by the nose, gives me the lie i' th' throat

  As deep as to the lungs? Who does me this?

  Ha, 'swounds, I should take it; for it cannot be

  But I am pigeon-livered and lack gall

519. *conceit* imagination.
529. *general* public.
534. *muddy-mettled* dull-spirited; *peak*

mope.
535. *unpregnant* not quickened to action.

To make oppression bitter, or ere this   545
I should 'a fatted all the region kites
With this slave's offal. Bloody, bawdy villain!
Remorseless, treacherous, lecherous, kindless villain!
Why, what an ass am I! This is most brave,
That I, the son of a dear father murdered,   550
Prompted to my revenge by heaven and hell,
Must like a whore unpack my heart with words,
And fall a-cursing like a very drab,
A stallion! Fie upon't! foh!
About, my brains. Hum—I have heard   555
That guilty creatures sitting at a play,
Have by the very cunning of the scene
Been struck so to the soul that presently
They have proclaimed their malefactions;
For murder, though it have no tongue, will speak   560
With most miraculous organ. I'll have these players
Play something like the murder of my father
Before mine uncle. I'll observe his looks.
I'll tent him to the quick. If 'a do blench,
I know my course. The spirit that I have seen   565
May be a devil, and the devil hath power
T' assume a pleasing shape, yea, and perhaps
Out of my weakness and my melancholy,
As he is very potent with such spirits,
Abuses me to damn me. I'll have grounds   570
More relative than this. The play's the thing
Wherein I'll catch the conscience of the king.   *Exit.*

[III.i]

> *Enter* KING, QUEEN, POLONIUS, OPHELIA, ROSENCRANTZ,
> GUILDENSTERN, LORDS.

KING. And can you by no drift of conference
Get from him why he puts on this confusion,
Grating so harshly all his days of quiet
With turbulent and dangerous lunacy?
ROS. He does confess he feels himself distracted,   5
But from what cause 'a will by no means speak.
GUIL. Nor do we find him forward to be sounded,

---

546. *region kites* kites of the air.
548. *kindless* unnatural. Following this line, *F* adds the words "Oh Vengeance!" Their inappropriateness to the occasion is noted by Professor Harold Jenkins (in his "Playhouse Interpolations in the Folio Text of Hamlet," *Studies in Bibliography*, XIII [1960], 37). Professor Jenkins remarks that the folio text, by introducing Hamlet's "call for vengeance while he is still absorbed in self-reproaches, both anticipates and misconstrues" the crisis of his passion and of the speech, which comes in fact at line 555 ("About, my brains"), when "he abandons his self-reproaches and plans action."
554. *stallion* prostitute (male or female).
558. *presently* immediately.
564. *tent* probe; *blench* flinch.
570. *Abuses* deludes.
571. *relative* relevant.

[III.i] 7. *forward* willing.

But with a crafty madness keeps aloof
When we would bring him on to some confession
Of his true state.
QUEEN.   Did he receive you well?   10
ROS. Most like a gentleman.
GUIL. But with much forcing of his disposition.
ROS. Niggard of question, but of our demands
  Most free in his reply.
QUEEN.   Did you assay him
  To any pastime?   15
ROS. Madam, it so fell out that certain players
  We o'er-raught on the way. Of these we told him,
  And there did seem in him a kind of joy
  To hear of it. They are here about the court,
  And as I think, they have already order   20
  This night to play before him.
POL.   'Tis most true,
  And he beseeched me to entreat your majesties
  To hear and see the matter.
KING. With all my heart, and it doth much content me
  To hear him so inclined.   25
  Good gentlemen, give him a further edge,
  And drive his purpose into these delights.
ROS. We shall, my lord. *Exeunt* ROSENCRANTZ *and* GUILDENSTERN.
KING.   Sweet Gertrude, leave us too,
  For we have closely sent for Hamlet hither,
  That he, as 'twere by accident, may here   30
  Affront Ophelia.
  Her father and myself (lawful espials)
  Will so bestow ourselves that, seeing unseen,
  We may of their encounter frankly judge,
  And gather by him, as he is behaved,   35
  If't be th' affliction of his love or no
  That thus he suffers for.
QUEEN.   I shall obey you.—
  And for your part, Ophelia, I do wish
  That your good beauties be the happy cause
  Of Hamlet's wildness. So shall I hope your virtues   40
  Will bring him to his wonted way again,
  To both your honors.
OPH.   Madam, I wish it may.   [*Exit* QUEEN.]
POL. Ophelia, walk you here.—Gracious, so please you,
  We will bestow ourselves.—[*to* OPHELIA] Read on this book,
  That show of such an exercise may color   45

14. *assay* try to win.
17. *o'er-raught* overtook.
26. *give him a further edge* sharpen his
inclination.
29. *closely* privately.

31. *Affront* meet face to face.
32. *espials* spies.
45. *exercise* act of devotion; *color* give
an appearance of naturalness to.

Your loneliness.—We are oft to blame in this,
'Tis too much proved, that with devotion's visage
And pious action we do sugar o'er
The devil himself.
KING. [*Aside*.]   O, 'tis too true.
How smart a lash that speech doth give my conscience!   50
The harlot's cheek, beautied with plast'ring art,
Is not more ugly to the thing that helps it
Than is my deed to my most painted word.
O heavy burden!
POL. I hear him coming. Let's withdraw, my lord.   55
                              [*Exeunt* KING *and* POLONIUS.]

          Enter HAMLET.
HAM. To be, or not to be, that is the question:
Whether 'tis nobler in the mind to suffer
The slings and arrows of outrageous fortune,
Or to take arms against a sea of troubles,
And by opposing end them. To die, to sleep—   60
No more; and by a sleep to say we end
The heartache, and the thousand natural shocks
That flesh is heir to. 'Tis a consumation
Devoutly to be wished—to die, to sleep—
To sleep, perchance to dream, ay there's the rub;   65
For in that sleep of death what dreams may come
When we have shuffled off this mortal coil
Must give us pause—there's the respect
That makes calamity of so long life.
For who would bear the whips and scorns of time,   70
Th' oppressor's wrong, the proud man's contumely,
The pangs of despised love, the law's delay,
The insolence of office, and the spurns
That patient merit of th' unworthy takes,
When he himself might his quietus make   75
With a bare bodkin? Who would fardels bear,
To grunt and sweat under a weary life,
But that the dread of something after death,
The undiscovered country, from whose bourn
No traveller returns, puzzles the will,   80
And makes us rather bear those ills we have
Than fly to others that we know not of?
Thus conscience does make cowards of us all;
And thus the native hue of resolution
Is sicklied o'er with the pale cast of thought,   85
And enterprises of great pitch and moment

52. *to* compared to.
65. *rub* obstacle (lit., obstruction encountered by bowler's ball).
67. *coil* bustle, turmoil.

75. *quietus* settlement.
76. *bodkin* dagger; *fardels* burdens.
79. *bourn* realm.
86. *pitch* height.

With this regard their currents turn awry
And lose the name of action.—Soft you now,
The fair Ophelia.—Nymph, in thy orisons
Be all my sins remembered.

OPH.   Good my lord,   90
How does your honor for this many a day?

HAM. I humbly thank you, well.

OPH. My lord, I have remembrances of yours
That I have longed long to re-deliver.
I pray you now receive them.

HAM.   No, not I,   95
I never gave you aught.

OPH. My honored lord, you know right well you did,
And with them words of so sweet breath composed
As made the things more rich. Their perfume lost,
Take these again, for to the noble mind   100
Rich gifts wax poor when givers prove unkind.
There, my lord.

HAM. Ha, ha! are you honest?

OPH. My lord?

HAM. Are you fair?   105

OPH. What means your lordship?

HAM. That if you be honest and fair, your honesty should admit
no discourse to your beauty.

OPH. Could beauty, my lord, have better commerce than with
honesty?   110

HAM. Ay, truly, for the power of beauty will sooner transform
honesty from what it is to a bawd than the force of honesty
can translate beauty into his likeness. This was sometime a
paradox, but now the time gives it proof. I did love you once.

OPH. Indeed, my lord, you made me believe so.   115

HAM. You should not have believed me, for virtue cannot so
inoculate our old stock but we shall relish of it. I loved you not.

OPH. I was the more deceived.

HAM. Get thee to a nunnery. Why wouldst thou be a breeder
of sinners? I am myself indifferent honest, but yet I could ac- 120
cuse me of such things that it were better my mother had not
borne me: I am very proud, revengeful, ambitious, with more
offences at my beck than I have thoughts to put them in,
imagination to give them shape, or time to act them in. What
should such fellows as I do crawling between earth and heaven? 125
We are arrant knaves all; believe none of us. Go thy ways to a
nunnery. Where's your father?

OPH. At home, my lord.

HAM. Let the doors be shut upon him, that he may play the fool

87. *regard* consideration.
89. *orisons* prayers.
103. *honest* chaste.

117. *inoculate* graft.
120. *indifferent honest* moderately respectable.

nowhere but in's own house. Farewell.   130
OPH. O, help him, you sweet heavens!
HAM. If thou dost marry, I'll give thee this plague for thy dowry:
be thou as chaste as ice, as pure as snow, thou shalt not escape
calumny. Get thee to a nunnery, farewell. Or if thou wilt
needs marry, marry a fool, for wise men know well enough 135
what monsters you make of them. To a nunnery, go, and
quickly too. Farewell.
OPH. Heavenly powers, restore him!
HAM. I have heard of your paintings well enough. God hath given
you one face, and you make yourselves another. You jig and 140
amble, and you lisp; you nickname God's creatures, and make
your wantonness your ignorance. Go to, I'll no more on't, it
hath made me mad. I say we will have no moe marriage. Those
that are married already, all but one, shall live. The rest shall
keep as they are. To a nunnery, go.   *Exit.* 145
OPH. O, what a noble mind is here o'erthrown!
The courtier's, soldier's, scholar's, eye, tongue, sword,
Th' expectancy and rose of the fair state,
The glass of fashion and the mould of form,
Th' observed of all observers, quite quite down!   150
And I of ladies most deject and wretched,
That sucked the honey of his musicked vows,
Now see that noble and most sovereign reason
Like sweet bells jangled, out of time and harsh;
That unmatched form and feature of blown youth   155
Blasted with ecstasy. O, woe is me
T' have seen what I have seen, see what I see!

    Enter KING *and* POLONIUS.

KING. Love! His affections do not that way tend,
Nor what he spake, though it lacked form a little,
Was not like madness. There's something in his soul   160
O'er which his melancholy sits on brood,
And I do doubt the hatch and the disclose
Will be some danger; which to prevent,
I have in quick determination
Thus set it down: he shall with speed to England   165
For the demand of our neglected tribute.
Haply the seas and countries different,
With variable objects, shall expel
This something-settled matter in his heart
Whereon his brains still beating puts him thus   170
From fashion of himself. What think you on't?

141–42. *make your wantonness your ignorance* excuse your wanton behavior with the plea that you don't know any better.
143. *moe* more.
148. *expectancy* hope.
149. *glass* mirror.
155. *blown* blooming.
156. *ecstasy* madness.
158. *affections* emotions.
162. *doubt* fear.

POL. It shall do well. But yet do I believe
The origin and commencement of his grief
Sprung from neglected love.—How now, Ophelia?
You need not tell us what Lord Hamlet said,   175
We heard it all.—My lord, do as you please,
But if you hold it fit, after the play
Let his queen-mother all alone entreat him
To show his grief. Let her be round with him,
And I'll be placed, so please you, in the ear   180
Of all their conference. If she find him not,
To England send him; or confine him where
Your wisdom best shall think.
KING.   It shall be so.
Madness in great ones must not unwatched go.   *Exeunt.*

[III.ii]

Enter HAMLET *and three of the* PLAYERS.

HAM. Speak the speech, I pray you, as I pronounced it to you,
trippingly on the tongue; but if you mouth it as many of our
players do, I had as lief the town-crier spoke my lines. Nor do
not saw the air too much with your hand thus, but use all
gently, for in the very torrent, tempest, and as I may say, whirl-   5
wind of your passion, you must acquire and beget a temperance
that may give it smoothness. O, it offends me to the soul to
hear a robustious periwig-pated fellow tear a passion to tatters,
to very rags, to split the ears of the groundlings, who for the
most part are capable of nothing but inexplicable dumb shows   10
and noise. I would have such a fellow whipped for o'erdoing
Termagant. It out-herods Herod. Pray you avoid it.
1 PLAY. I warrant your honour.
HAM. Be not too tame neither, but let your own discretion be
your tutor. Suit the action to the word, the word to the action,   15
with this special observance, that you o'erstep not the modesty
of nature; for anything so o'erdone is from the purpose of playing, whose end both at the first, and now, was and is, to hold as
'twere the mirror up to nature, to show virture her own feature, scorn her own image, and the very age and body of the   20
time his form and pressure. Now this overdone, or come tardy
off, though it makes the unskilful laugh, cannot but make the
judicious grieve, the censure of the which one must in your
allowance o'erweigh a whole theatre of others. O, there be
players that I have seen play—and heard others praise, and   25
that highly—not to speak it profanely, that neither having th'

---

179. *round* plain-spoken.

[III.ii] 9. *groundlings* spectators who
paid least and stood on the ground.
12. *Termagant* thought to be a Mohammedan deity, and represented in

medieval mystery plays as a violent
and ranting personage; *Herod* represented in the mystery plays as a blus-
tering tyrant.
23. *censure* judgment, opinion.

accent of Christians, nor the gait of Christian, pagan, nor
man, have so strutted and bellowed that I have thought some
of nature's journeymen had made men, and not made them
well, they imitated humanity so abominably.   30
1 PLAY. I hope we have reformed that indifferently with us.
HAM. O, reform it altogether. And let those that play your clowns
speak no more than is set down for them, for there be of them
that will themselves laugh, to set on some quantity of barren
spectators to laugh too, though in the meantime some neces-   35
sary question of the play be then to be considered. That's vil-
lainous, and shows a most pitiful ambition in the fool that
uses it. Go, make you ready.   [*Exeunt* PLAYERS.]

    Enter POLONIUS, GUILDENSTERN, *and* ROSENCRANTZ.
How now, my lord? Will the king hear this piece of work?
POL. And the queen too, and that presently.   40
HAM. Bid the players make haste.   [*Exit* POLONIUS.]
  Will you two help to hasten them?
ROS Ay, my lord.   *Exeunt they two.*
HAM. What, ho, Horatio!

    Enter HORATIO.
HOR. Here, sweet lord, at your service.   45
HAM. Horatio, thou art e'en as just a man
  As e'er my conversation coped withal.
HOR. O my dear lord!
HAM.   Nay, do not think I flatter,
  For what advancement may I hope from thee,
  That no revenue hast but thy good spirits   50
  To feed and clothe thee? Why should the poor be flattered?
  No, let the candied tongue lick absurd pomp,
  And crook the pregnant hinges of the knee
  Where thrift may follow fawning. Dost thou hear?
  Since my dear soul was mistress of her choice   55
  And could of men distinguish her election,
  S'hath sealed thee for herself, for thou hast been
  As one in suff'ring all that suffers nothing,
  A man that Fortune's buffets and rewards
  Hast ta'en with equal thanks; and blest are those   60
  Whose blood and judgment are so well comeddled
  That they are not a pipe for Fortune's finger
  To sound what stop she please. Give me that man
  That is not passion's slave, and I will wear him
  In my heart's core, ay, in my heart of heart,   65
  As I do thee. Something too much of this.
  There is a play to-night before the king.
  One scene of it comes near the circumstance

31. *indifferently* fairly well.   54. *thrift* profit.
47. *coped* encountered.   56. *election* choice.
53. *pregnant* ready.   61. *comeddled* mingled.

Which I have told thee of my father's death.
I prithee, when thou seest that act afoot,   70
Even with the very comment of thy soul
Observe my uncle. If his occulted guilt
Do not itself unkennel in one speech,
It is a damnéd ghost that we have seen,
And my imaginations are as foul   75
As Vulcan's stithy. Give him heedful note,
For I mine eyes will rivet to his face,
And after we will both our judgments join
In censure of his seeming.
HOR.   Well, my lord.
If 'a steal aught the whilst this play is playing,   80
And 'scape detecting, I will pay the theft.

Enter Trumpets and Kettledrums, KING, QUEEN, POLONIUS,
OPHELIA [ROSENCRANTZ, GUILDENSTERN, *and other* LORDS
attendant].

HAM. They are coming to the play. I must be idle.
Get you a place.
KING. How fares our cousin Hamlet?
HAM. Excellent, i' faith, of the chameleon's dish. I eat the air, 85
promise-crammed. You cannot feed capons so.
KING. I have nothing with this answer, Hamlet. These words are
not mine.
HAM. No, nor mine now. [*To* POLONIUS.] My lord, you played
once i' th' university, you say?   90
POL. That did I, my lord, and was accounted a good actor.
HAM. What did you enact?
POL. I did enact Julius Cæsar. I was killed i' th' Capitol; Brutus
killed me.
HAM. It was a brute part of him to kill so capital a calf there. Be 95
the players ready?
ROS. Ay, my lord, they stay upon your patience.
QUEEN. Come hither, my dear Hamlet, sit by me.
HAM. No, good mother, here's metal more attractive.
POL. [*To the* KING.] O, ho! do you mark that?   100
HAM. Lady, shall I lie in your lap?
                              [*Lying down at* OPHELIA'S *feet.*]
OPH. No, my lord.
HAM. I mean, my head upon your lap?
OPH. Ay, my lord.
HAM. Do you think I meant country matters?   105
OPH. I think nothing, my lord.
HAM. That's a fair thought to lie between maids' legs.

71. *the very comment of thy soul* with   76. *stithy* forge.
a keenness of observation that pene-   79. *censure* opinion.
trates to the very being.   82. *idle* crazy.
72. *occulted* hidden.   85. *chameleon's dish* the air, on which
73. *unkennel* reveal.   the chameleon was supposed to feed.

OPH. What is, my lord?

HAM. Nothing.

OPH. You are merry, my lord.   110

HAM. Who, I?

OPH. Ay, my lord.

HAM. O God, your only jig-maker! What should a man do but be merry? For look you how cheerfully my mother looks, and my father died within's two hours.   115

OPH. Nay, 'tis twice two months, my lord.

HAM. So long? Nay then, let the devil wear black, for I'll have a suit of sables. O heavens! die two months ago, and not forgotten yet? Then there's hope a great man's memory may outlive his life half a year, but by'r lady 'a must build churches 120 then, or else shall 'a suffer not thinking on, with the hobbyhorse, whose epitaph is 'For O, for O, the hobby-horse is forgot!'

The trumpets sound. Dumb Show follows.

Enter a KING *and a* QUEEN [*very lovingly*]; *the* QUEEN *embracing him and he her.* [*She kneels, and makes show of protestation unto him.*] *He takes her up, and declines his head upon her neck. He lies him down upon a bank of flowers; she, seeing him asleep, leaves him. Anon come in another man, takes off his crown, kisses it, pours poison in the sleeper's ears, and leaves him. The* QUEEN *returns, finds the King dead, makes passionate action. The* POISONER *with some three or four come in again, seem to condole with her. The dead body is carried away. The* POISONER *woos the* QUEEN *with gifts; she seems harsh awhile, but in the end accepts love.*   [*Exeunt.*]

OPH. What means this, my lord?

HAM. Marry, this is miching mallecho; it means mischief.   125

OPH. Belike this show imports the argument of the play.

Enter PROLOGUE.

HAM. We shall know by this fellow. The players cannot keep counsel; they'll tell all.

OPH. Will a' tell us what this show meant?

HAM. Ay, or any show that you will show him. Be not you 130 ashamed to show, he'll not shame to tell you what it means.

OPH. You are naught, you are naught. I'll mark the play.

PRO.

> For us, and for our tragedy,
> Here stooping to your clemency,
> We beg your hearing patiently.   [*Exit.*] 135

HAM. Is this a prologue, or the posy of a ring?

OPH. 'Tis brief, my lord.

121–22. *hobby-horse* the figure of a horse fastened round the waist of a morris dancer.
125. *miching mallecho* skulking or crafty crime.
132. *naught* naughty, lewd.
136. *posy* brief motto engraved on a finger-ring.

HAM. As woman's love.

        Enter [*the* PLAYER] KING *and* QUEEN.

P. KING. *Full thirty times hath Phœbus' cart gone round*
  Neptune's salt wash and Tellus' orbéd ground,   140
  And thirty dozen moons with borrowed sheen
  About the world have times twelve thirties been,
  Since love our hearts and Hymen did our hands
  Unite comutual in most sacred bands.

P. QUEEN. *So many journeys may the sun and moon*   145
  Make us again count o'er ere love be done!
  But woe is me, you are so sick of late,
  So far from cheer and from your former state,
  That I distrust you. Yet though I distrust,
  Discomfort you, my lord, it nothing must.   150
  For women's fear and love hold quantity,
  In neither aught, or in extremity.
  Now what my love is proof hath made you know,
  And as my love is sized, my fear is so.
  Where love is great, the littlest doubts are fear;   155
  Where little fears grow great, great love grows there.

P. KING. *Faith, I must leave thee, love, and shortly too;*
  My operant powers their functions leave to do.
  And thou shalt live in this fair world behind,
  Honored, beloved, and haply one as kind   160
  For husband shalt thou—

P. QUEEN.   *O, confound the rest!*
  Such love must needs be treason in my breast.
  In second husband let me be accurst!
  None wed the second but who killed the first.

HAM. That's wormwood.   165

P. QUEEN. *The instances that second marriage move*
  Are base respects of thrift, but none of love.
  A second time I kill my husband dead,
  When second husband kisses me in bed.

P. KING. *I do believe you think what now you speak,*   170
  But what we do determine oft we break.
  Purpose is but the slave to memory,
  Of violent birth, but poor validity;
  Which now, the fruit unripe, sticks on the tree,
  But fall unshaken when they mellow be.   175
  Most necessary 'tis that we forget
  To pay ourselves what to ourselves is debt.

139. *Phœbus' cart* the sun's chariot.
140. *Tellus' orbed ground* the earth (Tellus was the Roman goddess of the earth).
143. *Hymen* god of marriage.
149. *distrust* fear for.
151. *hold quantity* are proportional, weigh alike.
154. *as my love is sized* according to the greatness of my love.
158. *operant* vital.
166. *instances* motives.
173. *validity* endurance.

What to ourselves in passion we propose,
The passion ending, doth the purpose lose.
The violence of either grief or joy   180
Their own enactures with themselves destroy.
Where joy most revels, grief doth most lament;
Grief joys, joy grieves, on slender accident.
This world is not for aye, nor 'tis not strange
That even our loves should with our fortunes change;   185
For 'tis a question left us yet to prove,
Whether love lead fortune, or else fortune love.
The great man down, you mark his favourite flies;
The poor advanced makes friends of enemies;
And hitherto doth love on fortune tend,   190
For who not needs shall never lack a friend,
And who in want a hollow friend doth try,
Directly seasons him his enemy.
But orderly to end where I begun,
Our wills and fates do so contrary run   195
That our devices still are overthrown;
Our thoughts are ours, their ends none of our own.
So think thou wilt no second husband wed,
But die thy thoughts when thy first lord is dead.
P. QUEEN. *Nor earth to me give food, nor heaven light,*   200
Sport and repose lock from me day and night,
To desperation turn my trust and hope,
An anchor's cheer in prison be my scope,
Each opposite that blanks the face of joy
Meet what I would have well, and it destroy,   205
Both here and hence pursue me lasting strife,
If once a widow, ever I be wife!
HAM. If she should break it now!
P. KING. *'Tis deeply sworn. Sweet, leave me here awhile.*
My spirits grow dull, and fain I would beguile   210
The tedious day with sleep.   [*Sleeps.*]
P. QUEEN.   *Sleep rock thy brain,*
And never come mischance between us twain!   *Exit.*
HAM. Madam, how like you this play?
QUEEN. The lady doth protest too much, methinks.
HAM. O, but she'll keep her word.   215
KING. Have you heard the argument? Is there no offence in't?
HAM. No, no, they do but jest, poison in jest; no offence i' th'
world.
KING. What do you call the play?
HAM. 'The Mouse-trap.' Marry, how? Tropically. This play is the   220
image of a murder done in Vienna. Gonzago is the duke's
name; his wife, Baptista. You shall see anon. 'Tis a knavish

---

181. *enactures* enactments.
184. *aye* ever.

193. *seasons him* ripens him into.
203. *anchor's* anchorite's.

piece of work, but what of that? Your majesty, and we that
have free souls, it touches us not. Let the galled jade wince,
our withers are unwrung.   225

    Enter LUCIANUS.
This is one Lucianus, nephew to the king.
OPH. You are as good as a chorus, my lord.
HAM. I could interpret between you and your love, if I could
see the puppets dallying.
OPH. You are keen, my lord, you are keen.   230
HAM. It would cost you a groaning to take off mine edge.
OPH. Still better, and worse.
HAM. So you mis-take your husbands.—Begin, murderer. Leave
thy damnable faces and begin. Come, the croaking raven
doth bellow for revenge.   235
LUC. *Thoughts black, hands apt, drugs fit, and time agreeing,*
Confederate season, else no creature seeing,
Thou mixture rank, of midnight weeds collected,
With Hecate's ban thrice blasted, thrice infected,
Thy natural magic and dire property   240
On wholesome life usurps immediately.
                  [*Pours the poison in his ears.*]
HAM. 'A poisons him i' th' garden for his estate. His name's
Gonzago. The story is extant, and written in very choice
Italian. You shall see anon how the murderer gets the love
of Gonzago's wife.   245
OPH. The king rises.
HAM. What, frighted with false fire?
QUEEN. How fares my lord?
POL. Give o'er the play.
KING. Give me some light. Away!   250
POL. Lights, lights, lights! *Exeunt all but* HAMLET *and* HORATIO.
HAM.   Why, let the strucken deer go weep,
        The hart ungalléd play.
    For some must watch while some must sleep;
        Thus runs the world away.   255

Would not this, sir, and a forest of feathers—if the rest of
my fortunes turn Turk with me—with two Provincial roses on
my razed shoes, get me a fellowship in a cry of players?
HOR. Half a share.
HAM. A whole one, I.   260

    For thou dost know, O Damon dear,
      This realm dismantled was
    Of Jove himself, and now reigns here

224. *galled jade* sorebacked horse.
239. *Hecate* goddess of witchcraft; *blasted* fallen under a blight.
256. *feathers* plumes for actors' costumes.
257. *Provincial roses* ribbon rosettes (Provençal roses).
258. *cry* company.

A very, very—peacock.

HOR. You might have rhymed.   265

HAM. O good Horatio, I'll take the ghost's word for a thousand
pound. Didst perceive?

HOR. Very well, my lord.

HAM. Upon the talk of the poisoning.

HOR. I did very well note him.   270

HAM. Ah, ha! Come, some music. Come, the recorders.

For if the king like not the comedy,
Why then, belike he likes it not, perdy.
Come, some music.

Enter ROSENCRANTZ *and* GUILDENSTERN.

GUIL. Good my lord, vouchsafe me a word with you.   275

HAM. Sir, a whole history.

GUIL. The king, sir—

HAM. Ay, sir, what of him?

GUIL. Is in his retirement marvellous distempered.

HAM. With drink, sir?   280

GUIL. No, my lord, rather with choler.

HAM. Your wisdom should show itself more richer to signify this
to the doctor, for for me to put him to his purgation would
perhaps plunge him into more choler.

GUIL. Good my lord, put your discourse into some frame, and   285
start not so wildly from my affair.

HAM. I am tame, sir. Pronounce.

GUIL. The queen your mother, in most great affliction of spirit,
hath sent me to you.

HAM. You are welcome.   290

GUIL. Nay, good my lord, this courtesy is not of the right breed.
If it shall please you to make me a wholesome answer, I will
do your mother's commandment. If not, your pardon and my
return shall be the end of my business.

HAM. Sir, I cannot.   295

ROS. What, my lord?

HAM. Make you a wholesome answer; my wit's diseased. But, sir,
such answer as I can make, you shall command, or rather, as
you say, my mother. Therefore no more, but to the matter.
My mother, you say—   300

ROS. Then thus she says: your behavior hath struck her into
amazement and admiration.

HAM. O wonderful son, that can so stonish a mother! But is there
no sequel at the heels of this mother's admiration? Impart.

ROS. She desires to speak with you in her closet ere you go to   305
bed.

---

281. *choler* one of the four bodily   292. *wholesome* reasonable.
humors, an excess of which gave rise   302. *admiration* wonder.
to anger.

HAM. We shall obey, were she ten times our mother. Have you any further trade with us?

ROS. My lord, you once did love me.

HAM. And do still, by these pickers and stealers.   310

ROS. Good my lord, what is your cause of distemper? You do surely bar the door upon your own liberty, if you deny your griefs to your friend.

HAM. Sir, I lack advancement.

ROS. How can that be, when you have the voice of the king him- 315
self for your succession in Denmark?

HAM. Ay, sir, but 'while the grass grows'—the proverb is something musty.

Enter the PLAYERS *with recorders.*

O, the recorders! Let me see one. To withdraw with you—why do you go about to recover the wind of me, as if you would 320
drive me into a toil?

GUIL. O my lord, if my duty be too bold, my love is too unmannerly.

HAM. I do not well understand that. Will you play upon this pipe?   325

GUIL. My lord, I cannot.

HAM. I pray you.

GUIL. Believe me, I cannot.

HAM. I do beseech you.

GUIL. I know no touch of it, my lord.   330

HAM. It is as easy as lying. Govern these ventages with your fingers and thumb, give it breath with your mouth, and it will discourse most eloquent music. Look you, these are the stops.

GUIL. But these cannot I command to any utt'rance of harmony. I have not the skill.   335

HAM. Why, look you now, how unworthy a thing you make of me! You would play upon me, you would seem to know my stops, you would pluck out the heart of my mystery, you would sound me from my lowest note to the top of my compass; and there is much music, excellent voice, in this little organ, yet 340
cannot you make it speak. 'Sblood, do you think I am easier to be played on than a pipe? Call me what instrument you will, though you can fret me, you cannot play upon me.

Enter POLONIUS.

God bless you, sir!

POL. My lord, the queen would speak with you, and presently. 345

HAM. Do you see yonder cloud that's almost in shape of a camel?

POL. By th' mass, and 'tis like a camel indeed.

310. *pickers and stealers* hands.
317. *"while the grass grows"* a proverb ending "the horse starves."
319. *withdraw* step aside for private conversation.

321. *toil* net, snare.
331. *ventages* holes or stops in the recorder.
343. *fret* (1) a stop on the fingerboard of a guitar (2) annoy.

HAM. Methinks it is like a weasel.

POL. It is backed like a weasel.

HAM. Or like a whale.

350

POL. Very like a whale.

HAM. Then I will come to my mother by and by. [*Aside.*] They
fool me to the top of my bent.—I will come by and by.

POL. I will say so.   [*Exit* POLONIUS.]

HAM. 'By and by' is easily said. Leave me, friends.   355

[*Exeunt all but* HAMLET.]

'Tis now the very witching time of night,
When churchyards yawn, and hell itself breathes out
Contagion to this world. Now could I drink hot blood,
And do such bitter business as the day
Would quake to look on. Soft, now to my mother.   360
O heart, lose not thy nature; let not ever
The soul of Nero enter this firm bosom.
Let me be cruel, not unnatural;
I will speak daggers to her, but use none.
My tongue and soul in this be hypocrites—   365
How in my words somever she be shent,
To give them seals never, my soul, consent!   *Exit.*

[III.iii]

Enter KING, ROSENCRANTZ, *and* GUILDENSTERN.

KING. I like him not, nor stands it safe with us
To let his madness range. Therefore prepare you.
I your commission will forthwith dispatch,
And he to England shall along with you.
The terms of our estate may not endure   5
Hazard so near's as doth hourly grow
Out of his brows.

GUIL.   We will ourselves provide.
Most holy and religious fear it is
To keep those many many bodies safe
That live and feed upon your majesty.   10

ROS. The single and peculiar life is bound
With all the strength and armor of the mind
To keep itself from noyance, but much more
That spirit upon whose weal depends and rests
The lives of many. The cess of majesty   15
Dies not alone, but like a gulf doth draw
What's near it with it. It is a massy wheel
Fixed on the summit of the highest mount,
To whose huge spokes ten thousand lesser things

362. *Nero* Roman emperor who murdered his mother.
366. *somever* soever; *shent* reproved,
abused.

[III.iii] 5. *terms of our estate* conditions required for our rule as king.
7. *brows* effronteries.
11. *peculiar* private.
13. *noyance* harm.
15. *cess* cessation, extinction.

Are mortised and adjoined, which when it falls,   20
Each small annexment, petty consequence,
Attends the boist'rous ruin. Never alone
Did the king sigh, but with a general groan.
KING. Arm you, I pray you, to this speedy voyage,
For we will fetters put about this fear,   25
Which now goes too free-footed.
ROS.   We will haste us.
                                   Exeunt Gentlemen.

        Enter POLONIUS.
POL. My lord, he's going to his mother's closet.
Behind the arras I'll convey myself
To hear the process. I'll warrant she'll tax him home,
And as you said, and wisely was it said,   30
'Tis meet that some more audience than a mother,
Since nature makes them partial, should o'erhear
The speech, of vantage. Fare you well, my liege.
I'll call upon you ere you go to bed,
And tell you what I know.
KING.   Thanks, dear my lord.   35
                                   Exit [POLONIUS].
O, my offence is rank, it smells to heaven;
It hath the primal eldest curse upon't,
A brother's murder. Pray can I not,
Though inclination be as sharp as will.
My stronger guilt defeats my strong intent,   40
And like a man to double business bound,
I stand in pause where I shall first begin,
And both neglect. What if this cursèd hand
Were thicker than itself with brothers' blood,
Is there not rain enough in the sweet heavens   45
To wash it white as snow? Whereto serves mercy
But to confront the visage of offence?
And what's in prayer but this twofold force,
To be forestallèd ere we come to fall,
Or pardoned being down? Then I'll look up.   50
My fault is past. But, O, what form of prayer
Can serve my turn? 'Forgive me my foul murder'?
That cannot be, since I am still possessed
Of those effects for which I did the murder—
My crown, mine own ambition, and my queen.   55
May one be pardoned and retain th' offence?
In the corrupted currents of this world
Offence's gilded hand may shove by justice,
And oft 'tis seen the wicked prize itself
Buys out the law. But 'tis not so above.   60

20. *mortised* jointed (as with mortise   for listening.
and tenon).   39. *will* carnal desire.
33. *of vantage* from a convenient place

There is no shuffling; there the action lies
In his true nature, and we ourselves compelled,
Even to the teeth and forehead of our faults,
To give in evidence. What then? What rests?
Try what repentance can. What can it not?   65
Yet what can it when one can not repent?
O wretched state! O bosom black as death!
O liméd soul, that struggling to be free
Art more engaged! Help, angels! Make assay.
Bow, stubborn knees, and heart with strings of steel,   70
Be soft as sinews of the new-born babe.
All may be well.   [*He kneels.*]

     Enter HAMLET.

HAM. Now might I do it pat, now 'a is a-praying,
And now I'll do't—and so 'a goes to heaven,
And so am I revenged. That would be scanned.   75
A villain kills my father, and for that,
I, his sole son, do this same villain send
To heaven.
Why, this is hire and salary, not revenge.
'A took my father grossly, full of bread,   80
With all his crimes broad blown, as flush as May;
And how his audit stands who knows save heaven?
But in our circumstance and course of thought
'Tis heavy with him; and am I then revenged
To take him in the purging of his soul,   85
When he is fit and seasoned for his passage?
No.
Up, sword, and know thou a more horrid hent.
When he is drunk asleep, or in his rage,
Or in th' incestuous pleasure of his bed,   90
At game a-swearing, or about some act
That has no relish of salvation in't—
Then trip him, that his heels may kick at heaven,
And that his soul may be as damned and black
As hell, whereto it goes. My mother stays.   95
This physic but prolongs thy sickly days.   *Exit.*
KING. [*Rising.*] My words fly up, my thoughts remain below.
Words without thoughts never to heaven go.   *Exit.*

[III.iv]

     Enter [QUEEN] GERTRUDE *and* POLONIUS.

POL. 'A will come straight. Look you lay home to him.

---

61. *shuffling* doubledealing; *action* legal action.
68. *liméd soul* caught by sin as the bird by lime.
69. *assay* trial.

80. *grossly* unprepared spiritually.
81. *as flush as May* in full flower.
83. *in our circumstance* considering all evidence; *course* beaten way, habit.
88. *hent* occasion, opportunity.

Tell him his pranks have been too broad to bear with,
And that your grace hath screen'd and stood between
Much heat and him. I'll silence me even here.
Pray you be round.
QUEEN.   I'll warrant you. Fear me not.   5
  Withdraw, I hear him coming.

[POLONIUS goes behind the arras.]

      Enter HAMLET.
HAM. Now, mother, what's the matter?
QUEEN. Hamlet, thou hast thy father much offended.
HAM. Mother, you have my father much offended.
QUEEN. Come, come, you answer with an idle tongue.   10
HAM. Go, go, you question with a wicked tongue.
QUEEN. Why, how now, Hamlet?
HAM.   What's the matter now?
QUEEN. Have you forgot me?
HAM.   No, by the rood, not so.
  You are the queen, your husband's brother's wife,
  And would it were not so, you are my mother.   15
QUEEN. Nay, then I'll set those to you that can speak.
HAM. Come, come, and sit you down. You shall not budge.
  You go not till I set you up a glass
  Where you may see the inmost part of you.
QUEEN. What wilt thou do? Thou wilt not murder me?   20
  Help, ho!
POL. [*Behind.*] What, ho! help!
HAM. [*Draws.*] How now, a rat?
  Dead for a ducat, dead!

[Kills POLONIUS with a pass through the arras.]

POL. [*Behind.*] O, I am slain!   25
QUEEN. O me, what hast thou done?
HAM.   Nay, I know not.
  Is it the king?
QUEEN. O, what a rash and bloody deed is this!
HAM. A bloody deed!—almost as bad, good mother,
  As kill a king and marry with his brother.   30
QUEEN. As kill a king?
HAM.   Ay, lady, it was my word.

[Parting the arras.]

  Thou wretched, rash, intruding fool, farewell!
  I took thee for thy better. Take thy fortune.

[III.iv] 5. Following Polonius's "Pray you be round" (which in *F* reads "Pray you be round with him"), *F* adds the line: "*Ham. within.* Mother, mother, mother." Of which Professor Jenkins remarks (*SB*, XIII, 35), "What sort of prince is this who cannot come to his mother's chamber without announc- ing his arrival by calling 'Mother' three times in the corridor?" A similar instance where the *F* text supplies off- stage calls in support of onstage ref- erences to a character's approach occurs at IV.ii.1.
13. *rood* cross.

Thou find'st to be too busy is some danger.—
Leave wringing of your hands. Peace, sit you down   35
And let me wring your heart, for so I shall
If it be made of penetrable stuff,
If damnéd custom have not brazed it so
That it be proof and bulwark against sense.

QUEEN. What have I done that thou dar'st wag thy tongue   40
In noise so rude against me?

HAM.   Such an act
That blurs the grace and blush of modesty,
Calls virtue hypocrite, takes off the rose
From the fair forehead of an innocent love,
And sets a blister there, makes marriage-vows   45
As false as dicers' oaths. O, such a deed
As from the body of contraction plucks
The very soul, and sweet religion makes
A rhapsody of words. Heaven's face does glow
O'er this solidity and compound mass   50
With heated visage, as against the doom—
Is thought-sick at the act.

QUEEN.   Ay me, what act,
That roars so loud and thunders in the index?

HAM. Look here upon this picture and on this,
The counterfeit presentment of two brothers.   55
See what a grace was seated on this brow:
Hyperion's curls, the front of Jove himself,
An eye like Mars, to threaten and command,
A station like the herald Mercury
New lighted on a heaven-kissing hill—   60
A combination and a form indeed
Where every god did seem to set his seal,
To give the world assurance of a man.
This was your husband. Look you now what follows.
Here is your husband, like a mildewed ear   65
Blasting his wholesome brother. Have you eyes?
Could you on this fair mountain leave to feed,
And batten on this moor? Ha! have you eyes?
You cannot call it love, for at your age
The heyday in the blood is tame, it's humble,   70
And waits upon the judgment, and what judgment
Would step from this to this? Sense sure you have,
Else could you not have motion, but sure that sense

38. *brazed* plated it as with brass.
39. *proof* impenetrable, as of armor.
47. *contraction* the contract of marriage.
50. *this solidity and compound mass* the earth, as compounded of the four elements.
51. *doom* Judgment Day.

53. *index* table of contents; thus, indication of what is to follow.
55. *counterfeit presentment* portrait.
57. *front* brow.
59. *station* bearing, figure.
68. *batten* feed like an animal.
70. *heyday* ardor.
72. *sense* feeling.

Is apoplexed for madness would not err,
Nor sense to ecstasy was ne'er so thralled   75
But it reserved some quantity of choice
To serve in such a difference. What devil was't
That thus hath cozened you at hoodman-blind?
Eyes without feeling, feeling without sight,
Ears without hands or eyes, smelling sans all,   80
Or but a sickly part of one true sense
Could not so mope. O shame! where is thy blush?
Rebellious hell,
If thou canst mutine in a matron's bones,
To flaming youth let virtue be as wax   85
And melt in her own fire. Proclaim no shame
When the compulsive ardor gives the charge,
Since frost itself as actively doth burn,
And reason panders will.
QUEEN.   O Hamlet, speak no more!
Thou turn'st my eyes into my very soul;   90
And there I see such black and grainéd spots
As will not leave their tinct.
HAM.   Nay, but to live
In the rank sweat of an enseaméd bed,
Stewed in corruption, honeying and making love
Over the nasty sty—
QUEEN.   O, speak to me no more!   95
These words like daggers enter in my ears;
No more, sweet Hamlet.
HAM.   A murderer and a villain,
A slave that is not twentieth part the tithe
Of your precedent lord, a vice of kings,
A cutpurse of the empire and the rule,   100
That from a shelf the precious diadem stole
And put it in his pocket—
QUEEN. No more.

        Enter GHOST.
HAM. A king of shreds and patches—
Save me and hover o'er me with your wings,   105
You heavenly guards! What would your gracious figure?
QUEEN. Alas, he's mad.
HAM. Do you not come your tardy son to chide,
That lapsed in time and passion lets go by
Th' important acting of your dread command?   110
O, say!

75. *ecstasy* madness.
78. *hoodman-blind* blindman's bluff.
80. *sans* without.
82. *mope* act without full use of one's
wits.
89. *will* desire.

91. *grainéd spots* indelible stains.
92. *tinct* color.
93. *enseamed* greasy.
99. *vice* a character in the morality
plays, presented often as a buffoon
(here, a caricature).

GHOST. Do not forget. This visitation
Is but to whet thy almost blunted purpose.
But look, amazement on thy mother sits.
O, step between her and her fighting soul!   115
Conceit in weakest bodies strongest works.
Speak to her, Hamlet.
HAM. How is it with you, lady?
QUEEN.   Alas, how is't with you,
That you do bend your eye on vacancy,
And with th' incorporal air do hold discourse?   120
Forth at your eyes your spirits wildly peep,
And as the sleeping soldiers in th' alarm,
Your bedded hairs like life in excrements
Start up and stand an end. O gentle son,
Upon the heat and flame of thy distemper   125
Sprinkle cool patience. Whereon do you look?
HAM. On him, on him! Look you how pale he glares.
His form and cause conjoined, preaching to stones,
Would make them capable.—Do not look upon me,
Lest with this piteous action you convert   130
My stern effects. Then what I have to do
Will want true color—tears perchance for blood.
QUEEN. To whom do you speak this?
HAM. Do you see nothing there?
QUEEN. Nothing at all, yet all that is I see.   135
HAM. Nor did you nothing hear?
QUEEN. No, nothing but ourselves.
HAM. Why, look you there. Look how it steals away.
My father, in his habit as he lived!
Look where he goes even now out at the portal.   *Exit* GHOST. 140
QUEEN. This is the very coinage of your brain.
This bodiless creation ecstasy
Is very cunning in.
HAM. My pulse as yours doth temperately keep time,
And makes as healthful music. It is not madness   145
That I have uttered. Bring me to the test,
And I the matter will re-word, which madness
Would gambol from. Mother, for love of grace,
Lay not that flattering unction to your soul,
That not your trespass but my madness speaks.   150
It will but skin and film the ulcerous place
Whiles rank corruption, mining all within,
Infects unseen. Confess yourself to heaven,

---

116. *conceit* imagination.
123. *excrements* nails, hair (whatever
grows out of the body).
124. *an* on.
129 *capable* able to respond.
132. *want* lack.

148. *gambol* leap or start, as a shying
horse.
149. *unction* ointment; hence, soothing
notion.
152. *mining* undermining.

Repent what's past, avoid what is to come,
And do not spread the compost on the weeds,   155
To make them ranker. Forgive me this my virtue,
For in the fatness of these pursy times
Virtue itself of vice must pardon beg,
Yea, curb and woo for leave to do him good.
QUEEN. O Hamlet, thou hast cleft my heart in twain.   160
HAM. O, throw away the worser part of it,
And live the purer with the other half.
Good night—but go not to my uncle's bed.
Assume a virtue, if you have it not.
That monster custom, who all sense doth eat,   165
Of habits devil, is angel yet in this,
That to the use of actions fair and good
He likewise gives a frock or livery
That aptly is put on. Refrain to-night,
And that shall lend a kind of easiness   170
To the next abstinence; the next more easy;
For use almost can change the stamp of nature,
And either curb the devil, or throw him out
With wondrous potency. Once more, good night,
And when you are desirous to be blest,   175
I'll blessing beg of you. For this same lord
I do repent; but heaven hath pleased it so,
To punish me with this, and this with me,
That I must be their scourge and minister.
I will bestow him and will answer well   180
The death I gave him. So, again, good night.
I must be cruel only to be kind.
Thus bad begins and worse remains behind.
One word more, good lady.
QUEEN.   What shall I do?
HAM. Not this, by no means, that I bid you do: 185
Let the bloat king tempt you again to bed,
Pinch wanton on your cheek, call you his mouse,
And let him, for a pair of reechy kisses,
Or paddling in your neck with his damned fingers,
Make you to ravel all this matter out,   190
That I essentially am not in madness,
But mad in craft. 'Twere good you let him know,
For who that's but a queen, fair, sober, wise,
Would from a paddock, from a bat, a gib,

---

157. *fatness* grossness, slackness; *pursy* corpulent.
166. *Of habits devil* being a devil in, or in respect of, habits (with a play on "habits," as meaning both settled practices and garments, whereby devilish practices contrast with "actions fair and good," line 167, and devilish garments contrast with the "frock or livery" of line 168, which custom in its angelic aspect provides).
188. *reechy* dirty.
191. *essentially* in fact.
194. *paddock* toad; *gib* tom-cat.

Such dear concernings hide? Who would do so?   195
No, in despite of sense and secrecy,
Unpeg the basket on the house's top,
Let the birds fly, and like the famous ape,
To try conclusions, in the basket creep
And break your own neck down.   200
QUEEN. Be thou assured, if words be made of breath
And breath of life, I have no life to breathe
What thou hast said to me.
HAM. I must to England; you know that?
QUEEN.   Alack,
I had forgot. 'Tis so concluded on.   205
HAM. There's letters sealed, and my two school-fellows,
Whom I will trust as I will adders fanged,
They bear the mandate; they must sweep my way
And marshal me to knavery. Let it work,
For 'tis the sport to have the engineer   210
Hoist with his own petar; and't shall go hard
But I will delve one yard below their mines
And blow them at the moon. O, 'tis most sweet
When in one line two crafts directly meet.
This man shall set me packing.   215
I'll lug the guts into the neighbour room.
Mother, good night. Indeed, this counsellor
Is now most still, most secret, and most grave,
Who was in life a foolish prating knave.
Come sir, to draw toward an end with you.   220
Good night, mother.
[*Exit the* QUEEN. *Then*] *exit* [HAMLET *tugging in* POLONIUS].

[IV.i]

        Enter KING *and* QUEEN, *with* ROSENCRANTZ *and* GUILDEN-
        STERN.
KING. There's matter in these sighs, these profound heaves,
You must translate; 'tis fit we understand them.
Where is your son?
QUEEN. Bestow this place on us a little while.
            [*Exeunt* ROSENCRANTZ *and* GUILDENSTERN.]
Ah, mine own lord, what have I seen to-night!   5
KING. What, Gertrude? How does Hamlet?
QUEEN. Mad as the sea and wind when both contend
Which is the mightier. In his lawless fit,

197–200. *Unpeg the basket * * * neck down* the story is lost (in it, apparently, the ape carries a cage of birds to the top of a house, releases them by accident, and, surprised at their flight, imagines he can imitate it by first creeping into the basket and then leaping out. The moral of the story, for the queen, is not to expose herself to destruction by making public what good sense decrees should be kept secret.).
211. *petar* a bomb or charge for blowing in gates.

[IV.i] 2. *translate* explain.

Behind the arras hearing something stir,
Whips out his rapier, cries 'A rat, a rat!'   10
And in this brainish apprehension kills
The unseen good old man.
KING.   O heavy deed!
It had been so with us had we been there.
His liberty is full of threats to all—
To you yourself, to us, to every one.   15
Alas, how shall this bloody deed be answered?
It will be laid to us, whose providence
Should have kept short, restrained, and out of haunt,
This mad young man. But so much was our love,
We would not understand what was most fit;   20
But, like the owner of a foul disease,
To keep it from divulging, let it feed
Even on the pith of life. Where is he gone?
QUEEN. To draw apart the body he hath killed,
O'er whom his very madness, like some ore   25
Among a mineral of metals base,
Shows itself pure: 'a weeps for what is done.
KING. O Gertrude, come away!
The sun no sooner shall the mountains touch
But we will ship him hence, and this vile deed   30
We must with all our majesty and skill
Both countenance and excuse. Ho, Guildenstern!

          Enter ROSENCRANTZ *and* GUILDENSTERN.
Friends both, go join you with some further aid.
Hamlet in madness hath Polonius slain,
And from his mother's closet hath he dragged him. 35
Go seek him out; speak fair, and bring the body
Into the chapel. I pray you haste in this.
            [*Exeunt* ROSENCRANTZ *and* GUILDENSTERN.]
Come, Gertrude, we'll call up our wisest friends
And let them know both what we mean to do
And what's untimely done; so haply slander—   40
Whose whisper o'er the world's diameter,
As level as the cannon to his blank,
Transports his poisoned shot—may miss our name,
And hit the woundless air. O, come away!
My soul is full of discord and dismay.   *Exeunt.* 45

[IV.ii]

          Enter HAMLET.
HAM. Safely stowed.—But soft, what noise? Who calls on Hamlet? O, here they come.

11. *brainish apprehension* headstrong,
or passionate conception.
18. *out of haunt* away from society.
42. *As level* as sure of aim; *blank* the

white spot in the center of a target.

[IV.ii] 1. After the words "Safely
stowed," F adds the line: *"Gentlemen*

[*Enter*] ROSENCRANTZ, [GUILDENSTERN,] *and* OTHERS.

ROS. What have you done, my lord, with the dead body?

HAM. Compounded it with dust, whereto 'tis kin.

ROS. Tell us where 'tis, that we may take it thence   5
And bear it to the chapel.

HAM. Do not believe it.

ROS. Believe what?

HAM. That I can keep your counsel and not mine own. Besides,
to be demanded of a sponge—what replication should be   10
made by the son of a king?

ROS. Take you me for a sponge, my lord?

HAM. Ay, sir, that soaks up the king's countenance, his rewards,
his authorities. But such officers do the king best service in the
end. He keeps them like an apple in the corner of his jaw,   15
first mouthed to be last swallowed. When he needs what you
have gleaned, it is but squeezing you and, sponge, you shall be
dry again.

ROS. I understand you not, my lord.

HAM. I am glad of it. A knavish speech sleeps in a foolish ear.   20

ROS. My lord, you must tell us where the body is, and go with us
to the king.

HAM. The body is with the king, but the king is not with the
body. The king is a thing—

GUIL. A thing, my lord!   25

HAM. Of nothing. Bring me to him. Hide fox, and all after.

                                                    Exeunt.

[IV.iii]

        Enter KING, *and two or three.*

KING. I have sent to seek him, and to find the body.
How dangerous is it that this man goes loose!
Yet must not we put the strong law on him.
He's loved of the distracted multitude,
Who like not in their judgment but their eyes,   5
And where 'tis so, th' offender's scourge is weighed,
But never the offence. To bear all smooth and even,
This sudden sending him away must seem
Deliberate pause. Diseases desperate grown
By desperate appliance are relieved,   10
Or not at all.

        Enter ROSENCRANTZ, [GUILDENSTERN,] *and all the rest.*
                How now! what hath befall'n?

ROS. Where the dead body is bestowed, my lord,

within. Hamlet, Lord *Hamlet.*" Here,
as at III.iv.5, "when a character speaks
of hearing someone coming, *F* provides, though *Q* does not, for the
audience to hear it too" (Jenkins, *SB*,

XIII, 35).

10. *replication* reply.

[IV.iii] 9. *deliberate pause* carefully
considered.

We cannot get from him.
KING.   But where is he?
ROS. Without, my lord; guarded, to know your pleasure.
KING. Bring him before us.
ROS.   Ho! bring in the lord.   15

They enter [*with* HAMLET].
KING. Now, Hamlet, where's Polonius?
HAM. At supper.
KING. At supper? Where?
HAM. Not where he eats, but where 'a is eaten. A certain con-
    vocation of politic worms are e'en at him. Your worm is your   20
    only emperor for diet. We fat all creatures else to fat us, and
    we fat ourselves for maggots. Your fat king and your lean
    beggar is but variable service—two dishes, but to one table.
    That's the end.
KING. Alas, alas!   25
HAM. A man may fish with the worm that hath eat of a king,
    and eat of the fish that hath fed of that worm.
KING. What dost thou mean by this?
HAM. Nothing but to show you how a king may go a progress
    through the guts of a beggar.   30
KING. Where is Polonius?
HAM. In heaven. Send thither to see. If your messenger find him
    not there, seek him i' th' other place yourself. But if, indeed,
    you find him not within this month, you shall nose him as you
    go up the stairs into the lobby.   35
KING. [*To* ATTENDANTS.] Go seek him there.
HAM. 'A will stay till you come.   [*Exeunt* ATTENDANTS.]
KING. Hamlet, this deed, for thine especial safety—
    Which we do tender, as we dearly grieve
    For that which thou hast done—must send thee hence   40
    With fiery quickness. Therefore prepare thyself.
    The bark is ready, and the wind at help,
    Th' associates tend, and everything is bent
    For England.
HAM.   For England?
KING.   Ay, Hamlet.
HAM.   Good.
KING. So is it, if thou knew'st our purposes.   45
HAM. I see a cherub that sees them. But come, for England!
    Farewell, dear mother.
KING. Thy loving father, Hamlet.
HAM. My mother. Father and mother is man and wife, man and
    wife is one flesh. So, my mother. Come, for England.   *Exit.* 50
KING. Follow him at foot; tempt him with speed aboard.

28. *progress* the state journey of a
ruler.
39. *tender* value.

46. *cherub* one of the cherubim, the
watchmen or sentinels of heaven, and
thus endowed with the keenest vision.

Delay it not; I'll have him hence to-night.
Away! for everything is sealed and done
That else leans on th' affair. Pray you make haste.
[Exeunt all but the KING.]
And, England, if my love thou hold'st at aught—   55
As my great power thereof may give thee sense,
Since yet thy cicatrice looks raw and red
After the Danish sword, and thy free awe
Pays homage to us—thou mayst not coldly set
Our sovereign process, which imports at full   60
By letters congruing to that effect
The present death of Hamlet. Do it, England,
For like the hectic in my blood he rages,
And thou must cure me. Till I know 'tis done,
Howe'er my haps, my joys were ne'er begun.   *Exit.* 65

[IV.iv]

    Enter FORTINBRAS *with his* ARMY *over the stage.*
FORT. Go, captain, from me greet the Danish king.
  Tell him that by his licence Fortinbras
  Craves the conveyance of a promised march
  Over his kingdom. You know the rendezvous.
  If that his majesty would aught with us,   5
  We shall express our duty in his eye,
  And let him know so.
CAP.   I will do't, my lord.
FORT. Go softly on.   *[Exeunt all but the* CAPTAIN.]

    Enter HAMLET, ROSENCRANTZ, [GUILDENSTERN,] *and*
    OTHERS.
HAM. Good sir, whose powers are these?
CAP. They are of Norway, sir.   10
HAM. How purposed, sir, I pray you?
CAP. Against some part of Poland.
HAM. Who commands them, sir?
CAP. The nephew to old Norway, Fortinbras.
HAM. Goes it against the main of Poland, sir,   15
  Or for some frontier?
CAP. Truly to speak, and with no addition,
  We go to gain a little patch of ground
  That hath in it no profit but the name.
  To pay five ducats, five, I would not farm it;   20
  Nor will it yield to Norway or the Pole

---

57. *cicatrice* scar, used here of memory of a defeat.
59. *coldly* with indifference.
60. *process* mandate.
61. *congruing* according.
63. *hectic* consumptive fever.

65. *haps* fortunes.

[IV.iv] 3. *conveyance* conduct.
15. *main* chief part.
17. *addition* exaggeration.

A ranker rate should it be sold in fee.
HAM. Why, then the Polack never will defend it.
CAP. Yes, it is already garrisoned.
HAM. Two thousand souls and twenty thousand ducats   25
    Will not debate the question of this straw.
    This is th' imposthume of much wealth and peace,
    That inward breaks, and shows no cause without
    Why the man dies. I humbly thank you, sir.
CAP. God buy you, sir.   [*Exit.*]
ROS.   Will't please you go, my lord?   30
HAM. I'll be with you straight. Go a little before.
                    [*Exeunt all but* HAMLET.]
    How all occasions do inform against me,
    And spur my dull revenge! What is a man,
    If his chief good and market of his time
    Be but to sleep and feed? A beast, no more.   35
    Sure he that made us with such large discourse,
    Looking before and after, gave us not
    That capability and godlike reason
    To fust in us unused. Now, whether it be
    Bestial oblivion, or some craven scruple   40
    Of thinking too precisely on th' event—
    A thought which, quartered, hath but one part wisdom
    And ever three parts coward—I do not know
    Why yet I live to say 'This thing's to do',
    Sith I have cause, and will, and strength, and means,   45
    To do't. Examples gross as earth exhort me.
    Witness this army of such mass and charge,
    Led by a delicate and tender prince,
    Whose spirit, with divine ambition puffed,
    Makes mouths at the invisible event,   50
    Exposing what is mortal and unsure
    To all that fortune, death, and danger dare,
    Even for an eggshell. Rightly to be great
    Is not to stir without great argument,
    But greatly to find quarrel in a straw   55
    When honor's at the stake. How stand I then,
    That have a father killed, a mother stained,
    Excitements of my reason and my blood,
    And let all sleep, while to my shame I see
    The imminent death of twenty thousand men   60
    That for a fantasy and trick of fame
    Go to their graves like beds, fight for a plot
    Whereon the numbers cannot try the cause,

22. *a ranker rate* a greater price; *sold in fee* sold with absolute and perpetual possession.
27. *imposthume* abscess.
32. *inform* take shape.
34. *market* profit.
36. *discourse* power of reasoning.
39. *fust* grow musty.
50. *mouths* grimaces.
63. *try the cause* settle by combat.

Which is not tomb enough and continent
To hide the slain? O, from this time forth,   65
My thoughts be bloody, or be nothing worth!   *Exit.*

[IV.v]

        Enter HORATIO, [QUEEN] GERTRUDE, *and a* GENTLEMAN.

QUEEN. I will not speak with her.
GENT. She is importunate, indeed distract.
  Her mood will needs be pitied.
QUEEN.   What would she have?
GENT. She speaks much of her father, says she hears
  There's tricks i' th' world, and hems, and beats her heart,   5
  Spurns enviously at straws, speaks things in doubt
  That carry but half sense. Her speech is nothing,
  Yet the unshaped use of it doth move
  The hearers to collection; they aim at it,
  And botch the words up fit to their own thoughts,   10
  Which, as her winks and nods and gestures yield them,
  Indeed would make one think there might be thought,
  Though nothing sure, yet much unhappily.
HOR. 'Twere good she were spoken with, for she may strew
  Dangerous conjectures in ill-breeding minds.   15
QUEEN. Let her come in.   [*Exit* GENTLEMAN.]
  [*Aside.*] To my sick soul, as sin's true nature is,
  Each toy seems prologue to some great amiss.
  So full of artless jealousy is guilt,
  It spills itself in fearing to be split.   20

        Enter OPHELIA [*distracted*].

OPH. Where is the beauteous majesty of Denmark?
QUEEN. How now, Ophelia!
OPH.   How should I your true love know   *She sings.*
         From another one?
        By his cockle hat and staff,   25
        And his sandal shoon.
QUEEN. Alas, sweet lady, what imports this song?
OPH. Say you? Nay, pray you mark.

        He is dead and gone, lady,   (*Song.*)
          He is dead and gone;   30
        At his head a grass-green turf,
        At his heels a stone.

---

64. *continent* receptacle.

[IV.v] 6. *Spurns enviously at straws*
takes exception, spitefully, to trifles.
7. *nothing* nonsense.
8. *unshaped use* disordered manner.
9. *collection* attempts at shaping meaning; *aim* guess.
13. *sure* certain.

18. *toy* trifle.
19. *artless jealousy* ill-concealed suspicion.
20. *spills* destroys.
25. *cockle hat* hat bearing a cockle
shell, worn by a pilgrim who had been
to the shrine of St. James of Compos-
tella, in Spain.
26. *shoon* shoes.

O, ho!

QUEEN. Nay, but, Ophelia—

OPH.   Pray you mark.

[*Sings.*] White his shroud as the mountain snow—   35

     Enter KING.

QUEEN. Alas, look here, my lord.

OPH.   Larded all with sweet flowers;   (*Song.*)
         Which bewept to the grave did not go
           With true-love showers.

KING. How do you, pretty lady?   40

OPH. Well, God dild you! They say the owl was a baker's daughter. Lord, we know what we are, but know not what we may be.
God be at your table!

KING. Conceit upon her father.

OPH. Pray let's have no words of this, but when they ask you   45
what it means, say you this:

         To-morrow is Saint Valentine's day,   (*Song.*)
           All in the morning betime,
         And I a maid at your window,
           To be your Valentine.   50
         Then up he rose, and donn'd his clo'es,
           And dupped the chamber-door,
         Let in the maid, that out a maid
           Never departed more.

KING. Pretty Ophelia!   55

OPH. Indeed, without an oath, I'll make an end on't.

[*Sings.*]   By Gis and by Saint Charity,
          Alack, and fie for shame!
         Young men will do't, if they come to't;
          By Cock, they are to blame.   60
         Quoth she 'Before you tumbled me,
          You promised me to wed'.

He answers:

         'So would I 'a done, by yonder sun,
          An thou hadst not come to my bed'.   65

KING. How long hath she been thus?

OPH. I hope all will be well. We must be patient, but I cannot
choose but weep to think they would lay him i' th' cold
ground. My brother shall know of it, and so I thank you for

---

41. *dild* yield, repay.
41–42. *They say the owl was a baker's
daughter* allusion to a folktale in which
a baker's daughter was transformed
into an owl because of her ungenerous
behavior (giving short measure) when
Christ asked for bread in the baker's

shop.
44. *Conceit upon her father* i.e., obsessed with her father's death.
48. *betime* early.
52. *dupped* opened.
57. *Gis* Jesus.

your good counsel. Come, my coach! Good night, ladies, good 70
night. Sweet ladies, good night, good night. [*Exit.*]
KING. Follow her close; give her good watch, I pray you.
[*Exeunt* HORATIO *and* GENTLEMAN.]
O, this is the poison of deep grief; it springs
All from her father's death, and now behold!
O Gertrude, Gertrude! 75
When sorrows come, they come not single spies,
But in battalions: first, her father slain;
Next, your son gone, and he most violent author
Of his own just remove; the people muddied,
Thick and unwholesome in their thoughts and whispers 80
For good Polonius' death; and we have done but greenly
In hugger-mugger to inter him; poor Ophelia
Divided from herself and her fair judgment,
Without the which we are pictures, or mere beasts;
Last, and as much containing as all these, 85
Her brother is in secret come from France,
Feeds on his wonder, keeps himself in clouds,
And wants not buzzers to infect his ear
With pestilent speeches of his father's death,
Wherein necessity, of matter beggared, 90
Will nothing stick our person to arraign
In ear and ear. O my dear Gertrude, this,
Like to a murd'ring piece, in many places
Gives me superfluous death. Attend, *A noise within.*

Enter a MESSENGER.
Where are my Switzers? Let them guard the door. 95
What is the matter?
MESS. Save yourself, my lord.
The ocean, overpeering of his list,
Eats not the flats with more impiteous haste
Than young Laertes, in a riotous head,
O'erbears your officers. The rabble call him lord, 100
And as the world were now but to begin,
Antiquity forgot, custom not known,
The ratifiers and props of every word,
They cry 'Choose we, Laertes shall be king'.
Caps, hands, and tongues, applaud it to the clouds, 105
'Laertes shall be king, Laertes king'.

79. *remove* banishment, departure; *muddied* stirred up and confused.
81. *greenly* without judgment.
82. *hugger-mugger* secrecy and disorder.
88. *wants* lacks.
90. *of matter beggared* lacking good cause.
91. *nothing stick* in no way hesitate.
93. *murd'ring piece* cannon loaded with shot meant to scatter.
94. *F* omits the King's "Attend," but substitutes, by way of drawing attention to the "noise within," what Jenkins (*SB*, XIII, 36) terms "a more obvious exclamation from the Queen: 'Alacke, what noyse is this?' "
95. *Switzers* Swiss bodyguard.
97. *list* bound.
99. *riotous head* turbulent mob.

QUEEN. How cheerfully on the false trail they cry! *A noise within.*
O, this is counter, you false Danish dogs!
KING. The doors are broke.

     Enter LAERTES, *with* OTHERS.
LAER. Where is this king?—Sirs, stand you all without.   110
ALL. No, let's come in.
LAER.   I pray you give me leave.
ALL. We will, we will.   [*Exeunt his followers.*]
LAER. I thank you. Keep the door.—O thou vile king,
Give me my father!
QUEEN.   Calmly, good Laertes.
LAER. That drop of blood that's calm proclaims me bastard,   115
Cries cuckold to my father, brands the harlot
Even here between the chaste unsmirchéd brow
Of my true mother.
KING.   What is the cause, Laertes,
That thy rebellion looks so giant-like?
Let him go, Gertrude. Do not fear our person.   120
There's such divinity doth hedge a king
That treason can but peep to what it would,
Acts little of his will. Tell me, Laertes,
Why thou art thus incensed. Let him go, Gertrude.
Speak, man.   125
LAER. Where is my father?
KING.   Dead.
QUEEN.   But not by him.
KING.   Let him demand his fill.
LAER. How came he dead? I'll not be juggled with.
To hell allegiance, vows to the blackest devil,
Conscience and grace to the profoundest pit!   130
I dare damnation. To this point I stand,
That both the worlds I give to negligence,
Let come what comes, only I'll be revenged
Most throughly for my father.
KING. Who shall stay you?
LAER.   My will, not all the world's.   135
And for my means, I'll husband them so well
They shall go far with little.
KING.   Good Laertes,
If you desire to know the certainty
Of your dear father, is't writ in your revenge
That, swoopstake, you will draw both friend and foe,   140
Winner and loser?
LAER.   None but his enemies.
KING. Will you know them, then?

---

108. *counter* hunting backward on the trail.
120. *fear* fear for.

134. *throughly* thoroughly.
140. *swoopstake* sweepstake, taking all the stakes on the gambling table.

LAER. To his good friends thus wide I'll ope my arms,
    And like the kind life-rend'ring pelican,
    Repast them with my blood.
KING.   Why, now you speak   145
    Like a good child and a true gentleman.
    That I am guiltless of your father's death,
    And am most sensibly in grief for it,
    It shall as level to your judgment 'pear
    As day does to your eye.
                        A noise within: 'Let her come in.' 150
LAER. How now? What noise is that?

    Enter OPHELIA.
    O, heat dry up my brains! tears seven times salt
    Burn out the sense and virtue of mine eye!
    By heaven, thy madness shall be paid with weight
    Till our scale turn the beam. O rose of May,   155
    Dear maid, kind sister, sweet Ophelia!
    O heavens! is't possible a young maid's wits
    Should be as mortal as an old man's life?
    Nature is fine in love, and where 'tis fine
    It sends some precious instance of itself   160
    After the thing it loves.
OPH.   They bore him barefac'd on the bier;   (*Song.*)
         Hey non nonny, nonny, hey nonny;
         And in his grave rain'd many a tear—

    Fare you well, my dove!   165
LAER. Hadst thou thy wits, and didst persuade revenge,
    It could not move thus.
OPH. You must sing 'A-down, a-down, and you call him a-down-
    a.' O, how the wheel becomes it! It is the false steward, that
    stole his master's daughter.   170
LAER. This nothing's more than matter.
OPH. There's rosemary, that's for remembrance. Pray you, love,
    remember. And there is pansies, that's for thoughts.
LAER. A document in madness, thoughts and remembrance fitted.
OPH. There's fennel for you, and columbines. There's rue for you, 175
    and here's some for me. We may call it herb of grace a Sun-
    days. O, you must wear your rue with a difference. There's a
    daisy. I would give you some violets, but they withered all
    when my father died. They say 'a made a good end.

[*Sings.*]   For bonny sweet Robin is all my joy.   180

144. *pelican* supposed to feed her young with her own blood.
149. *level* plain.
153. *virtue* power.
159. *fine* refined to purity.
169. *wheel* burden, refrain.

175. *fennel* symbol of flattery; *columbines* symbol of thanklessness (?); *rue* symbol of repentance.
178. *daisy* symbol of dissembling; *violets* symbol of faithfulness.

LAER. Thought and affliction, passion, hell itself,
    She turns to favor and to prettiness.
OPH.   And will 'a not come again?   (*Song.*)
                    And will 'a not come again?
                        No, no, he is dead,   185
                        Go to thy death-bed,
                    He never will come again.

                    His beard was as white as snow,
                    All flaxen was his poll;
                        He is gone, he is gone,   190
                        And we cast away moan:
                    God-a-mercy on his soul!

    And of all Christian souls, I pray God. God buy you.   [*Exit.*]
LAER. Do you see this, O God?
KING. Laertes, I must commune with your grief,   195
    Or you deny me right. Go but apart,
    Make choice of whom your wisest friends you will,
    And they shall hear and judge 'twixt you and me.
    If by direct or by collateral hand
    They find us touched, we will our kingdom give,   200
    Our crown, our life, and all that we call ours,
    To you in satisfaction; but if not,
    Be you content to lend your patience to us,
    And we shall jointly labor with your soul
    To give it due content.
LAER.   Let this be so.   205
    His means of death, his obscure funeral—
    No trophy, sword, nor hatchment, o'er his bones,
    No noble rite nor formal ostentation—
    Cry to be heard, as 'twere from heaven to earth,
    That I must call't in question.
KING.   So you shall;   210
    And where th' offence is, let the great axe fall.
    I pray you go with me.   *Exeunt.*

[IV.vi]

        Enter HORATIO *and* OTHERS.
HOR. What are they that would speak with me?
GENTLEMAN. Sea-faring men, sir. They say they have letters for
    you.
HOR. Let them come in.   [*Exit* GENTLEMAN.]
    I do not know from what part of the world   5
    I should be greeted, if not from Lord Hamlet.

        Enter SAILORS.
SAIL. God bless you, sir.

207. *hatchment* coat of arms.

HOR. Let him bless thee too.

SAIL. 'A shall, sir, an't please him. There's a letter for you, sir—
it came from th' ambassador that was bound for England—if 10
your name be Horatio, as I am let to know it is.

HOR. [*Reads.*] 'Horatio, when thou shalt have overlooked this,
give these fellows some means to the king. They have letters
for him. Ere we were two days old at sea, a pirate of very warlike appointment gave us chase. Finding ourselves too slow of 15
sail, we put on a compelled valor, and in the grapple I boarded
them. On the instant they got clear of our ship, so I alone became their prisoner. They have dealt with me like thieves of
mercy, but they knew what they did; I am to do a good turn
for them. Let the king have the letters I have sent, and repair 20
thou to me with as much speed as thou wouldest fly death.
I have words to speak in thine ear will make thee dumb; yet
are they much too light for the bore of the matter. These good
fellows will bring thee where I am. Rosencrantz and Guildenstern hold their course for England. Of them I have much to 25
tell thee. Farewell.

> He that thou knowest thine, HAMLET.'

Come, I will give you way for these your letters,
And do't the speedier that you may direct me
To him from whom you brought them.   *Exeunt.* 30

[IV.vii]

> *Enter* KING *and* LAERTES.

KING. Now must your conscience my acquittance seal,
And you must put me in your heart for friend,
Sith you have heard, and with a knowing ear,
That he which hath your noble father slain
Pursued my life.

LAER.   It well appears. But tell me   5
Why you proceeded not against these feats,
So crimeful and so capital in nature,
As by your safety, greatness, wisdom, all things else,
You mainly were stirred up.

KING.   O, for two special reasons,
Which may to you, perhaps, seem much unsinewed,   10
But yet to me th'are strong. The queen his mother
Lives almost by his looks, and for myself—
My virtue or my plague, be it either which—
She is so conjunctive to my life and soul
That, as the star moves not but in his sphere,   15
I could not but by her. The other motive,
Why to a public count I might not go,

[IV.vi] 23. *bore* literally, caliber of a
gun; hence, size, importance.
[IV.vii] 7. *capital* punishable by death.

10. *unsinewed* weak.
14. *conjunctive* closely joined.

Is the great love the general gender bear him,
Who, dipping all his faults in their affection,
Work like the spring that turneth wood to stone,   20
Convert his gyves to graces; so that my arrows,
Too slightly timbered for so loud a wind,
Would have reverted to my bow again,
But not where I have aimed them.
LAER. And so have I a noble father lost,   25
A sister driven into desp'rate terms,
Whose worth, if praises may go back again,
Stood challenger on mount of all the age
For her perfections. But my revenge will come.
KING. Break not your sleeps for that. You must not think   30
That we are made of stuff so flat and dull
That we can let our beard be shook with danger,
And think it pastime. You shortly shall hear more.
I loved your father, and we love our self,
And that, I hope, will teach you to imagine—   35

     Enter a MESSENGER *with letters.*
MESS. These to your majesty; this to the queen.
KING. From Hamlet! Who brought them?
MESS. Sailors, my lord, they say. I saw them not.
They were given me by Claudio; he received them
Of him that brought them.
KING.   Laertes, you shall hear them.—   40
Leave us.   [*Exit* MESSENGER.]
    [*Reads.*] 'High and mighty, you shall know I am set naked
on your kingdom. To-morrow shall I beg leave to see your
kingly eyes; when I shall, first asking your pardon thereunto,
recount the occasion of my sudden and more strange return.
                            HAMLET.'   45
What should this mean? Are all the rest come back?
Or is it some abuse, and no such thing?
LAER. Know you the hand?
KING. 'Tis Hamlet's character. 'Naked'!
And in a postscript here, he says 'alone'.   50
Can you devise me?
LAER. I am lost in it, my lord. But let him come.

18. *general gender* common people.
21. *gyves* fetters.
35. Following the entrance of the Messenger, the King says in *F* "How now? What Newes?" and the Messenger replies, "Letters my Lord from *Hamlet.*" Jenkins comments (*SB*, XIII, 36): "In *Q* the King is not told the letters come from Hamlet; he is left to find this out as he reads, and his cry 'From *Hamlet*' betokens his astonishment on doing so. I think Hamlet would not have approved of the *F* messenger who robs his bomb of the full force of its explosion. Shakespeare's messenger did not even know he carried such a bomb, for the letters had reached him via sailors who were ignorant of their sender. They took him for 'th' Embassador that was bound for *England*' (IV.vi.10). *F*, with its too knowledgeable messenger, by seeking to enhance the effect, destroys it."
51. *devise* explain to.

It warms the very sickness in my heart
That I shall live and tell him to his teeth
'Thus didest thou'.
KING.   If it be so, Laertes—   55
As how should it be so, how otherwise?—
Will you be ruled by me?
LAER.   Ay, my lord,
So you will not o'errule me to a peace.
KING. To thine own peace. If he be now returned,
As checking at his voyage, and that he means   60
No more to undertake it, I will work him
To an exploit now ripe in my device,
Under the which he shall not choose but fall;
And for his death no wind of blame shall breathe
But even his mother shall uncharge the practice   65
And call it accident.
LAER.   My lord, I will be ruled;
The rather if you could devise it so
That I might be the organ.
KING.   It falls right.
You have been talked of since your travel much,
And that in Hamlet's hearing, for a quality   70
Wherein they say you shine. Your sum of parts
Did not together pluck such envy from him
As did that one, and that, in my regard,
Of the unworthiest siege.
LAER.   What part is that, my lord?
KING. A very riband in the cap of youth,   75
Yet needful too, for youth no less becomes
The light and careless livery that it wears
Than settled age his sables and his weeds,
Importing health and graveness. Two months since
Here was a gentleman of Normandy.   80
I have seen myself, and served against, the French,
And they can well on horseback, but this gallant
Had witchcraft in't. He grew unto his seat,
And to such wondrous doing brought his horse,
As had he been incorpsed and demi-natured   85
With the brave beast. So far he topped my thought
That I, in forgery of shapes and tricks,
Come short of what he did.
LAER.   A Norman was't?

60. *checking at* turning aside from (like a falcon turning from its quarry for other prey).
65. *uncharge the practice* regard the deed as free from villainy.
68. *organ* instrument.
74. *siege* rank.

78. *weeds* garments.
85. *incorpsed* made one body; *deminatured* like a centaur, half man half horse.
86. *topped* excelled.
87. *forgery* invention.

KING. A Norman.
LAER. Upon my life, Lamord.
KING.   The very same.   90
LAER. I know him well. He is the brooch indeed
    And gem of all the nation.
KING. He made confession of you,
    And gave you such a masterly report
    For art and exercise in your defence,   95
    And for your rapier most especial,
    That he cried out 'twould be a sight indeed
    If one could match you. The scrimers of their nation
    He swore had neither motion, guard, nor eye,
    If you opposed them. Sir, this report of his   100
    Did Hamlet so envenom with his envy
    That he could nothing do but wish and beg
    Your sudden coming o'er, to play with you.
    Now out of this—
LAER.   What out of this, my lord?
KING. Laertes, was your father dear to you?   105
    Or are you like the painting of a sorrow,
    A face without a heart?
LAER.   Why ask you this?
KING. Not that I think you did not love your father,
    But that I know love is begun by time,
    And that I see in passages of proof,   110
    Time qualifies the spark and fire of it.
    There lives within the very flame of love
    A kind of wick or snuff that will abate it,
    And nothing is at a like goodness still,
    For goodness, growing to a plurisy,   115
    Dies in his own too much. That we would do,
    We should do when we would; for this 'would' changes,
    And hath abatements and delays as many
    As there are tongues, are hands, are accidents,
    And then this 'should' is like a spendthrift's sigh   120
    That hurts by easing. But to the quick of th' ulcer—
    Hamlet comes back; what would you undertake
    To show yourself in deed your father's son
    More than in words?
LAER.   To cut his throat i' th' church.
KING. No place indeed should murder sanctuarize;   125
    Revenge should have no bounds. But, good Laertes,
    Will you do this? Keep close within your chamber.
    Hamlet returned shall know you are come home.

98. *scrimers* fencers.   115. *plurisy* excess.
110. *passages of proof* incidents of ex-   121. *quick* sensitive flesh.
perience.   125. *sanctuarize* give sanctuary to.
111. *qualifies* weakens.

We'll put on those shall praise your excellence,
And set a double varnish on the fame   130
The Frenchman gave you, bring you in fine together,
And wager on your heads. He, being remiss,
Most generous, and free from all contriving,
Will not peruse the foils, so that with ease,
Or with a little shuffling, you may choose   135
A sword unbated, and in a pass of practice
Requite him for your father.

LAER.   I will do't,
And for that purpose I'll anoint my sword.
I bought an unction of a mountebank,
So mortal that but dip a knife in it,   140
Where it draws blood no cataplasm so rare,
Collected from all simples that have virtue
Under the moon, can save the thing from death
That is but scratched withal. I'll touch my point
With this contagion, that if I gall him slightly,   145
It may be death.

KING.   Let's further think of this,
Weigh what convenience both of time and means
May fit us to our shape. If this should fail,
And that our drift look through our bad performance,
'Twere better not assayed. Therefore this project   150
Should have a back or second that might hold
If this did blast in proof. Soft, let me see.
We'll make a solemn wager on your cunnings—
I ha't.
When in your motion you are hot and dry—   155
As make your bouts more violent to that end—
And that he calls for drink, I'll have preferred him
A chalice for the nonce, whereon but sipping,
If he by chance escape your venomed stuck,
Our purpose may hold there.—But stay, what noise?   160

Enter QUEEN.

QUEEN. One woe doth tread upon another's heel,
So fast they follow. Your sister's drowned, Laertes.

LAER. Drowned? O, where?

QUEEN. There is a willow grows askant the brook
That shows his hoar leaves in the glassy stream.   165

---

132. *remiss* careless.
134. *peruse* inspect.
136. *unbated* not blunted; *pass of practice* treacherous thrust.
141. *cataplasm* poultice.
142. *simples* medicinal herbs.
148. *shape* plan.
149. *drift* scheme.
151. *back or second* something in support.
152. *blast in proof* burst during trial (like a faulty cannon).
155. *motion* exertion.
158. *nonce* occasion.
159. *stuck* thrust.
164. *askant* alongside.
165. *hoar* gray.

Therewith fantastic garlands did she make
Of crowflowers, nettles, daisies, and long purples
That liberal shepherds give a grosser name,
But our cold maids do dead men's fingers call them.
There on the pendent boughs her crownet weeds   170
Clamb'ring to hang, an envious sliver broke,
When down her weedy trophies and herself
Fell in the weeping brook. Her clothes spread wide,
And mermaid-like awhile they bore her up,
Which time she chanted snatches of old lauds,   175
As one incapable of her own distress,
Or like a creature native and indued
Unto that element. But long it could not be
Till that her garments, heavy with their drink,
Pulled the poor wretch from her melodious lay   180
To muddy death.
LAER.   Alas, then she is drowned?
QUEEN. Drowned, drowned.
LAER. Too much of water hast thou, poor Ophelia,
And therefore I forbid my tears; but yet
It is our trick; nature her custom holds,   185
Let shame say what it will. When these are gone,
The woman will be out. Adieu, my lord.
I have a speech o' fire that fain would blaze
But that this folly drowns it.   *Exit.*
KINC.   Let's follow, Gertrude.
How much I had to do to calm his rage!   190
Now fear I this will give it start again;
Therefore let's follow.   *Exeunt.*

[V.i]
      Enter two CLOWNS.
CLOWN. Is she to be buried in Christian burial when she wilfully
    seeks her own salvation?
OTHER. I tell thee she is. Therefore make her grave straight.
    The crowner hath sat on her, and finds it Christian burial.
CLOWN. How can that be, unless she drowned herself in her own   5
    defence?
OTHER. Why, 'tis found so.
CLOWN. It must be 'se offendendo'; it cannot be else. For here
    lies the point: if I drown myself wittingly, it argues an act,
    and an act hath three branches—it is to act, to do, to perform;   10
    argal, she drowned herself wittingly.

---

168. *liberal* free-spoken, licentious.
169. *cold* chaste.
170. *crownet* coronet.
171. *envious* malicious.
176. *incapable of* insensible to.
177. *indued* endowed.

187. *woman* unmanly part of nature.

[V.i] 4. *crowner* coroner.
8. *se offendendo* the Clown's blunder
for *se defendendo* ("in self-defense").
11. *argal* therefore (corrupt form of

OTHER. Nay, but hear you, Goodman Delver.

CLOWN. Give me leave. Here lies the water; good. Here stands
the man; good. If the man go to this water and drown himself,
it is, will he, nill he, he goes—mark you that. But if the water 15
come to him and drown him, he drowns not himself. Argal,
he that is not guilty of his own death shortens not his own life.

OTHER. But is this law?

CLOWN. Ay, marry, is't; crowner's quest law.

OTHER. Will you ha' the truth on't? If this had not been a gentle- 20
woman, she should have been buried out o' Christian burial.

CLOWN. Why, there thou say'st. And the more pity that great
folk should have count'nance in this world to drown or hang
themselves more than their even-Christen. Come, my spade.
There is no ancient gentlemen but gard'ners, ditchers, and 25
grave-makers. They hold up Adam's profession.

OTHER. Was he a gentleman?

CLOWN. 'A was the first that ever bore arms.

OTHER. Why, he had none.

CLOWN. What, art a heathen? How dost thou understand the 30
Scripture? The Scripture says Adam digged. Could he dig without arms? I'll put another question to thee. If thou answerest
me not to the purpose, confess thyself—

OTHER. Go to.

CLOWN. What is he that builds stronger than either the mason, 35
the shipwright, or the carpenter?

OTHER. The gallows-maker, for that frame outlives a thousand
tenants.

CLOWN. I like thy wit well, in good faith. The gallows does well.
But how does it well? It does well to those that do ill. Now 40
thou dost ill to say the gallows is built stronger than the
church. Argal, the gallows may do well to thee. To't again,
come.

OTHER. Who builds stronger than a mason, a shipwright, or a carpenter?

CLOWN. Ay, tell me that, and unyoke. 45

OTHER. Marry, now I can tell.

CLOWN. To't.

OTHER. Mass, I cannot tell.

CLOWN. Cudgel thy brains no more about it, for your dull ass 50
will not mend his pace with beating. And when you are asked
this question next, say 'a grave-maker'. The houses he makes
lasts till doomsday. Go, get thee in, and fetch me a stoup of
liquor.   [*Exit* OTHER CLOWN.]

    Enter HAMLET *and* HORATIO [*as* CLOWN *digs and sings*].

    In youth, when I did love, did love,   (*Song.*) 55

ergo).

19. *quest* inquest.

24. *even-Christen* fellow Christian.

46. *tell me that, and unyoke* answer
the question and then you can relax.

53. *stoup* tankard.

    Methought it was very sweet,
To contract the time for-a my behove,
  O, methought there-a was nothing-a meet.

HAM. Has this fellow no feeling of his business, that 'a sings in
grave-making?   60

HOR. Custom hath made it in him a property of easiness.

HAM. 'Tis e'en so. The hand of little employment hath the
dantier sense.

CLOWN.   But age, with his stealing steps,   (*Song.*)
           Hath clawed me in his clutch,   65
    And hath shipped me intil the land,
    As if I had never been such.
                                [*Throws up a skull.*]

HAM. That skull had a tongue in it, and could sing once. How
the knave jowls it to the ground, as if 'twere Cain's jawbone,
that did the first murder! This might be the pate of a politi- 70
cian, which this ass now o'erreaches; one that would circumvent
God, might it not?

HOR. It might, my lord.

HAM. Or of a courtier, which could say 'Good morrow, sweet
lord! How dost thou, sweet lord?' This might be my Lord 75
Such-a-one, that praised my Lord Such-a-one's horse, when 'a
went to beg it, might it not?

HOR. Ay, my lord.

HAM. Why, e'en so, and now my Lady Worm's, chapless, and
knock'd about the mazzard with a sexton's spade. Here's fine 80
revolution, an we had the trick to see't. Did these bones cost
no more the breeding but to play at loggats with them? Mine
ache to think on't.

CLOWN.   A pick-axe and a spade, a spade,   (*Song.*)
           For and a shrouding sheet: 85
    O, a pit of clay for to be made
    For such a guest is meet.
                       [*Throws up another skull.*]

HAM. There's another. Why may not that be the skull of a
lawyer? Where be his quiddities now, his quillets, his cases,
his tenures, and his tricks? Why does he suffer this mad knave 90
now to knock him about the sconce with a dirty shovel, and
will not tell him of his action of battery? Hum! This fellow
might be in's time a great buyer of land, with his statutes, his
recognizances, his fines, his double vouchers, his recoveries. Is

---

61. *a property of easiness* a habit that
comes easily to him.
66. *intil* into.
69. *jowls* hurls.
71. *circumvent* cheat.
79. *chapless* with lower jaw missing.
80. *mazzard* head.
82. *loggats* small logs of wood for
throwing at a mark.
89. *quiddities* subtle distinctions; *quillets* quibbles.
94. *recognizances* legal bonds, defining
debts; *vouchers* persons vouched or
called on to warrant a title; *recoveries*
legal processes to break an entail.

this the fine of his fines, and the recovery of his recoveries, to 95
have his fine pate full of fine dirt? Will his vouchers vouch
him no more of his purchases, and double ones too, than the
length and breadth of a pair of indentures? The very conveyances of his lands will scarcely lie in this box, and must th'
inheritor himself have no more, ha? 100

HOR. Not a jot more, my lord.

HAM. Is not parchment made of sheepskins?

HOR. Ay, my lord, and of calves' skins too.

HAM. They are sheep and calves which seek out assurance in that.
I will speak to this fellow. Whose grave's this, sirrah? 105

CLOWN. Mine, sir.

>[*Sings.*] O, a pit of clay for to be made—

HAM. I think it be thine indeed, for thou liest in't.

CLOWN. You lie out on't, sir, and therefore 'tis not yours. For my
part, I do not lie in't, yet it is mine. 110

HAM. Thou dost lie in't, to be in't and say it is thine. 'Tis for the
dead, not for the quick; therefore thou liest.

CLOWN. 'Tis a quick lie, sir; 'twill away again from me to you.

HAM. What man dost thou dig it for?

CLOWN. For no man, sir. 115

HAM. What woman, then?

CLOWN. For none neither.

HAM. Who is to be buried in't?

CLOWN. One that was a woman, sir; but, rest her soul, she's dead.

HAM. How absolute the knave is! We must speak by the card, or 120
equivocation will undo us. By the Lord, Horatio, this three
years I have took note of it, the age is grown so picked that the
toe of the peasant comes so near the heel of the courtier, he
galls his kibe. How long hast thou been a grave-maker?

CLOWN. Of all the days i' th' year, I came to't that day that our 125
last King Hamlet overcame Fortinbras.

HAM. How long is that since?

CLOWN. Cannot you tell that? Every fool can tell that. It was
that very day that young Hamlet was born—he that is mad, and
sent into England. 130

HAM. Ay, marry, why was he sent into England?

CLOWN. Why, because 'a was mad. 'A shall recover his wits there;
or, if 'a do not, 'tis no great matter there.

HAM. Why?

CLOWN. 'Twill not be seen in him there. There the men are as 135
mad as he.

HAM. How came he mad?

---

98. *pair of indentures* deed or legal
agreement in duplicate; *conveyances*
deeds by which property is transferred.
120. *absolute* positive; *card* card on
which the points of the mariner's compass are marked (i.e., absolutely to the
point).
122. *picked* fastidious.
124. *kibe* chilblain.

CLOWN. Very strangely, they say.

HAM. How strangely?

CLOWN. Faith, e'en with losing his wits. 140

HAM. Upon what ground?

CLOWN. Why, here in Denmark. I have been sexton here, man and boy, thirty years.

HAM. How long will a man lie i' th' earth ere he rot?

CLOWN. Faith, if 'a be not rotten before 'a die—as we have many 145 pocky corses now-a-days that will scarce hold the laying in—'a will last you some eight year or nine year. A tanner will last you nine year.

HAM. Why he more than another?

CLOWN. Why, sir, his hide is so tanned with his trade that 'a will 150 keep out water a great while; and your water is a sore decayer of your whoreson dead body. Here's a skull now hath lien you i' th' earth three and twenty years.

HAM. Whose was it?

CLOWN. A whoreson mad fellow's it was. Whose do you think it 155 was?

HAM. Nay, I know not.

CLOWN. A pestilence on him for a mad rogue! 'A poured a flagon of Rhenish on my head once. This same skull, sir, was, sir, Yorick's skull, the king's jester. 160

HAM. [*Takes the skull.*] This?

CLOWN. E'en that.

HAM. Alas, poor Yorick! I knew him, Horatio—a fellow of infinite jest, of most excellent fancy. He hath bore me on his back a thousand times, and now how abhorred in my imagina- 165 tion it is! My gorge rises at it. Here hung those lips that I have kissed I know not how oft. Where be your gibes now, your gambols, your songs, your flashes of merriment that were wont to set the table on a roar? Not one now to mock your own grinning? Quite chap-fall'n? Now get you to my lady's 170 chamber, and tell her, let her paint an inch thick, to this favor she must come. Make her laugh at that. Prithee, Horatio, tell me one thing.

HOR. What's that, my lord?

HAM. Dost thou think Alexander looked o' this fashion i' th' 175 earth?

HOR. E'en so.

HAM. And smelt so? Pah! [*Throws down the skull.*]

HOR. E'en so, my lord.

HAM. To what base uses we may return, Horatio! Why may not 180 imagination trace the noble dust of Alexander till 'a find it stopping a bung-hole?

HOR. 'Twere to consider too curiously to consider so.

146. *pocky* infected with pox (syphilis).

159. *Rhenish* Rhine wine.

183. *too curiously* over ingeniously.

HAM. No, faith, not a jot, but to follow him thither with modesty enough, and likelihood to lead it. Alexander died, Alexander 185 was buried, Alexander returneth to dust; the dust is earth; of earth we make loam; and why of that loam whereto he was converted might they not stop a beer-barrel?

> Imperious Cæsar, dead and turned to clay,
> Might stop a hole to keep the wind away.   190
> O, that that earth which kept the world in awe
> Should patch a wall t' expel the winter's flaw!

But soft, but soft awhile! Here comes the king,
The queen, the courtiers.

> *Enter* KING, QUEEN, LAERTES, *and the Corse* [*with a Doctor of Divinity as* PRIEST *and* LORDS *attendant*].
>   Who is this they follow?
And with such maimed rites? This doth betoken   195
The corse they follow did with desperate hand
Fordo it own life. 'Twas of some estate.
Couch we awhile and mark.   [*Retires with* HORATIO.]
LAER. What ceremony else?
HAM. That is Laertes, a very noble youth. Mark.   200
LAER. What ceremony else?
DOCTOR. Her obsequies have been as far enlarged
As we have warranty. Her death was doubtful,
And but that great command o'ersways the order,
She should in ground unsanctified been lodged   205
Till the last trumpet. For charitable prayers,
Shards, flints, and pebbles, should be thrown on her.
Yet here she is allowed her virgin crants,
Her maiden strewments, and the bringing home
Of bell and burial.   210
LAER. Must there no more be done?
DOCTOR.   No more be done.
We should profane the service of the dead
To sing a requiem and such rest to her
As to peace-parted souls.
LAER.   Lay her i' th' earth,
And from her fair and unpolluted flesh   215
May violets spring! I tell thee, churlish priest,
A minist'ring angel shall my sister be
When thou liest howling.
HAM.   What, the fair Ophelia!
QUEEN. Sweets to the sweet. Farewell!   [*Scatters flowers.*]
I hoped thou shouldst have been my Hamlet's wife.   220
I thought thy bride-bed to have decked, sweet maid,

---

192. *flaw* gust.
197. *Fordo* destroy; *it* its.

207. *Shards* bits of broken pottery.
208. *crants* garland.

And not have strewed thy grave.

LAER.   O, treble woe
Fall ten times treble on that curséd head
Whose wicked deed thy most ingenious sense
Deprived thee of! Hold off the earth awhile,   225
Till I have caught her once more in mine arms.
                                        [*Leaps into the grave.*]
Now pile your dust upon the quick and dead,
Till of this flat a mountain you have made
T' o'er-top old Pelion or the skyish head
Of blue Olympus.

HAM. [*Coming forward.*] What is he whose grief   230
Bears such an emphasis, whose phrase of sorrow
Conjures the wand'ring stars, and makes them stand
Like wonder-wounded hearers? This is I,
Hamlet the Dane.   [*Leaps into the grave.*]

LAER. The devil take thy soul!   [*Grappling with him.*]

HAM.   Thou pray'st not well.   235
I prithee take thy fingers from my throat,
For though I am not splenitive and rash,
Yet have I in me something dangerous,
Which let thy wisdom fear. Hold off thy hand.

KING. Pluck them asunder.   240

QUEEN. Hamlet! Hamlet!

ALL. Gentlemen!

HOR. Good my lord, be quiet.
    [*The* ATTENDANTS *part them, and they come out of the grave.*]

HAM. Why, I will fight with him upon this theme
Until my eyelids will no longer wag.   245

QUEEN. O my son, what theme?

HAM. I loved Ophelia. Forty thousand brothers
Could not with all their quantity of love
Make up my sum. What wilt thou do for her?

KING. O, he is mad, Laertes.   250

QUEEN. For love of God, forbear him.

HAM. 'Swounds, show me what th'owt do.
Woo't weep, woo't fight, woo't fast, woo't tear thyself,
Woo't drink up eisel, eat a crocodile?
I'll do't. Dost come here to whine?   255
To outface me with leaping in her grave?
Be buried quick with her, and so will I.

---

224. *most ingenious* of quickest apprehension.
228. *Pelion* a mountain in Thessaly, like Olympus, line 229, and Ossa, line 261 (the allusion is to the war in which the Titans fought the gods and, in their attempt to scale heaven, heaped Ossa and Olympus on Pelion. or Pelion and Ossa on Olympus).
231. *such an emphasis* so vehement an expression or display.
237. *splenitive* fiery-tempered (from the spleen, seat of anger).
253. *woo't* wilt (thou).
254. *eisel* vinegar.

And if thou prate of mountains, let them throw
Millions of acres on us, till our ground,
Singeing his pate against the burning zone,   260
Make Ossa like a wart! Nay, an thou'lt mouth,
I'll rant as well as thou.
QUEEN.   This is mere madness;
And thus awhile the fit will work on him.
Anon, as patient as the female dove
When that her golden couplets are disclosed,   265
His silence will sit drooping.
HAM.   Hear you, sir.
What is the reason that you use me thus?
I loved you ever. But it is no matter.
Let Hercules himself do what he may,
The cat will mew, and dog will have his day.   270
KING. I pray thee, good Horatio, wait upon him.
                              Exit Hamlet and Horatio.
[*To* LAERTES.] Strengthen your patience in our last night's
  speech.
We'll put the matter to the present push.—
Good Gertrude, set some watch over your son.—
This grave shall have a living monument.   275
An hour of quiet shortly shall we see;
Till then in patience our proceeding be.   *Exeunt.*

[V.ii]
            Enter HAMLET *and* HORATIO.
HAM. So much for this, sir; now shall you see the other.
  You do remember all the circumstance?
HOR. Remember it, my lord!
HAM. Sir, in my heart there was a kind of fighting
  That would not let me sleep. Methought I lay   5
  Worse than the mutines in the bilboes. Rashly,
  And praised be rashness for it—let us know,
  Our indiscretion sometime serves us well,
  When our deep plots do pall; and that should learn us
  There's a divinity that shapes our ends,   10
  Rough-hew them how we will—
HOR.   That is most certain.
HAM. Up from my cabin,
  My sea-gown scarfed about me, in the dark
  Groped I to find out them, had my desire,
  Fingered their packet, and in fine withdrew   15
  To mine own room again, making so bold,
  My fears forgetting manners, to unseal

265. *couplets* newly-hatched pair.   fetters.
                                             9. *pall* fail.
[V.ii] 6. *mutines* mutineers; *bilboes*   15. *fingered* filched.

Their grand commission; where I found, Horatio—
Ah, royal knavery!—an exact command,
Larded with many several sorts of reasons,   20
Importing Denmark's health, and England's too,
With, ho! such bugs and goblins in my life,
That on the supervise, no leisure bated,
No, not to stay the grinding of the axe,
My head should be struck off.

HOR.   Is't possible?   25

HAM. Here's the commission; read it at more leisure.
    But wilt thou hear now how I did proceed?

HOR. I beseech you.

HAM. Being thus benetted round with villainies,
    Or I could make a prologue to my brains,   30
    They had begun the play. I sat me down,
    Devised a new commission, wrote it fair.
    I once did hold it, as our statists do,
    A baseness to write fair, and labored much
    How to forget that learning; but sir, now   35
    It did me yeoman's service. Wilt thou know
    Th' effect of what I wrote?

HOR.   Ay, good my lord.

HAM. An earnest conjuration from the king,
    As England was his faithful tributary,
    As love between them like the palm might flourish,   40
    As peace should still her wheaten garland wear
    And stand a comma 'tween their amities,
    And many such like as's of great charge,
    That on the view and knowing of these contents,
    Without debatement further more or less,   45
    He should those bearers put to sudden death,
    Not shriving-time allowed.

HOR.   How was this sealed?

HAM. Why, even in that was heaven ordinant,
    I had my father's signet in my purse,
    Which was the model of that Danish seal,   50
    Folded the writ up in the form of th' other,
    Subscribed it, gave't th' impression, placed it safely,
    The changeling never known. Now, the next day
    Was our sea-fight, and what to this was sequent
    Thou knowest already.   55

HOR. So Guildenstern and Rosencrantz go to't.

20. *Larded* garnished.
22. *bugs and goblins* imaginary horrors (here, horrendous crimes attributed to Hamlet, and represented as dangers should he be allowed to live).
23. *supervise* perusal; *bated* deducted, allowed.
24. *stay* await.
30. *Or* ere.
33. *statists* statesmen.
42. *comma* connective.
43. *charge* (1) importance (2) burden (the double meaning fits the play that makes "as's" into "asses").
48. *ordinant* guiding.
52. *Subscribed* signed.

HAM. Why, man, they did make love to this employment.
  They are not near my conscience; their defeat
  Does by their own insinuation grow.
  'Tis dangerous when the baser nature comes   60
  Between the pass and fell incensèd points
  Of mighty opposites.
HOR.   Why, what a king is this!
HAM. Does it not, think thee, stand me now upon—
  He that hath killed my king and whored my mother,
  Popped in between th' election and my hopes,   65
  Thrown out his angle for my proper life,
  And with such coz'nage—is't not perfect conscience
  To quit him with this arm? And is't not to be damned
  To let this canker of our nature come
  In further evil?   70
HOR. It must be shortly known to him from England
  What is the issue of the business there.
HAM. It will be short; the interim is mine.
  And a man's life's no more than to say 'one'.
  But I am very sorry, good Horatio,   75
  That to Laertes I forgot myself;
  For by the image of my cause I see
  The portraiture of his. I'll court his favours.
  But sure the bravery of his grief did put me
  Into a tow'ring passion.
HOR.   Peace; who comes here?   80

        Enter [OSRIC] *a courtier.*

OSR. Your lordship is right welcome back to Denmark.
HAM. I humbly thank you, sir. [*Aside to* HORATIO.] Dost know
  this water-fly?
HOR. [*Aside to* HAMLET.] No, my good lord.
HAM. [*Aside to* HORATIO.] Thy state is the more gracious, for 'tis 85
  a vice to know him. He hath much land, and fertile. Let a
  beast be lord of beasts, and his crib shall stand at the king's
  mess. 'Tis a chough, but as I say, spacious in the possession of
  dirt.
OSR. Sweet lord, if your lordship were at leisure, I should impart 90
  a thing to you from his majesty.
HAM. I will receive it, sir, with all diligence of spirit. Put your
  bonnet to his right use. 'Tis for the head.
OSR. I thank your lordship, it is very hot.
HAM. No, believe me, 'tis very cold; the wind is northerly.   95
OSR. It is indifferent cold, my lord, indeed.

59. *insinuation* intrusion.
61. *pass* thrust; *fell* fierce.
63. *Does it not * * * stand me now upon* is it not incumbent upon me.
65. *election* i.e., to the kingship, Denmark being an elective monarchy.
66. *angle* fishing line; *proper* own.
68. *quit* repay.
79. *bravery* ostentatious display.
88. *mess* table; *chough* jackdaw; thus, a chatterer.
96. *indifferent* somewhat.

HAM. But yet methinks it is very sultry and hot for my complexion.

OSR. Exceedingly, my lord; it is very sultry, as 'twere—I cannot tell how. My lord, his majesty bade me signify to you that 'a 100 has laid a great wager on your head. Sir, this is the matter—

HAM. I beseech you, remember.

[HAMLET *moves him to put on his hat.*]

OSR. Nay, good my lord; for my ease, in good faith. Sir, here is newly come to court Laertes; believe me, an absolute gentleman, full of most excellent differences, of very soft society and 105 great showing. Indeed, to speak feelingly of him, he is the card or calendar of gentry, for you shall find in him the continent of what part a gentleman would see.

HAM. Sir, his definement suffers no perdition in you, though I know to divide him inventorially would dozy th' arithmetic of 110 memory, and yet but yaw neither in respect of his quick sail. But in the verity of extolment, I take him to be a soul of great article, and his infusion of such dearth and rareness as, to make true diction of him, his semblable is his mirror, and who else would trace him, his umbrage, nothing more. 115

OSR. Your lordship speaks most infallibly of him.

HAM. The concernancy sir? Why do we wrap the gentleman in our more rawer breath?

OSR. Sir?

HOR. Is't not possible to understand in another tongue? You 120 will to't, sir, really.

HAM. What imports the nomination of this gentleman?

OSR. Of Laertes?

HOR. [*Aside.*] His purse is empty already. All's golden words are spent. 125

HAM. Of him, sir.

OSR. I know you are not ignorant—

HAM. I would you did, sir; yet, in faith, if you did, it would not much approve me. Well, sir.

OSR. You are not ignorant of what excellence Laertes is— 130

HAM. I dare not confess that, lest I should compare with him in excellence; but to know a man well were to know himself.

OSR. I mean, sir, for his weapon; but in the imputation laid on him by them, in his meed he's unfellowed.

HAM. What's his weapon? 135

97. *complexion* temperament.
105. *differences* distinguishing qualities.
106. *great showing* distinguished appearance; *card* map.
107. *continent* all-containing embodiment.
109. *definement* definition.
110. *divide him inventorially* classify him in detail; *dozy* dizzy.
111. *yaw* hold to a course unsteadily like a ship that steers wild.

113. *article* scope, importance; *infusion* essence; *dearth* scarcity.
114. *semblable* likeness.
115. *trace* (1) draw (2) follow; *umbrage* shadow.
117. *concernancy* import, relevance.
121. *to't* i.e., get to an understanding.
122. *nomination* mention.
129. *approve* commend.
131. *compare* compete.
134. *meed* pay; *unfellowed* unequaled.

OSR. Rapier and dagger.

HAM. That's two of his weapons—but well.

OSR. The king, sir, hath wagered with him six Barbary horses, against the which he has impawned, as I take it, six French rapiers and poniards, with their assigns, as girdle, hangers, and so. Three of the carriages, in faith, are very dear to fancy, very responsive to the hilts, most delicate carriages, and of very liberal conceit. 140

HAM. What call you the carriages?

HOR. [*Aside to* HAMLET.] I knew you must be edified by the margent ere you had done. 145

OSR. The carriages, sir, are the hangers.

HAM. The phrase would be more germane to the matter if we could carry a cannon by our sides. I would it might be hangers till then. But on! Six Barbary horses against six French swords, their assigns, and three liberal conceited carriages; that's the French bet against the Danish. Why is this all impawned, as you call it? 150

OSR. The king, sir, hath laid, sir, that in a dozen passes between yourself and him he shall not exceed you three hits; he hath laid on twelve for nine, and it would come to immediate trial if your lordship would vouchsafe the answer. 155

HAM. How if I answer no?

OSR. I mean, my lord, the opposition of your person in trial.

HAM. Sir, I will walk here in the hall. If it please his majesty, it is the breathing time of day with me. Let the foils be brought, the gentleman willing, and the king hold his purpose; I will win for him an I can. If not, I will gain nothing but my shame and the odd hits. 160

OSR. Shall I deliver you so? 165

HAM. To this effect, sir, after what flourish your nature will.

OSR. I commend my duty to your lordship.

HAM. Yours. [*Exit* OSRIC.] He does well to commend it himself; there are no tongues else for's turn.

HOR. This lapwing runs away with the shell on his head. 170

HAM. 'A did comply, sir, with his dug before 'a sucked it. Thus has he, and many more of the same bevy that I know the drossy age dotes on, only got the tune of the time; and out of an habit of encounter, a kind of yesty collection which carries

---

139. *impawned* staked.
140. *assigns* appendages.
142. *carriages* an affected word for *hangers*, i.e., straps from which the weapon was hung.
143. *liberal conceit* elaborate design.
146. *margent* margin (where explanatory notes were printed).
161. *breathing time* time for taking exercise.
163. *an* if.

170. *lapwing* a bird reputedly so precocious as to run as soon as hatched.
171. *comply* observe the formalities of courtesy; *dug* mother's nipple.
172. *bevy* a covey of quails or lapwings; *drossy* frivolous.
174. *encounter* manner of address or accosting; *yesty collection* a frothy and superficial patchwork of terms from the conversation of others.

them through and through the most fanned and winnowed 175
opinions; and do but blow them to their trial, the bubbles are
out.

    Enter a LORD.

LORD. My lord, his majesty commended him to you by young
    Osric, who brings back to him that you attend him in the hall.
    He sends to know if your pleasure hold to play with Laertes, or 180
    that you will take longer time.
HAM. I am constant to my purposes; they follow the king's pleas-
    ure. If his fitness speaks, mine is ready; now or whensoever,
    provided I be so able as now.
LORD. The king and queen and all are coming down.   185
HAM. In happy time.
LORD. The queen desires you to use some gentle entertainment
    to Laertes before you fall to play.
HAM. She well instructs me.   [*Exit* LORD.]
HOR. You will lose this wager, my lord.   190
HAM. I do not think so. Since he went into France I have been
    in continual practice. I shall win at the odds. But thou wouldst
    not think how ill all's here about my heart. But it is no matter.
HOR. Nay, good my lord—
HAM. It is but foolery, but it is such a kind of gaingiving as would 195
    perhaps trouble a woman.
HOR. If your mind dislike anything, obey it. I will forestall their
    repair hither, and say you are not fit.
HAM. Not a whit, we defy augury. There is special providence in
    the fall of a sparrow. If it be now, 'tis not to come; if it be not 200
    to come, it will be now; if it be not now, yet it will come. The
    readiness is all. Since no man of aught he leaves knows, what
    is't to leave betimes? Let be.

A table prepared. [*Enter*] TRUMPETS, DRUMS, *and* OFFICERS *with*
cushions; KING, QUEEN, [OSRIC] *and all the the* STATE, [*with*]
foils, daggers, and LAERTES.

KING. Come, Hamlet, come, and take this hand from me.
            [*The king puts* LAERTES's *hand into* HAMLET's.]
HAM. Give me your pardon, sir. I have done you wrong,   205
    But pardon 't as you are a gentleman.
    This presence knows, and you must needs have heard,
    How I am punished with a sore distraction.
    What I have done
    That might your nature, honor, and exception,   210
    Roughly awake, I here proclaim was madness.
    Was 't Hamlet wronged Laertes? Never Hamlet.
    If Hamlet from himself be ta'en away,
    And when he's not himself does wrong Laertes,

---

175. *winnowed* tested, freed from inferior elements.

183. *fitness* convenience, inclination.
195. *gaingiving* misgiving.

Then Hamlet does it not, Hamlet denies it.   215
Who does it then? His madness. If't be so,
Hamlet is of the faction that is wronged;
His madness is poor Hamlet's enemy.
Sir, in this audience,
Let my disclaiming from a purposed evil   220
Free me so far in your most generous thoughts
That I have shot my arrow o'er the house
And hurt my brother.

LAER.   I am satisfied in nature,
Whose motive in this case should stir me most
To my revenge. But in my terms of honor   225
I stand aloof, and will no reconcilement
Till by some elder masters of known honor
I have a voice and precedent of peace
To keep my name ungored. But till that time
I do receive your offered love like love,   230
And will not wrong it.

HAM.   I embrace it freely,
And will this brother's wager frankly play.
Give us the foils.

LAER.   Come, one for me.

HAM. I'll be your foil, Laertes. In mine ignorance
Your skill shall, like a star i' th' darkest night,   235
Stick fiery off indeed.

LAER.   You mock me, sir.

HAM. No, by this hand.

KING. Give them the foils, young Osric. Cousin Hamlet,
You know the wager?

HAM.   Very well, my lord;
Your Grace has laid the odds o' th' weaker side.   240

KING. I do not fear it, I have seen you both;
But since he is bettered, we have therefore odds.

LAER. This is too heavy; let me see another.

HAM. This likes me well. These foils have all a length?
                        [*They prepare to play.*]

OSR. Ay, my good lord.   245

KING. Set me the stoups of wine upon that table.
If Hamlet give the first or second hit,
Or quit in answer of the third exchange,
Let all the battlements their ordnance fire.
The king shall drink to Hamlet's better breath,   250
And in the cup an union shall he throw,

228. *voice and precedent* authoritative statement justified by precedent.
234. *foil* (1) setting for gem (2) weapon.
242. *bettered* perfected through training.
244. *have all a length* are all of the same length.
248. *quit in answer* literally, give as good as he gets (i.e., if the third bout is a draw).
251. *union* pearl.

Richer than that which four successive kings
In Denmark's crown have worn. Give me the cups,
And let the kettle to the trumpet speak,
The trumpet to the cannoneer without, 255
The cannons to the heavens, the heaven to earth,
'Now the king drinks to Hamlet'. Come, begin—
Trumpets the while.
And you, the judges, bear a wary eye.
HAM. Come on, sir.
LAER.   Come, my lord.   [*They play.*]
HAM.   One.
LAER.   No.
HAM.   Judgment?
OSR. A hit, a very palpable hit. 260
Drums, trumpets and shot. Flourish; a piece goes off.
LAER. Well, again.
KING. Stay, give me drink. Hamlet, this pearl is thine.
Here's to thy health. Give him the cup.
HAM. I'll play this bout first; set it by awhile.
Come.   [*They play.*] 265
Another hit; what say you?
LAER. I do confess't.
KING. Our son shall win.
QUEEN.   He's fat, and scant of breath.
Here, Hamlet, take my napkin, rub thy brows.
The queen carouses to thy fortune, Hamlet. 270
HAM. Good madam!
KING. Gertrude, do not drink.
QUEEN. I will, my lord; I pray you pardon me.
KING. [*Aside.*] It is the poisoned cup; it is too late.
HAM. I dare not drink yet, madam; by and by. 275
QUEEN. Come, let me wipe thy face.
LAER. My lord, I'll hit him now.
KING.   I do not think't.
LAER. [*Aside.*] And yet it is almost against my conscience.
HAM. Come, for the third, Laertes. You do but dally.
I pray you pass with your best violence; 280
I am afeard you make a wanton of me.
LAER. Say you so? Come on.   [*They play.*]
OSR. Nothing, neither way.
LAER. Have at you now! [LAERTES *wounds* HAMLET: *then, in
scuffling, they change rapiers, and* HAMLET *wounds* LAERTES.]
KING. Part them. They are incensed. 285
HAM. Nay, come again.   [*The* QUEEN *falls.*]
OSR. Look to the queen there, ho!
HOR. They bleed on both sides. How is it, my lord?

268. *fat* sweaty.
281. *make a wanton of me* trifle with me.

OSR. How is't, Laertes?

LAER. Why, as a woodcock to mine own springe, Osric.   290
   I am justly killed with mine own treachery.

HAM. How does the queen?

KING. She swoons to see them bleed.

QUEEN. No, no, the drink, the drink! O my dear Hamlet!
   The drink, the drink! I am poisoned.   [*Dies.*] 295

HAM. O, villainy! Ho! let the door be locked.
   Treachery! seek it out.   [LAERTES *falls.*]

LAER. It is here, Hamlet. Hamlet, thou art slain;
   No med'cine in the world can do thee good.
   In thee there is not half an hour's life.   300
   The treacherous instrument is in thy hand,
   Unbated and envenomed. The foul practice
   Hath turned itself on me. Lo, here I lie,
   Never to rise again. Thy mother's poisoned.
   I can no more. The king, the king's to blame.   305

HAM. The point envenomed too?
   Then, venom, to thy work.   [*Hurts the* KING.]

ALL. Treason! treason!

KING. O, yet defend me, friends. I am but hurt.

HAM. Here, thou incestuous, murd'rous, damned Dane,   310
   Drink off this potion. Is thy union here?
   Follow my mother.   [KING *dies.*]

LAER.   He is justly served.
   It is a poison tempered by himself.
   Exchange forgiveness with me, noble Hamlet.
   Mine and my father's death come not upon thee,   315
   Nor thine on me!   [*Dies.*]

HAM. Heaven make thee free of it! I follow thee.
   I am dead, Horatio. Wretched queen, adieu!
   You that look pale and tremble at this chance,
   That are but mutes or audience to this act,   320
   Had I but time, as this fell sergeant Death
   Is strict in his arrest, O, I could tell you—
   But let it be. Horatio, I am dead:
   Thou livest; report me and my cause aright
   To the unsatisfied.

HOR.   Never believe it.   325
   I am more an antique Roman than a Dane.
   Here's yet some liquor left.

HAM.   As th'art a man,
   Give me the cup. Let go. By heaven, I'll ha't.
   O God, Horatio, what a wounded name,
   Things standing thus unknown, shall live behind me!   330

290. *springe* trap.
302. *unbated* unblunted; *practice* plot.
321. *fell* cruel; *sergeant* an officer
whose duty is to summon persons to
appear before a court.

If thou didst ever hold me in thy heart,
Absent thee from felicity awhile,
And in this harsh world draw thy breath in pain,
To tell my story.   *A march afar off.*
             What warlike noise is this?
OSR. Young Fortinbras, with conquest come from Poland,   335
   To th' ambassadors of England gives
   This warlike volley.
HAM.   O, I die, Horatio!
   The potent poison quite o'er-crows my spirit.
   I cannot live to hear the news from England,
   But I do prophesy th' election lights   340
   On Fortinbras. He has my dying voice.
   So tell him, with th' occurrents, more and less,
   Which have solicited—the rest is silence.   [*Dies.*]
HOR. Now cracks a noble heart. Good night, sweet prince,
   And flights of angels sing thee to thy rest! [*March within.*] 345
   Why does the drum come hither?

       Enter FORTINBRAS, *with the* AMBASSADORS [*and with drum,*
          colors, and ATTENDANTS].

FORT. Where is this sight?
HOR.   What is it you would see?
   If aught of woe or wonder, cease your search.
FORT. This quarry cries on havoc. O proud death,
   What feast is toward in thine eternal cell   350
   That thou so many princes at a shot
   So bloodily hast struck?
AMB.   The sight is dismal;
   And our affairs from England come too late.
   The ears are senseless that should give us hearing
   To tell him his commandment is fulfilled,   355
   That Rosencrantz and Guildenstern are dead.
   Where should we have our thanks?
HOR.   Not from his mouth,
   Had it th' ability of life to thank you.
   He never gave commandment for their death.
   But since, so jump upon this bloody question,   360
   You from the Polack wars, and you from England,
   Are here arrived, give order that these bodies
   High on a stage be placéd to the view,
   And let me speak to th' yet unknowing world
   How these things came about. So shall you hear   365
   Of carnal, bloody, and unnatural acts;
   Of accidental judgments, casual slaughters;

338. *o'er-crows* triumphs over.   349. *quarry* pile of dead.
341. *voice* vote.   350. *toward* impending.
342. *more and less* great and small.   360. *jump* exactly.
343. *solicited* incited, prompted.

Of deaths put on by cunning and forced cause;
And, in this upshot, purposes mistook
Fall'n on th' inventors' heads. All this can I   370
Truly deliver.
FORT.   Let us haste to hear it,
And call the noblest to the audience.
For me, with sorrow I embrace my fortune.
I have some rights of memory in this kingdom,
Which now to claim my vantage doth invite me.   375
HOR. Of that I shall have also cause to speak,
And from his mouth whose voice will draw on more.
But let this same be presently performed,
Even while men's minds are wild, lest more mischance
On plots and errors happen.
FORT.   Let four captains   380
Bear Hamlet like a soldier to the stage,
For he was likely, had he been put on,
To have proved most royal; and for his passage
The soldier's music and the rite of war
Speak loudly for him.   385
Take up the bodies. Such a sight as this
Becomes the field, but here shows much amiss.
Go, bid the soldiers shoot.

            Exeunt [*marching. A peal of ordnance shot off*].

368. *put on* instigated; *forced cause* by   382. *put on* set to perform in office.
reason of compulsion.   383. *passage* death.

Textual Commentary

The first edition of Hamlet was printed in quarto in 1603. It was published apparently without authorization—not surprisingly in view of the fact that it presents a pirated text of the play. This so-called "bad" quarto (Q1) is a reported text, put together from memory by a group of actors who had either seen the play performed, or who had themselves performed in it, on the London stage. Their purpose, presumably, was to furnish themselves with an acting version of the play to take on tour in the provinces. Most of their memories seem to have been drawn from the Shakespearean version of the tragedy, though it appears likely that memories of the pre-Shakespearean *Hamlet* have been incorporated at several points into the Q1 text. In it, Polonius is named Corambis (he is called Corambus in *Der Bestrafte Brudermord*), Reynaldo is Montano, and the nunnery scene occurs in Act II, immediately after Polonius/Corambis has made his suggestion to "loose" his daughter to Hamlet. In the Q1 version of the scene in Gertrude's chamber, the Queen explicitly denies having been a party to her husband's murder (thereby clearing up a point that is not clear in the more authoritative editions, and which Coleridge and other critics have wondered about), and she pledges herself to assist her son in his revenge. Q1 presents just the sort of garbled text that memorial reconstructions regularly do. The line of the action as we know it from the later editions is roughly preserved, though it is greatly simplified and vulgarized; and the Shakespearean language is thoroughly dissipated.

An authorized version of the play was duly published in the following year (the title pages of some copies of the second quarto bear the date 1604, others are dated 1605). All the evidence—especially that of the stage directions—suggests that this second quarto (Q2) was printed from Shakespeare's own manuscript. It is the fullest text of the play that survives (almost 3800 lines, as opposed to the 2220 type-lines of Q1), and the most authoritative, though its authority is somewhat diminished as a result of the many compositorial errors and omissions made in the process of printing, and also as a result of the fact that the bad first quarto was frequently consulted, for whatever reason, during the early stages of the printing of Q2, so that what should be, and in most respects is, the most authoritative text of the play has been contaminated at sundry points throughout the first act from the reported text of Q1.

A third quarto (Q3), printed from Q2, was published in 1611; and sometime between then and 1623 a fourth quarto (Q4, undated), printed from Q3, appeared. Neither Q3 nor Q4 has any independent textual authority.

The text of *Hamlet* which appeared in the folio collection (F) of Shakespeare's complete works in 1623 is generally supposed to have been printed from—or at least to have had behind it, if it were not directly printed from—the official theatrical promptbook. Thus it presumably represents the play as it had come to be acted by the King's Men some twenty years after its original production. It omits some 230 lines found in Q2, though it contains some 80 lines that are missing from Q2. There are numerous verbal differences between the two texts. Many of these are compositorial errors, occasioned when either the Q2 or the F workmen misread their manuscript. Examples are such variants as "cap" (F), "lap" (Q2), at II.ii.224; "loneliness" (F), "lowliness" (Q2), at III.i.46; "feature" (F), "stature" (Q2), at III.i.155; "so loud a wind" (F), "so loved Arm'd" (Q2), at IV.vii.22; "argal" (F), "or all" (Q2), at V.i.11, where in each case, F gives a correct reading for what is a literal misprint in Q2. But the folio has its share of compositorial misreadings as well. The "time" (Q2), "tune" (F) variant at III.i.154 is an example of one which has long been received into editions of the play. The famous case of the "sallied" (Q2) vs. the "solid" (F) flesh which Hamlet wishes, at I.ii.129, would melt, is almost certainly another.[1]

Not all the instances where F displays a word or phrase different from the corresponding reading in Q2 are due, however, to compositorial misreadings. There is no reason to suppose that the folio text represents a Shakespearean revision of the play as it appears in Q2. And assuming that the folio text derives from the official promptbook, and thus reflects theatrical practices, there is good reason to suppose that, where F departs from Q2 and a compositor is not responsible, the F variants represent verbal changes that had come to be made in the text by the actors themselves, over the years during which the play was performed. The folio text of *Hamlet* exhibits, in fact, just the sort of changes that one might expect to take place in the language of a play that had been in an active theatrical repertory for two decades. By comparison with the text of Q2, the actors can be seen taking certain liberties with their lines. Verbal substitutions have been made, catch words and phrases are repeated, and most troublesome of all perhaps, as Professor Harold Jenkins has pointed out in an important article,[2] the actors have interpolated a number of "gag lines" into their parts, of which the "Oh Vengeance" which F (but not Q2) interjects midway through Hamlet's soliloquy at the close of the second act is the most egregious.

For all its typographical imperfections, the second quarto gives us a text of *Hamlet* which must be regarded as superior to that of the folio, not only because it is fuller, but because it is closer to a Shakespearean manuscript source. It is the basis of the present edition. The folio text has been regularly consulted, and readings from it have been received into

1. For persuasive arguments that both Q2 readings here are the right ones, see G. W. Williams, "Hamlet's Reason, Jangled out of Time: III.i.166," *Notes and Queries*, Vol. 205 (1960), 329–331; and F. T. Bowers, "Hamlet's 'Sullied' or 'Solid' Flesh. A Bibliographical Case-History," *Shakespeare Survey*, 9 (1956), 44–47.
2. "Playhouse Interpolations in the Folio Text of *Hamlet*," *Studies in Bibliography*, Vol. XIII (1960), 31–47.

the present edition to supply Q2 omissions of words and phrases, to correct Q2 misprints, and to emend other corruptions in the Q2 text. The folio is, of course, the authority for the longer passages omitted from Q2 (as, for instance, at II.ii.233–260; II.ii.322–342; V.ii.68–80). The precise extent of my use of the folio text, and of all other editions of the play apart from Q2, is shown in the Textual Notes, where all substantive departures from the text of the second quarto are recorded. The Q2 spelling has been modernized for the present edition, and the punctuation has been silently emended where intelligibility has seemed to require it. I have sought, however, to retain wherever possible the relatively light Q2 system of pointing, which is often highly revealing, chiefly, one would like to suppose, because it reflects at a not too distant remove Shakespeare's own intentions. The stage directions of this edition are those of the second quarto. Editorial additions to them are enclosed in square brackets. Strong preterit verb endings are marked with an acute accent (') in verse passages where the meter requires that they be stressed.

TEXTUAL NOTES

Emendations of the second quarto text received into the present edition are printed inside the square bracket with—to the right of the bracket—an abbreviated reference to the edition in which the emendation first appears. The rejected Q2 reading follows. *om.* means *omitted*. Editions are referred to by the following abbreviations:

Q1 Quarto, 1603
Q2 Quarto, 1604–5
Q3 Quarto, 1611
Q4 Quarto, Undated
Q5 Quarto, 1637
F   Folio, 1623

The following later editions are also cited in the notes, by name: Rowe (1709); Pope (1723–25); Theobald (1733); Hanmer (1744); Warburton (1747); Johnson (1765); Capell (1767–68); Malone (1790); Collier (1842–44); Keightley (1867); Furness (1877); New Cambridge (1934).

[I.i] 16. soldier]*F;* souldiers *Q2.* 44. harrows]*F;* horrowes *Q2.* 45. Question it]*F;* Speak to it *Q2.* 73. why]*F;* with *Q2.* 73. cast]*F;* cost *Q1–2.* 88. those]*F;* these *Q2.* 91. return'd]*F;* returne *Q2.* 94. design'd] *Pope;* desseigne *Q2;* designe *F.* 112. mote]*Q4;* moth *Q2; om. F.* 121. fear'd]*Collier;* feare *Q2; om. F.* 138. you]*Q1, F;* your *Q2.* 140. at]*F; om. Q2.*
[I.ii] s.d. Councillors] Counsaile: as *Q2.* 58. He]*Q1,3,F; om. Q2.* 67. Not so. my]*F;* Not so much my *Q2.* 77.

good]*F;* coold *Q2.* 82. shapes]*Q3;* chapes *Q2;* shewes *F.* 137. come to this]*F;* come thus *Q2.* 143. would] *Q1,F;* should *Q2.* 149. even she]*F; om. Q2.* 175. you to drink deep ere] *Q1,F;* you for to drink ere *Q2.* 178. see]*Q1,F; om. Q2.* 236. hundred]*Q1,F;* hundreth *Q2.* 254. Foul]*Q1,F;* fonde *Q2.*
[I.iii] 3. is]*F;* in *Q2.* 18. For he * * * birth]*F; om. Q2.* 49. like]*F; om. Q2.* 74. Are]*Q1,F;* Or *Q2.* 75. be]*F;* boy *Q2.* 76. loan]*F;* loue *Q2.*

83. invites]*F;* inuests *Q2.* 109. Running]*Collier;* tendring *Q1;* Wrong *Q2;* Roaming *F.* 115. springes]*Q1,F;* springs *Q2.* 125. tether]*F;* tider *Q2.* 130. bawds]*Theobald;* bonds *Q2,F.* 131. beguile]*Q3,F;* beguide *Q2.*

[I.iv] 2 a]*F; om. Q2.* 19. clepe]*Q5;* clip *Q2; om. F.* 27. the]*Pope;* their *Q2; om. F.* 36. evil]*Keightley;* eale *Q2; om. F.* 37. often dout]*Collier;* of a doubt *Q2; om. F.*

[I.v.] 20. fretful]*Q1,F;* fearefull *Q2.* 33. rots]*F;* roots *Q1–2.* 47. a]*F; om. Q2.* 55. lust]*Q1,F;* but *Q2.* 56. sate]*Q1,F;* sort *Q2.* 95. stiffly]*F;* swiftly *Q2.* 116. bird]*F;* and *Q2.* 122. my lord]*Q1,F; om. Q2.*

[II.i] s.d. with his man]with his man or two *Q2.* 28. no]*F; om. Q2.* warrant]*F;* wit *Q2.* 40. i' th']*F;* with *Q2.* 63. takes]*F;* take *Q2.*

[II.ii] 57. o'erhasty]*F;* hastie *Q2.* 90. since]*F; om. Q2.* 125. above]*F;* about *Q2.* 136. winking]*F;* working *Q2.* 142. his]*Q3,F;* her *Q2.* 148. a]*F; om. Q2.* 150. 'tis]*F; om. Q2.* 180. god] *Warburton;* good *Q2,F.* 207. sanity]*F;* sanctity *Q2.* 208–9. suddenly * * * between him and]*F; om. Q2.* 211. will more]*Q1,F;* will not more *Q2.* 220. excellent]*Q3,F;* extent *Q2.* 223. overhappy]*F;* euer happy *Q2.* 224. cap]*F;* lap *Q2.* 232. that]*F; om. Q2.* 233–60. Let me question * * * dreadfully attended]*F; om. Q2.* 269. Why]*F; om. Q2.* 292. What a piece]*F;* What peece *Q2.* 309–10. the clown * * * sere]*F,* where "tickle" reads "tickled"; *om. Q2.* 322–42. How comes it * * * load too]*F; om. Q2.* 351. lest]*F;* let *Q2.* 351. my]*Q3,F;* me *Q2.* 374–75. tragical-historical . . . pastoral]*F; om. Q2.* 399. By'r]*F;* by *Q2.* 403–4. French falconers]*Q1,F;* friendly Fankners *Q2.* 415. affectation]*F;* affection *Q2.* 445. Then * * * Ilium]*F; om. Q2.* 453. And like]*F;* Like *Q2.* 466. fellies] *Furness;* follies *Q2;* fallies *F.* 507. for a need]*Q1,F;* for need *Q2.* 508. dozen or]*Q1,F;* dosen lines, or *Q2.* 527. the cue for]*F;* that for *Q2.* 550. father] *Q3; om. Q2,F.*

[III.i] 32. lawful espials]*F; om. Q2.* 33. will]*F;* wee'le *Q2.* 46. loneliness]*F;* lowlines *Q2.* 55. Let's]*F; om. Q2.* 83. of us all]*F; om. Q2.* 99. the]*F;* these *Q2.* 107. your honesty should]*F;* you should *Q2.* 119. to]*F; om. Q2.* 126. all]*F; om. Q2.* 141. lisp]*F;* list *Q2.* 142. your ignorance]*F;* ignorance *Q2.* 148. expectancy]*F;* expectation *Q2.* 153. that]*F;* what *Q2.* 155. feature]*F;* stature *Q2.*

[III.ii] 19–20. own feature]*F;* feature *Q2.* 23. the which]*F;* which *Q2.* 25. praise]*F;* praysd *Q2.* 103–4. I mean * * * lord]*F; om. Q2.* 125. this is miching mallecho]*F;* this munching

Mallico Q2. 127. counsel]*F; om. Q2.* 140. orbed ground]*F;* orb'd the ground *Q2.* 150–51. must. / For women's]*F;* must. / For women feare too much, euen as they loue, / And womens *Q2.* 152. In neither aught]*F;* Eyther none, in neither ought *Q2.* 153. love]*F;* Lord *Q2.* 183. joys]*F;* joy *Q2.* 207. once a widow]*F;* once I be a widdow *Q2.* 207. be wife]*Q4,F1;* be a wife *Q2.* 237. Confederate]*Q1,F;* Considerat *Q2.* 239. infected]*Q1,F;* inuected *Q2.* 247. What * * * fire] *Q1.F; om. Q2.* 257. two]*F; om. Q2.* 264. peacock]*Pope;* paiock *Q2;* Paiocke *F.* 294. my]*F; om. Q2.* 332. thumb]*F;* the vmber *Q2.* 339. the top of]*F; om. Q2.* 343. can fret me]*F;* fret me not *Q2.* 354–55. *Pol.* I long say so. / *Ham.* 'By and by' is easily said. Leave me, friends.]*F; Ham.* * * * / Leaue me friends. / I will, say so. By and by is easily said, *Q2.* 357. breathes]*F;* breakes *Q2.* 359. bitter business as the day]*F;* business as the bitter day *Q2.* 364. daggers]*F;* dagger *Q2.*

[III.iii] 17. It is]*F;* or it is *Q2.* 19. huge]*F;* hough *Q2.* 22. ruin]*F;* raine *Q2.* 23. with]*F; om. Q2.* 50. pardoned]*F;* pardon *Q2.* 58. shove]*F;* showe *Q2.* 73. pat]*F;* but *Q2.* 79. hire and salary]*F;* base and silly *Q2.*

[III.iv] 5. warrant]*F;* wait *Q2.* 19. inmost]*F;* most *Q2.* 53. That roars * * * index]*F;* line assigned to Hamlet in *Q2.* 60. a heaven-kissing]*F;* a heaue, a kissing *Q2.* 89. panders]*F;* pardons *Q2.* 90. eyes into my very soul]*F;* very eyes into my soule *Q2.* 91. grained]*F;* greeued *Q2.* 92. will not leave their tinct]*F;* will leaue there their tinct *Q2.* 98. tithe]*F;* kyth *Q2.* 123. hairs]*Rowe;* haire *Q2, F.* 147. I]*F; om. Q2.* 169. Refrain tonight]*F;* to refraine night *Q2.* 173. curb] *Malone; om. Q2,F.* 219. a foolish]*F;* a most foolish *Q2.*

[IV.i] 40. so * * * slander]*Capell; om. Q2,F.*

[IV.ii] 4. Compounded]*Q3,F;* Compound *Q2.* 26. Hide * * * after]*F; om. Q2.*

[IV.iii] 41. With * * * quickness] *F; om. Q2.* 65. begun]*F;* begin *Q2.*

[IV.v] 9. aim]*F;* yawn *Q2.* 16. *Queen.* Let her come in.]*F;* speech assigned to Horatio in *Q2.* 38. grave]*F;* ground *Q2.* 80. their]*F; om. Q2.* 87. his]*F;* this *Q2.* 95. are]*Q3,F;* is *Q2.* 104. They]*F;* The *Q2.* 140. swoopstake]*Q1;* soopstake *Q2,F.* 150. Let her come in]*F;* assigned to Laertes in *Q2.* 158. an old]*F;* a poor *Q2.* 159–61. Nature * * * it loves]*F; om. Q2.* 163. Hey * * * hey nonny]*F; om. Q2.* 177. O, you must]*F;* you may *Q2.* 181. affliction]*F;* afflictions *Q2.* 189.

All] *F; om. Q2.* 193. 1 pray God]*F; om. Q2.* 194. see]*F; om. Q2.*
[IV.vi] 19. good]*F; om. Q2.* 23. bore]*F;* bord *Q2.* 27. He]*F;* So *Q2.* 28. give]*F; om. Q2.*
[IV.vii] 6. proceeded]*F;* proceede *Q2.* 14. conjunctive]*F;* concliue *Q2.* 22. so loud a wind]*F;* so loued Arm'd *Q2.* 44. and more strange]*F; om. Q2.* 54. shall]*F; om. Q2.* 60. As checking]*F;* As the King *Q2.* 86. my]*F;* me *Q2.* 132. on]*F;* ore *Q2.* 138. that] *F; om. Q2.* 165. hoar]*F;* horry *Q2.* 169. cold]*F;* cull-cold *Q2.*
[V.i] 8. "se offendendo"]*F;* so offended *Q2.* 11. argal]*F;* or all *Q2.* 29–32. *Other.* Why, he had none. / *Clown.* What, * * * without arms?] *F; om. Q2.* 37. frame]*F; om. Q2.* 53. stoup]*F;* soope *Q2.* 59. that]*F; om. Q2.* 66. intil]*F;* into *Q2.* 80. mazzard] *F;* massene *Q2.* 94–95. Is this the fine of his fines, and the recovery of his recoveries]*F; om. Q2.* 96. Will his vouchers]*F;* will vouchers *Q2.* 97. double ones too]*F;* doubles *Q2.* 107. O]*F;* or *Q2.* 124. a]*Q3,F; om. Q2.* 125. all]*F; om. Q2.* 146. now-a-days] *F; om. Q2.* 153. three and twenty years]*F;* 23 years *Q2.* 171. chamber] *F;* table *Q2.* 192. winter's]*F;* waters *Q2.* 207. Shards]*F; om. Q2.* 223. times treble]*F;* times double *Q2.* 237. and]

F; om. Q2. 263. thus]*F;* this *Q2.* 276. shortly]*F;* thereby *Q2.*
[V.ii] 9. pall]*F;* fall *Q2.* 17. unseal]*F;* unfold *Q2.* 43. as's]*F;* as sir *Q2.* 57. Why, man * * * employment] *F; om. Q2.* 68–80. To quit * * * comes here]*F; om. Q2.* 73. interim is] *Hanmer;* interim's *F.* 92. Put]*F; om. Q2.* 97. sultry]*Q3,F;* sully *Q2.* 97. for]*F;* or *Q2.* 121. to't]*Johnson;* doo't *Q2; om. F.* 133. his]*Q1676;* this *Q2.* 140. hangers]*F;* hanger *Q2.* 149. might be]*Q3,F;* be might *Q2.* 152. impawned] *New Cambridge; om. Q2;* impon'd *F.* 152. as]*F; om. Q2.* 168. He]*F; om. Q2.* 171. comply]*F;* so *Q2.* 172. bevy] *F;* breede *Q2.* 174. yesty]*F;* histy *Q2.* 175. fanned]*Warburton;* prophane *Q2;* fond *F.* 175. winnowed]*F;* trennowed *Q2.* 190. this wager]*F; om. Q2.* 200. be now, 'tis]*F;* be, tis *Q2.* 219. Sir, in this audience]*F; om. Q2.* 229. keep]*F; om. Q2.* 229. till]*F;* all *Q2.* 242. bettered]*F;* better *Q2.* 251. union]*F;* Onixe *Q2.* 281. afeard]*F;* sure *Q2.* 298. Hamlet, thou]*F;* thou *Q2.* 301. thy]*F;* my *Q2.* 310. murd'rous]*F; om. Q2.* 311. thy union]*F;* the Onixe *Q2.* 330. shall live]*F;* shall I leaue *Q2.* 364. th' yet]*Q3,F;* yet *Q2.* 368. forced]*F;* for no *Q2.* 377. on]*F;* no *Q2.*

Intellectual Backgrounds
and
Extracts from the Sources

Intellectual Backgrounds

MELANCHOLY

PETER DE LA PRIMAUDAYE: The French Academy[1]

Of the blood and of other humors in the body . . .

We understand by a *Humor*, a liquid and running body into which the food is converted in the liver, to this end: that bodies might be nourished and preserved by them. And as there are four elements of which our bodies are compounded, so there are four sorts of humors answerable to their natures, being all mingled together with the blood, as we may see by experience in blood let out of one's body. For uppermost we see as it were a little skim like to the flower or working of new wine, or of other wine when it is poured forth. Next, we may see as it were small streams of water mingled with the blood. And in the bottom is seen a black and thicker humor, like to the lees of wine in a wine vessel. So that if we know how to consider wisely of these things, it will be easy for us to understand the distinction of these sundry humors, and their nature. Now, concerning the first of them, we are to know that the proper nature of blood is to be hot and moist, wherein it answereth to the nature of air. It is temperate, sweet, and fatty, as also the best and chiefest part of nourishment. For albeit all the other humors do nourish likewise, and are carried of the blood, nevertheless that humor which is properly called blood is the chiefest part of nourishment. * * * Next, that thin skim which is seen on the top of it, resembling the flower of wine, is that humor that is called yellow choler, or the choleric humor, which is hot and dry, of a bitter taste, and answerable to the nature of fire. * * * Moreover, those small streams of water which we see mingled in the blood proceed of the phlegmatic humor that is cold and moist, like to water of whose nature it holdeth * * * and without taste, or as some affirm, it is somewhat brackish, but not fatty. Lastly, the black humor and most earthy, which looketh like the very bottom of a deep, red, and thick wine, or like the lees

1. Translated by "T. B. C.," London, 1594. The first extract is from II.lxiv (pp. 358–59); the second from II.lxviii (pp. 380–82).

in a vessel full of wine or oil, is the melancholic humor, or as some term it, black choler, being cold and dry like to the earth, with which it hath some agreement, and of taste somewhat sharp.

Of the diverse temperatures and complexions of men, according to the humors that bear most sway in them . . .

* * * But we account those natures to be well tempered which approach nearest to the perfect temperature. And as every humor ruleth more or less in every one, so he is called either sanguine, or phlegmatic, or choleric, or melancholic. Again, as the other humors bear sway next unto the principal, so is a man said to be either phlegmatic-sanguine, choleric-sanguine, or melancholic-sanguine. The like may be said of the other humors according to their temperature, as also of the affections which have some agreement with them. Hereof it is that, when there is excess of the phlegmatic humor in men, their natures are commonly slothful, they shun labor and give themselves to bodily pleasures, they love dainties, and delicate meats and drinks, they are tender and effeminate, and clean contrary to stout and valiant men. And if there be excess of the choleric humor, their natures are easily provoked and stirred up to wrath, but their anger is as a fire of thorns that, being soon kindled and making a great noise, is by and by quenched again. Their gestures also are more quick and vehement, and their hastiness is commonly foolish and turbulent. They babble much, and are like to vessels full of holes, unable to hold in and keep any secret matter. They are fierce in assailing, but inconstant in sustaining the assault, in some sort resembling the nature of dogs, which bark and bite if they can, and afterward fly away. And if there be excess of the melancholic humor, the natures of such are sad, still hard to please, suspicious, conceited,[2] obstinate, some more and some less. And if the choleric and melancholic humors be corrupt and mingled together, their natures become monstrous, proud, full of envy, fraud, subtilities, venemous and poisonful, hateful and diabolical. And when the malignant spirits know men's nature thus disposed, no doubt but they take occasion thereby to intermingle themselves, if God permit them, and propose to use them for the punishing of men: I say they will join themselves unto them, and make them their instruments, as God on the other side useth those natures that are most moderate and best tempered, making them instruments of his glory.

Now, we may call to mind what we learned before almost to

2. Ingenious.

the same end, touching the means whereby evil spirits might trouble the imagination, fantasy and minds of men. We may say as much of the humors of the body, whose motions and nature they know very well. Whereby they can so much the more easily abuse them in their damnable work—and will, as we may judge by the example of him that was possessed and lunatic, of whom the Evangelists make mention.[3] * * * And by that which they wrote of him, it seemeth that he was subject to the falling sickness, that returneth oftentimes according to the course of the moon, which naturally hath great affinity with the humors, and great power over them. And therefore it is very likely that the evil spirit which tormented this poor lunatic watched the occasions of his disease to afflict him the more, and to cause him to fall either in the fire or in the water, as he did indeed, thereby to work his death. * * * Which example showeth unto us what is the malice of the devil, what pleasure he taketh in hurting of men, what means and what occasions he seeketh for and maketh choice of, and what access unto us we may offer him through our corrupt nature, through our vices and sins, and through our inclinations and manners that are naturally evil and perverse, if God letteth him loose the bridle by his just judgment. * * * For this cause, we ought to take good heed that we give not our common enemy those occasions that he seeketh to have from us, to the end that he abuse us not, nor anything that is ours, and which God hath bestowed upon us. This is the reason why the consideration of our temperature, complexion, and natural inclination is very necessary for us: because the knowledge hereof affordeth unto us many good instruments that may stand us in great stead throughout our whole life, as well for the preservation of the health of our bodies, as for the rule and government of our affections and manners, as also in regard of the familiarity and acquaintance which we have one with another. For through the contemplation hereof, we may know, not only the causes of health and sickness, of the life and death of the body, but also of that of the soul. For as the good humors corrupt in our bodies according as we have heard, and breed in them sundry diseases, which finally lead them unto death; even so by means of sin all those good and natural affections, which ought to be the seeds of virtue in us, are corrupted and turn into vices, that are the diseases of the soul, and bring unto it the second and eternal death: as, contrariwise, virtues are the health and life thereof.

3. See Matthew xvii.14–18, Mark ix.14–29, Luke ix.37–42.

TIMOTHY BRIGHT: A Treatise of Melancholy[4]
How melancholy altereth those actions which rise out of the brain.

Touching actions which rise from the brain, melancholy causeth dullness of conceit,[5] both by reason the substance of the brain in such persons is more gross, and their spirit not so prompt and subtle as is requisite for ready understanding. Again, almost all the senses standing in a kind of passive nature, a substance cold and dry—and by consequent hard—is not so meet thereto; which, as it serveth well to retain that which is once engraven, so like adamant it keepeth, in comparison of other tempers, that which once it hath received: whereby as they are unfit to commit readily to memory, so retain they that is committed in surer custody. Sometime it falleth out that melancholy men are found very witty, and quickly discern, either because the humor of melancholy with some heat is so made subtle that, as from the driest wood riseth the clearest flame, and from the lees of wine is distilled a strong and burning aqua vitae, in like sort their spirits, both from the dryness of the matter, and straining of the gross substance from which they pass, receiving a pureness, are instruments of such sharpness, which is the dry light that Heraclitus approved. To this, other reasons may be added, as: exercise of their wits, wherein they be indefatigable, which maketh them seem to have that of a natural readiness which custom of exercise, and use hath found in them. Moreover, while their passions be not yet vehement, whereby they might be overcarried, melancholy breedeth a jealousy of doubt in that they take in deliberation, and causeth them to be the more exact and curious in pondering the very moments of things. To these reasons may be added the vehemancy of their affections once raised: which carrieth them, with all their faculties thereto belonging, into the depth of that they take pleasure to inter-meddle in. For though the melancholy man be not so easily affected with any other passion as with those of fear, sadness, and jealousy, yet being once thoroughly heat with a contrary passion, retaineth the fervency thereof far longer time than any other complexion, and more fervently boileth therewith, by reason his heart and spirit hath more solidity of substance to entertain deeply the passion, which in a more rare and thin sooner vanisheth away. Thus greediness of desire in those things which they affect maketh them diligent and

4. London, 1586. This extract is from   5. Apprehension.
Chapter XXII, pp. 129–31.

painful, wary and circumspect, and so in actions of brain and
sense not inferior to the best tempers; as also it maketh them stiff
in opinion. Their resolution riseth of long deliberation, because
of doubt and distrust which, as it is not easily bred, so it is also
hard to remove. Such persons are doubtful, suspicious, and thereby
long in deliberation, because those domestical fears, or that internal obscurity, causeth an opinion of danger in outward affairs
where there is no cause of doubt. Their dreams are fearful, partly
by reason of their fancy, waking, is most occupied about fears and
terrors, which retaineth the impression in sleep; and partly through
black and dark fumes of melancholy rising up to the brain, whereof
the fantasy forgeth objects, and disturbeth the sleep of melancholy
persons. * * *

DEMONOLOGY

LEWES LAVATER: Of Ghosts and Spirits Walking by Night[1]

Melancholic persons and mad men imagine many things which
in very deed are not.

There have been very many in all ages which have utterly denied
that there be any spirits or strange sights. The philosophers of
Epicurus's sect did jest and laugh at all those things which were
reported of them, and counted them as feigned and counterfeit,
by the which only children and fools and plain simple men were
made afraid. * * * True it is that many men do sadly[2] persuade
themselves that they see or hear ghosts: for that which they imagine
they see or hear proceedeth either of melancholy, madness, weakness of the senses, fear, or of some other perturbation; or else when
they see or hear beasts, vapors, or some other natural things, then
they vainly suppose they have seen sights I wot not what. * * *

There is no doubt but that almost all those things which the
common people judge to be wonderful sights are nothing less than
so.[3] But in the mean season it can not be denied but that strange
sights, and many other such like things, are sometimes heard and
also seen.

And first it can not be denied but that some men which, either

1. Translated into English by "R. H.,"
London, 1572. The extracts here
printed are from I.ii (pp. 9–10), II.ii
(pp. 102–9), II.iv (p. 114), II.xiii
(pp. 159–61), and II.xv (p. 163).
2. Seriously.
3. I.e., delusions.

by dispositions of nature or for that[4] they have sustained great misery, are now become heavy and full of melancholy, imagine many times with themselves, being alone, miraculous and strange things. Sometimes they affirm in great sooth that they verily hear and see this or that thing, which not withstanding neither they nor yet any other man did once see or hear: which thing we sometimes see by experience to be true in those men which be troubled with great headaches or subject to other diseases of the body, or cannot take rest in the night, or are distraughted of their wits. Those which dwell with such kind of men, when they hear them tell such absurd tales, such strange things, and such marvelous visions, albeit they pity their unfortunate estate, yet can they not many times contain themselves from laughing. * * *

The Papists' doctrine touching the souls of dead men, and the appearing of them.

The papists in former times have publicly both taught and written that those spirits which men sometime see and hear be either good or bad angels, or else the souls of those which either live in everlasting bliss, or in purgatory, or in the place of damned persons; and that divers of them are those souls that crave aid and deliverance of men. * * *

Of this place, to wit, purgatory, popish writers teach marvelous things. Some of them say that purgatory is also under the earth as hell is. Some say that hell and purgatory are both one place, albeit the pains be divers according to the deserts of souls. * * * Some of them say that the pain of purgatory is all one with the punishment of hell, and that they differ only in this, that the one hath an end, the other no end: and that it is far more easy to endure all the pains of this world which all men since Adam's time have sustained, even unto the day of the last judgment, than to bear one day's space the least of those two punishments. * * *

Hereunto they add that the spirits, as well of the good as the ill, do come and are sent unto men living, from hell; and that by the common law of justice, all men at the day of judgment shall come to their trial from hell; and that none before that time can come from thence. Farther they teach that by God's license and dispensation, certain, yea before the day of judgment, are permitted to come out of hell, and that not forever, but only for a season, for the instructing and terrifying of the living. * * *

But as concerning the time and place when and where spirits do proffer themselves to be seen, they say no certain rule can be given, for this standeth wholly in God's pleasure, who if he list to de-

4. Because.

liver any, suffereth him to make his appearance forthwith even in such places as he may be well heard in. And that spirits do not always appear under a visible shape, but sometimes invisibly, insomuch that sometimes nothing else is heard of them but sneezing, spitting, sighing, and clapping of hands, etc. * * * And wheresoever these spirits be, they say that they endure punishment. Besides that souls do not appear nor answer unto every man's interrogatories, but that of a great number they scantly appear unto one. And therefore they teach whensoever such visions of spirits are showed, men should use fasting and prayer or ever they demand any question of them. * * * Besides this, shrift and massing[5] should be used ere we question with them: farther, that we should not give credit as soon as we hear but one sign, but await to hear the same thrice repeated, which in the first book of Samuel and third chapter is read to have been done by Samuel being yet a child: for otherwise the divel may delude and deceive us, as he doth very often. * * *

* * * This [the use of some form of prayer] done, we should, as they teach, fall to questioning with them, and say: "Thou spirit, we beseech thee by Christ Jesus, tell us what thou art, and if there be any amongst us to whom thou wouldst gladly make answer, name him, or by some sign declare so much." After this, the question is to be moved, each man there present being recited,[6] whether he would answer unto this or that man. And if at the name of any he speak, or make a noise, all other demands remaining should be made unto him, as these and such like: What man's soul he is? For what cause he is come, and what he doth desire? Whether he require any aid by prayers and suffrages? Whether by massing or alms-giving he may be released? * * *

Moreover, popish writers teach us to discern good spirits from evil by four means. First, they say that if he be a good spirit, he will at the beginning somewhat terrify men, but again soon revive and comfort them. * * * Their second note is to descry them by their outward and visible shape. For if they appear under the form of a lion, bear, dog, toad, serpent, cat, or black ghost, it may easily be gathered that it is an evil spirit. And that, on the other side, good spirits do appear under the shape of a dove, a man, a lamb, or in the brightness and clear light of the sun.

We must also consider whether the voice which we hear be sweet, lowly, sober, sorrowful, or otherwise terrible and full of reproach, for so they term it.

Thirdly, we must note whether the spirit teach ought that doth vary from the doctrine of the apostles, and other doctors approved

5. Saying of masses.   6. Called by name.

by the church's censure; or whether he utter anything that doth dissent from the faith, good manners, and ceremonies of the church, according to the cannonical rites or decrees of councils, and against the laws of the holy Church of Rome.

Fourthly, we must take diligent heed whether in his words, deeds, and gestures, he do show forth any humility, acknowledging or confessing of his sins and punishments, or whether we hear of him any groaning, weeping, complaint, boasting, threatening, slander or blasphemy. For as the beggar doth rehearse his own misery, so likewise do good spirits that desire any help or deliverance. * * *

Testimonies out of the word of God that neither the souls of the faithful nor of infidels do walk upon the earth after they are once parted from their bodies.

Now, that the souls neither of the faithful nor of infidels do wander any longer on the earth when they be once severed from the bodies, I will make it plain and evident unto you by these reasons following. First, certain it is that such as depart hence either die in faith or in unbelief. Touching those that go hence in a right belief, their souls are by and by in possession of life everlasting; and they that depart in unbelief do straightway become partakers of eternal damnation. The souls do not vanish away and die with the body, as the Epicures' opinion is, neither yet be in every place, as some do imagine. * * *

What those things are which men see and hear: and first, that good angels do sometimes appear.

But thou wilt say, "I do not yet clearly and plainly understand what manner of things those are whereof * * * historiographers, holy fathers, and others make mention: as that holy apostles, bishops, martyrs, confessors, virgins, and many other which died long ago, appeared unto certain men lying at the point of death, gave them warning, answered unto certain questions, commanded them to do this or that thing. * * *" You will say, "I hear and understand very well that these things are not men's souls, which continually remain in their appointed places. I pray you, then, what are they?" To conclude in few words: If it be not a vain persuasion proceeding through weakness of the senses, through fear, or some such like cause, or if it be not deceit of men, or some natural thing * * * it is either a good or evil angel, or some other forewarning sent by God. * * * For as servants stand before their masters to fulfill their commandments, even so are the angels pressed and ready to serve God. Isaiah the 63[:9]: "The angel of his face," that is, which standeth ready in his sight, "preserved them." And further, they which often stand in presence of their lords are acceptable unto them, and privy to their secrets. Out of this place of Matthew [18:10], Saint Jerome in his commentaries, and other fathers do conclude that God doth assign unto every soul as soon as he createth him his peculiar angel, which taketh care of him. But whether that everyone of the elect have his proper angel, or many angels be appointed unto him, it is not expressly set forth, yet this is most sure and certain, that God hath given his angels in charge to have regard and care over us.

That sometimes, yea and for the most part, evil angels do appear.

Contrariwise, evil angels are hurtful and enemies unto men; they follow them everywhere, to the end they may withdraw them from true worshipping of God, and from faith in his only son, Jesus Christ, unto sundry other things. These appear in divers shapes: for if the devil, as Paul doth witness, transformed himself into an angel of light, no less may he take the shape of a prophet, an apostle, evangelist, bishop, and martyr, and appear in their likeness; or so bewitch us, that we verily suppose we hear or see them in very deed. He taketh on him to tell of things to come, whether he hit them right or wrong. He affirmeth that he is this or that soul, that he may be delivered by this or that means, that by these means he may purchase credit and authority unto those things which have no ground of scripture.

G. GIFFORD: A Discourse of the Subtle Practices of Devils by Witches and Sorcerers[7]
Devils have no power to hurt men's bodies or goods, but upon special leave given unto them.

The reprobate angels are mighty, fierce and subtle. * * * They be instruments of God's vengeance, and executioners of his wrath. They do not exercise power and authority which is absolute, and at their own will and appointment, but so far as God leteth forth the chain to give them scope. Touching the reprobate,[8] which despise the ways of God and are disobedient, we are taught that God in righteous vengeance giveth them over into their[9] hands, for they would not love his laws, nor honor him as their God. Therefore they come under the tyranny of wicked devils, which work in

---

7. London, 1587; this extract appears on sig. D2.

8. I.e., reprobate humans.

9. I.e., of the reprobate angels.

them with power; their hearts do they harden; their eyes, even the eyes of their minds, do they blind; they kindle and stir up in them all filthy lusts, and carry them headlong into foul and abominable sins.

THE NATURE OF MAN

PETER DE LA PRIMAUDAYE: The French Academy[1]

Of Man

ASER. When I direct my flight now and then, my companions, even unto the heavens, and with the wings of contemplation behold their wonderful greatness; their terrible motions, being contrary and without ceasing; the lively brightness, rare beauty, and incomparable force of the sun and moon; their unchangeable course, one while cause of light, and by and by after of darkness; the infinite number of goodly stars, and of so many other celestial signs: and from this excellent and constant order of all these things, as one ravished and amazed, when I withdraw my spirit lower into the elementary region, to admire and wonder at the situation and spreading of the earth amidst the waters, both of them making one round mass or lump, which in the midst of this great firmament occupieth the room but of a prick or tittle in respect thereof: besides, when I acknowledge in this earth and water as many sundry and most beautiful plants, and kinds of earthy and watery creatures, as there are grains of sand on the sea banks: and when I delight myself in the variety of minerals and precious stones, considering the form, quality, and virtue of each of these things: briefly, when I admire the diversity of times and seasons, the continual spring of fountains, the certain course of rivers, and generally, so many wonderful works under the cope of heaven, I cannot marvel enough at the excellency of Man, for whom all these things were created, and are maintained and preserved in their being and moving, by one and the same divine providence always like unto itself.

AMANA. There is nothing more certain than this, that all things whatsoever either the eye can behold, or the ear hear, were created for the benefit, profit, and use of man, and that he was made excellent above all things to rule over them: yea, the very angels are

---

1. Translated by "T. B. C.," London, 1594. This extract is from I.i (pp. 9–17).

sent to minister for their sakes, which shall receive the inheritance of salvation.

ARAM. Oh unspeakable and heavenly goodness, which hast created man little lower than thyself, and crowned him with glory and worship! But tell us, I pray thee, Achitob, more particularly, what this great and principal work of nature—Man—is, to what end his being was given him, and how he hath showed forth the fruits thereof. For it must needs be that there is something in him greatly to be wondered at, seeing all things were created to serve and obey him.

ACHITOB. Truly ye have reason, companions, to begin our happy assembly with that knowledge which we ought to have of ourselves, as being the storehouse of all wisdom, and beginning of salvation: whereof we may have an assured testimony from that father of philosophy, Socrates, who beholding the first precept written at Delphos in that temple of Apollo, which was so renowned throughout Graecia, namely, *Know thy self*, was forthwith driven into a very deep cogitation, and being rapt with contemplation of spirit, he began from that time forward to doubt and to inquire of himself. * * * Ignorance of a man's self, saith Lactantius, and the want[2] of knowledge wherefore and to what end he is born, is the cause of error, of evil * * * of forsaking the light to walk in darkness. Now if we account it a shameful thing to be ignorant of those things which belong to the life of man, surely the not knowing of ourselves is much more dishonest. Let us then consider what man is, according to that mean knowledge, which by the grace of God we are endued withal. * * * Man is a creature made of God after his own image, just, holy, good and right by nature, and compounded of soul and body. I say of soul, which was inspired of God with spirit and life, and of a perfect natural body, framed of the earth by the same power of God. In this sort man had his being of the eternal workmaster of the whole world, of whom he was created by his incomprehensible goodness, to be made partaker of his immortality and permanent felicity, for this only end: to set forth the glory of his Creator, and to speak and do those things that are agreeable unto him, through the acknowledgment of his benefits. From which end man, being fallen of his own free will through ingratitude and disobedience, was bereaved of all those ornaments, which he had received before of God, and instead of righteousness and holiness, all iniquity, filthiness and uncleanness entered into him: whereby he was made the slave of sin and death, from whence all those miseries had their beginnings,

2. Lack.

wherewith the life of man is overwhelmed. His soul also was wrapped with infinite hurtful passions and perturbations, which work in it a continual disquietness, and his body became subject to innumerable travails, and violent untowardness. * * * Notwithstanding, God, whose goodness and mercy are endless, reestablished and assured the succession of his immortal inheritance unto those whom it pleased him by grace to make dead to sin and alive to himself, through the satisfaction of his wrath made by the innocency of his eternal son, purging them in his blood, and opening unto them by him the gates of heaven, after he hath renewed them in righteousness, holiness and innocency, that they may follow after godliness and religion. * * * Furthermore, the same heavenly grace blessing this holy desire of the man regenerate, causeth him to draw out of the doctrine of holy scriptures that wherewithal he may, if not heal perfectly his wicked inclinations, yet at the least contain and repress them in such sort that they break not out into any damnable execution. He teacheth him also to receive the infirmities of his flesh as fatherly chastisements for his sin, and as necessary means to exercise him, and to keep him in awe. And lastly, for the upshot and perfection of all happiness and felicity in this world, he instructeth him how he may lead a quiet and peaceable life in beholding the wonderful works of the divinity, which he is to adore and honor, and in the amendment and correction of his manners naturally corrupted, by squaring them after the pattern of virtue, that so he may be made worthy and fit to govern human affairs, for the profit of many: and at length attain to the perfection of a wise man, by joining together the active life with the contemplative in the certain hope and expectation of a second, immortal and most blessed life. * * *

MICHAEL DE MONTAIGNE: An Apology of Raymond Sebond[3]

Let us now but consider man alone, without other help, armed but with his own weapons, and unprovided of the grace and knowledge of God, which is all his honor, all his strength, and all the ground of his being. Let us see what holdfast, or freehold, he hath in this gorgeous and goodly equipage. Let him with the utmost power of his discourse make me understand upon what foundation he hath built those great advantages and odds he supposeth to have over other creatures. Who hath persuaded him that

3. *Essays*, in John Florio's translation, London, 1603; from II.xii (p. 258).

this admirable moving of heaven's vaults; that the eternal light of these lamps so fiercely rolling over his head; that the horror-moving and continual motion of this infinite vast ocean, were established, and continue so many ages, for his commodity and service? Is it possible to imagine anything so ridiculous as this miserable and wretched creature, which is not so much as master of himself, exposed and subject to the offenses of all things, and yet dareth call himself master and emperor of this universe? In whose power it is not to know the least part of it, much less to command the same. And the privilege, which he so fondly[4] challengeth, to be the only absolute creature in this huge world's frame, perfectly able to know the absolute beauty and several parts thereof, and that he is only of power[5] to yield the great Architect thereof due thanks for it, and to keep account both of the receipts and layings out of the world. Who hath sealed him this patent? Let him show us his letters of privilege for so noble and so great a charge.

DEATH

HIERONYMOUS CARDANUS: Comfort[1]

Therefore Socrates was wont to say that death might be resembled either to sound sleep, a long journey, or destruction, as is the death of brute beasts. If the soul doth live, and after death feeleth nothing, then is it like unto a sound sleep, because therein we rest without either feeling or understanding, and after a while return to the same exercises. Most assured it is that such sleeps are most sweet as be most sound. For those are the best wherein, like unto dead men, we dream nothing. The broken sleeps, the slumber and dreams full of visions, are commonly in them that have weak and sickly bodies. * * *
* * * But if thou compare death to long travel, and that the soul—being let loose from prison of the body—seeth all things and walketh everywhere, then what can be considered more happy. For the soul, being burdened with the body, is neither free nor rightly knoweth anything, but being overladen with cares, doth behold only the figure of things, and as it were through a web, or cloth, guesseth a sight, and certainly knoweth nothing; but being

4. Foolishly.
5. I.e., he alone has the power.
1. Translated by Thomas Bedingfield,

London, 1576. This extract is from Book II (sigs. Dii^r–Diii^v).

free, doth not only cast off all hindrance, but also beholdeth all things without interruption, which being true, who is he that willingly would eschew death? * * *

For there is nothing that doth better or more truly prophesy the end of life than when a man dreameth that he doth travel and wander into far countries, and chiefly if he imagineth himself to ride upon a white horse, that is swift; and that he traveleth in countries unknown without hope of return, in such sort naturally divining of that shortly will come to pass indeed. But if death be resembled to destruction—which, as is already proved, is most impossible—yet can it no ways be accompted[2] evil. Because whatsoever is not, cannot be evil, else we should lament for them that never were born, nor never were at all; and they that are not, can nothing suffer.

MICHAEL DE MONTAIGNE: An Apology of Raymond Sebond[3]

* * * In few, *there is no constant existence, neither of our being, nor of the objects.*[4] And we, and our judgment, and all mortal things else, do uncessantly roll, turn and pass away. Thus can nothing be certainly established, nor of the one, nor of the other; both the judging and the judged being in continual alteration and motion. We have no communication with being; for every human nature is ever in the middle between being born and dying; giving nothing of itself but an obscure appearance and shadow, and an uncertain and weak opinion. And if perhaps you fix your thought to take its being, it would be even as if one should go about to poison the water: for, how much the more he shall close and press that which by its own nature is ever gliding, so much the more he shall lose what he would hold and fasten. Thus, seeing all things are subject to pass from one change to another, reason, which therein seeketh a real subsistence, finds herself deceived, as unable to apprehend anything subsistent and permanent: forsomuch as each thing either cometh to a being, and is not yet altogether; or beginneth to die before it be born. * * *

And * * * we others do foolishly fear a kind of death whenas we have already passed, and daily pass, so many others. For not only, as Heraclitus said, the death of fire is a generation of air, and the death of air a generation of water; but also we may most

2. Accounted.
3. *Essays*, in John Florio's translation, London, 1603; from II.xii (pp. 350 and 351).
4. I.e., the material objects of the external world; "in few": in short.

evidently see it in ourselves. The flower of age dieth, fadeth and fleeteth, when age comes upon us; and youth endeth in the flower of a full grown man's age; childhood in youth, and the first age dieth in infancy; and yesterday endeth in this day, and today shall die in tomorrow. And *nothing remaineth or ever continueth in one state.* For to prove it, if we should ever continue one and the same, how is it then that now we rejoice at one thing, and now at another? How comes it to pass we love things contrary, or we hate them * * * or we blame them? How is it that we have different affections, holding no more the same sense in the same thought? For it is not likely that without alteration we should take other passions, and *what admitteth alterations, continueth not the same;* and if it be not one selfsame, then is it not; but rather with being all one, the simple being doth also change, ever becoming other from other. And by consequence, nature's senses are deceived and lie falsely; taking what appeareth for what is; for want of truly knowing what it is that is. But then what is it, that is indeed? That which is eternal, that is to say, that which never had birth, nor ever shall have end; and to which no time can bring change or cause alteration. * * *

MICHAEL DE MONTAIGNE: Of Physiognomy[5]

We trouble death with the care of life, and life with the care of death. The one annoyeth, the other affrights us. It is not against death we prepare ourselves; it is a thing too momentary. A quarter of an hour of passion without consequence and without annoyance deserves not particular precepts. To say truth, we prepare ourselves against the preparations of death. *Philosophy teacheth us ever to have death before our eyes, to foresee and consider it before it come;* then giveth us rules and precautions so to provide that such foresight and thought hurt us not. So do physicians, who cast us into diseases that they may employ their drugs and skill about them. If we have not known how to live, it is injustice to teach us how to die, and deform the end from all the rest. Have we known how to live constantly and quietly, we shall know how to die resolutely and reposedly. They may brag as much as they please * * * *The whole life of a philosopher is the meditation of his death.* But, methinks, it is indeed the end, yet not the scope of life. It is her last, it is her extremity; yet not her object. Herself must be unto herself, her aim, her drift and her design. Her direct study is to order, to direct and to suffer herself. In the number of

5. *Essays,* in John Florio's translation, London, 1603; from III.xii (pp. 626–27).

many other offices which the general and principal chapter, "To Know how to Live," containeth, is this special article, "To Know how to Die." And of the easiest, did not our own fear weigh it down. To judge them by their profit and by the naked truth, the lessons of simplicity yield not much to those which doctrine preacheth to the contrary unto us. Men are different in feeling, and diverse in force; they must be directed to their good according to themselves, and by divers ways. * * *

I never saw mean peasant of my neighbor's enter into cogitation, or care, with what assurance or countenance he should pass this last hour. Nature teacheth him never to muse on death but when he dieth. And then hath he a better grace in it than Aristotle, whom death perplexeth doubly, both by herself and by so long a premeditation. Therefore was it Caesar's opinion that *the least premeditated death was the happiest and the easiest * * * He grieves more than he need, that grieves before he need.* The sharpness of this imagination proceeds from our curiosity. Thus we ever hinder ourselves, desiring to forerun and sway natural prescriptions. It is but for doctors, being in health, to fare the worse by it, and to frown and startle at the image of death. The vulgar sort have neither need of remedy nor comfort but when the shock or stroke cometh, and justly considers no more of it than he feeleth. And is it not as we say, that the vulgars' stupidity and want of apprehension afford them this patience in present evils, and this deep carelessness of sinister future accidents? That their mind—being more gross, dull and blockish—is less penetrable and agitable? In God's name, if it be so, let us henceforth keep a school of brutality. It is the utmost fruit that sciences promise unto us, to which she so gently bringeth her disciples.

Extracts from the Sources

SAXO GRAMMATICUS
Amleth†

At this time Horwendil and Feng, whose father Gerwendil had been governor of the Jutes, were appointed in his place by Rorik to defend Jutland. But Horwendil held the monarchy for three years, and then, to win the height of glory, devoted himself to roving.[1] Then Koll, King of Norway, in rivalry of his great deeds and renown, deemed it would be a handsome deed if by his greater strength in arms he could bedim the far-famed glory of the rover; and, cruising about the sea, he watched for Horwendil's fleet and came us with it. There was an island lying in the middle of the sea, which each of the rovers, bringing his ships up on either side, was holding. The captains were tempted by the pleasant look of the beach, and the comeliness of the shores led them to look through the interior of the spring-tide woods, to go through the glades, and roam over the sequestered forests. It was here that the advance of Koll and Horwendil brought them face to face without any witness. Then Horwendil endeavoured to address the king first, asking him in what way it was his pleasure to fight, and declaring that one best which needed the courage of as few as possible. For, said he, the duel was the surest of all modes of combat for winning the meed of bravery, because it relied only upon native courage, and excluded all help from the hand of another. Koll marvelled at so brave a judgment in a youth, and said: "Since thou hast granted me the choice of battle, I think it is best to employ that kind which needs only the endeavours of two, and is free from all the tumult. Certainly it is more venturesome, and allows of a speedier award of the victory. * * * But since the issue remains doubtful, we must pay some regard to gentle dealing, and must not give way so

† Translated by Oliver Elton. From *The Sources of Hamlet*, edited by Israel Gollancz (London: Oxford University Press, 1926; reissued by Frank Cass & Company, Ltd.), pp. 95–131.
1. Literally, piracy ("piraticae incubuerat" in the Latin original).

far to our inclinations as to leave the last offices undone. * * * Let us, therefore, have this pious stipulation, that the conqueror shall give funeral rites to the conquered. For all allow that these are the last duties of human kind, from which no righteous man shrinks. Let each army lay aside its sternness and perform this function in harmony. Let jealousy depart at death, let the feud be buried in the tomb. * * *"

After mutually pledging their faiths to these terms, they began the battle. * * * Horwendil, in his too great ardour, became keener to attack his enemy than to defend his own body; and, heedless of his shield, had grasped his sword with both hands; and his boldness did not fail. For by his rain of blows he destroyed Koll's shield and deprived him of it, and at last hewed off his foot and drove him lifeless to the ground. Then, not to fail of his compact, he buried him royally, gave him a howe of lordly make and pompous obsequies. Then he pursued and slew Koll's sister Sela, who was a skilled warrior and experienced in roving.

He had now passed three years in valiant deeds of war; and, in order to win higher rank in Rorik's favour, he assigned to him the best trophies and the pick of the plunder. His friendship with Rorik enabled him to woo and win in marriage his daughter Gerutha, who bore him a son Amleth.

Such great good fortune stung Feng with jealousy, so that he resolved treacherously to waylay his brother, thus showing that goodness is not safe even from those of a man's own house. And behold, when a chance came to murder him, his bloody hand sated the deadly passion of his soul. Then he took the wife of the brother he had butchered, capping unnatural murder with incest. For whoso yields to one iniquity, speedily falls an easier victim to the next, the first being an incentive to the second. Also the man veiled the monstrosity of his deed with such hardihood of cunning, that he made up a mock pretence of goodwill to excuse his crime, and glossed over fratricide with a show of righteousness. Gerutha, said he, though so gentle that she would do no man the slightest hurt, had been visited with her husband's extremest hate; and it was all to save her that he had slain his brother; for he thought it shameful that a lady so meek and unrancorous should suffer the heavy disdain of her husband. Nor did his smooth words fail in their intent; for at courts, where fools are sometimes favoured and backbiters preferred, a lie lacks not credit. Nor did Feng keep from shameful embraces the hands that had slain a brother; pursuing with equal guilt both of his wicked and impious deeds.

Amleth beheld all this, but feared lest too shrewd a behaviour might make his uncle suspect him. So he chose to feign dulness, and pretend an utter lack of wits. This cunning course not only concealed his intelligence but ensured his safety. Every day he remained in his mother's house utterly listless and unclean, flinging himself on the ground, and bespattering his person with foul and filthy dirt. His discoloured face and visage smutched with slime denoted foolish and grotesque madness. All he said was of a piece with these follies; all he did savoured of utter lethargy. In a word, you would not have thought him a man at all, but some absurd abortion due to a mad fit of destiny. He used at times to sit over the fire, and, raking up the embers with his hands, to fashion wooden crooks, and harden them in the fire, shaping at their tips certain barbs, to make them hold more tightly to their fastenings. When asked what he was about, he said that he was preparing sharp javelins to avenge his father. This answer was not a little scoffed at, all men deriding his idle and ridiculous pursuit; but the thing helped his purpose afterwards. Now it was his craft in this matter that first awakened in the deeper observers a suspicion of his cunning. For his skill in a trifling art betokened the hidden talent of the craftsman; nor could they believe the spirit dull where the hand had acquired so cunning a workmanship. Lastly, he always watched with the most punctual care over his pile of stakes that he had pointed in the fire. Some people, therefore, declared that his mind was quick enough, and fancied that he only played the simpleton in order to hide his understanding, and veiled some deep purpose under a cunning feint. His wiliness (said these) would be most readily detected, if a fair woman were put in his way in some secluded place, who should provoke his mind to the temptations of love; all men's natural temper being too blindly amorous to be artfully dissembled, and this passion being also too impetuous to be checked by cunning. Therefore, if his lethargy were feigned, he would seize the opportunity, and yield straightway to violent delights. So men were commissioned to draw the young man in his rides into a remote part of the forest, and there assail him with a temptation of this nature. Among these chanced to be a foster-brother of Amleth, who had not ceased to have regard to their common nurture; and who esteemed his present orders less than the memory of their past fellowship. He attended Amleth among his appointed train, being anxious not to entrap, but to warn him; and was persuaded that he would suffer the worst if he showed the slightest glimpse of sound reason, and above all if he did the act of love openly. This was also plain enough to Amleth himself. For when he was bidden mount his horse, he deliberately set himself in such a fashion that he turned his back to the neck and faced about, fronting the tail; which he proceeded to encompass with the reins, just as if on that side he would check the horse in its furious pace. By this cunning thought he eluded the trick, and overcame the treachery of his uncle. The reinless steed galloping on, with the rider directing its tail, was ludicrous enough to behold.

Amleth went on, and a wolf crossed his path amid the thicket. When his companions told him that a young colt had met him, he retorted, that in Feng's stud there were too few of that kind fighting. This was a gentle but witty fashion of invoking a curse upon his uncle's riches. When they averred that he had given a cunning answer, he answered that he had spoken deliberately: for he was loth to be thought prone to lying about any matter, and wished to be held a stranger to falsehood; and accordingly he mingled craft and candour in such wise that, though his words did not lack truth, yet there was nothing to betoken the truth and betray how far his keenness went.

Again, as he passed along the beach, his companions found the rudder of a ship which had been wrecked, and said they had discovered a huge knife. "This," said he, "was the right thing to carve such a huge ham;" by which he really meant the sea, to whose infinitude, he thought, this enormous rudder matched. Also, as they passed the sandhills, and bade him look at the meal, meaning the sand, he replied that it had been ground small by the hoary tempests of the ocean. His companions praising his answer, he said that he had spoken it wittingly. Then they purposely left him, that he might pluck up more courage to practise wantonness. The woman whom his uncle had dispatched met him in a dark spot, as though she had crossed him by chance; and he took her and would have ravished her, had not his foster-brother, by a secret device, given him an inkling of the trap. For this man, while pondering the fittest way to play privily the prompter's part, and forestall the young man's hazardous lewdness, found a straw on the ground and fastened it underneath the tail of a gadfly that was flying past; which he then drove towards the particular quarter where he knew Amleth to be: an act which served the unwary prince exceedingly well. The token was interpreted as shrewdly as it had been sent. For Amleth saw the gadfly, espied with curiosity the straw which it wore embedded in its tail, and perceived that it was a secret warning to beware of treachery. Alarmed, scenting a trap, and fain to possess his desire in greater safety, he caught up the woman in his arms and dragged her off to a distant and impenetrable fen. Moreover, when they had lain together, he conjured her earnestly to disclose the matter to none, and the promise of silence was accorded as heartily as it was asked. For both of them had been under the same fostering in their childhood; and this early rearing in common had brought Amleth and the girl into great intimacy.

So, when he had returned home, they all jeeringly asked him whether he had given way to love, and he avowed that he had ravished the maid. When he was next asked where he did it, and what had been his pillow, he said that he had rested upon the hoof of a beast of burden, upon a cockscomb, and also upon a ceiling. For, when he was starting into temptation, he had gathered fragments of all these things, in order to avoid lying. And though his jest did not take aught of the truth out of the story, the answer was greeted with shouts of merriment from the bystanders. The maiden, too, when questioned on the matter, declared that he had done no such thing; and her denial was the more readily credited when it was found that the escort had not witnessed the deed. Then he who had marked the gadfly in order to give a hint, wishing to show Amleth that to his trick he owed his salvation, observed that latterly he had been singly devoted to Amleth. The young man's reply was apt. Not to seem forgetful of his informant's service, he said that he had seen a certain thing bearing a straw flit by suddenly, wearing a stalk of chaff fixed on its hinder parts. The cleverness of this speech, which made the rest split with laughter, rejoiced the heart of Amleth's friend.

Thus all were worsted, and none could open the secret lock of the young man's wisdom. But a friend of Feng, gifted more with assurance than judgment, declared that the unfathomable cunning of such a mind could not be detected by any vulgar plot, for the man's obstinacy was so great that it ought not to be assailed with any mild measures; there were many sides to his wiliness, and it ought not to be entrapped by any one method. Accordingly, said he, his own profounder acuteness had hit on a more delicate way, which was well fitted to be put in practice, and would effectually discover what they desired to know. Feng was purposely to absent himself, pretending affairs of great import. Amleth should be closeted alone with his mother in her chamber; but a man should first be commissioned to place himself in a concealed part of the room and listen heedfully to what they talked about. For if the son had any wits at all he would not hesitate to speak out in the hearing of his mother, or fear to trust himself to the fidelity of her who bore him. The speaker, loth to seem readier to devise than to carry out the plot, zealously proffered himself as the agent of the eavesdropping. Feng rejoiced at the scheme, and departed on pretence of a long journey. Now he who had given this counsel repaired privily to the room where

Amleth was shut up with his mother, and lay down skulking in the straw. But Amleth had his antidote for the treachery. Afraid of being overheard by some eavesdropper, he at first resorted to his usual imbecile ways, and crowed like a noisy cock, beating his arms together to mimic the flapping of wings. Then he mounted the straw and began to swing his body and jump again and again, wishing to try if aught lurked there in hiding. Feeling a lump beneath his feet, he drove his sword into the spot, and impaled him who lay hid. Then he dragged him from his concealment and slew him. Then, cutting his body into morsels, he seethed it in boiling water, and flung it through the mouth of an open sewer for the swine to eat, bestrewing the stinking mire with his hapless limbs. Having in this wise eluded the snare, he went back to the room. Then his mother set up a great wailing, and began to lament her son's folly to his face; but he said: "Most infamous of women! dost thou seek with such lying lamentations to hide thy most heavy guilt? Wantoning like a harlot, thou hast entered a wicked and abominable state of wedlock, embracing with incestuous bosom thy husband's slayer, and wheedling with filthy lures of blandishment him who had slain the father of thy son. This, forsooth, is the way that the mares couple with the vanquishers of their mates; for brute beasts are naturally incited to pair indiscriminately; and it would seem that thou, like them, hast clean forgot thy first husband. As for me, not idly do I wear the mask of folly; for I doubt not that he who destroyed his brother will riot as ruthlessly in the blood of his kindred. Therefore it is better to choose the garb of dulness than that of sense, and to borrow some protection from a show of utter frenzy. Yet the passion to avenge my father still burns in my heart; but I am watching the chances, I await the fitting hour. There is a place for all things; against so merciless and dark a spirit must be used the deeper devices of the mind. And thou, who hadst been better employed in lamenting thine own disgrace, know it is superfluity to bewail my witlessness; thou shouldst weep for the blemish in thine own mind, not for that in another's. On the rest see thou keep silence." With such reproaches he rent the heart of his mother and redeemed her to walk in the ways of virtue; teaching her to set the fires of the past above the seductions of the present.

When Feng returned, nowhere could he find the man who had suggested the treacherous espial; he searched for him long and carefully, but none said they had seen him anywhere. Amleth, among others, was asked in jest if he had come on any trace of him, and replied that the man had gone to the sewer, but had fallen through its bottom and been stifled by the floods of filth, and that he had been devoured by the swine that came up all about that place. This speech was flouted by those who heard; for it seemed senseless, though really it expressly avowed the truth.

Feng now suspected that his stepson was certainly full of guile, and desired to make away with him, but durst not do the deed for fear of the displeasure, not only of Amleth's grandsire Rorik, but also of his own wife. So he thought that the King of Britain should be employed to slay him, so that another could do the deed, and he be able to feign innocence. Thus, desirous to hide his cruelty, he chose rather to besmirch his friend than to bring disgrace on his own head. Amleth, on departing, gave secret orders to his mother to hang the hall with woven knots, and to perform pretended obsequies for him a year thence; promising that he would then return. Two retainers of Feng then accompanied him, bearing a letter graven on wood—a kind of writing material frequent in old times; this letter enjoined the king of the Britons to put to death the youth who was sent over to him. While they were reposing, Amleth searched their coffers, found the letter, and read the instructions therein. Whereupon he erased all the writing on the surface, substituted fresh characters, and so, changing the purport of the instructions, shifted his own doom upon his companions. Nor was he satisfied with removing from himself the sentence of death and passing the peril on to others, but added an entreaty that the King of Britain would grant his daughter in marriage to a youth of great judgment whom he was sending to him. Under this was falsely marked the signature of Feng.

* * *

[*In Britain, Amleth gains the confidence of the King, and is given his daughter as wife. When the King executes Amleth's companions, Amleth feigns indignation and receives from the King, as compensation, gold which he later melts in the fire, and conceals in some hollow sticks.*]

When he has passed a whole year with the king he obtained leave to make a journey, and returned to his own land, carrying away of all his princely wealth and state only the sticks which held the gold. On reaching Jutland, he exchanged his present attire for his ancient demeanour, which he had adopted for righteous ends, purposely assuming an aspect of absurdity. Covered with filth, he entered the banquet-room where his own obsequies were being held, and struck all men utterly aghast, rumour having falsely noised abroad his death. At last terror melted into mirth, and the guests jeered and taunted one another, that he whose last rites they were celebrating as though he were dead, should appear in the flesh. When he was asked concerning his comrades, he pointed to the sticks he was carrying, and said, "Here is both the one and the other." This he observed with equal truth and pleasantry; for his speech, though most thought it idle, yet departed not from the truth; for it pointed at the weregild of the slain as though it were themselves. Thereon, wishing to bring the company into a gayer mood, he joined the cupbearers, and diligently did the office of plying the drink. Then, to prevent his loose dress hampering his walk, he girded his sword upon his side, and purposely drawing it several times, pricked his fingers with its point. The bystanders accordingly had both sword and scabbard riveted across with an iron nail. Then, to smooth the way more safely to his plot, he went to the lords and plied them heavily with draught upon draught, and drenched them all so deep in wine, that their feet were made feeble with drunkenness, and they turned to rest within the palace, making their bed where they had revelled. Then he saw they were in a fit state for his plots, and thought that here was a chance offered to do his purpose. So he took out of his bosom the stakes he had long ago prepared, and went into the building, where the ground lay covered with the bodies of the nobles wheezing off their sleep and their debauch. Then, cutting away its supports, he brought down the hanging his mother had knitted, which covered the inner as well as the outer walls of the hall. This he flung upon the snorers, and then applying the crooked stakes, he knotted and bound them up in such insoluble intricacy, that not one of the men beneath, however hard he might struggle, could contrive to rise. After this he set fire to the palace. The flames spread, scattering the conflagration far and wide. It enveloped the whole dwelling, destroyed the palace, and burnt them all while they were either buried in deep sleep or vainly striving to arise. Then he went to the chamber of Feng, who had before this been conducted by his train into his pavilion; plucked up a sword that chanced to be hanging to the bed, and planted his own in its place. Then, awakening his uncle, he told him that his nobles were perishing in the flames, and that Amleth was here, armed with his old crooks to help him, and thirsting to exact the vengeance, now long overdue, for his father's murder. Feng, on hearing this, leapt from his couch, but was cut down while, deprived of his own sword, he strove in vain to draw the strange one. O valiant Amleth, and worthy of immortal fame, who being shrewdly armed with a feint of folly, covered a wisdom too high for human wit under a marvellous disguise of silliness! and not only found in his subtlety means to protect his own safety, but also by its guidance found opportunity to avenge his father. By this skilful defence of himself, and strenuous revenge for his parent, he has left it doubtful whether we are to think more of his wit or his bravery. * * *

BELLEFOREST

The Hystorie of Hamblet, Prince of Denmarke.[1]

Chapter I. How Horuendile and Fengon were made Gouernours of the Prouince of Ditmarse, and how Horuendile marryed Geruth, daughter to Roderick chief K. of Denmark: by whom he had Hamblet: and how after his marriage his brother Fengon slewe him trayterously, and marryed his brothers wife, and what followed.

* * * King Rodericke as then raigning in Denmarke, after hee had appeased the troubles in the countrey, and driuen the Sweathlanders and Slaueans from thence; he diuided the kingdom into diuers Prouinces, placing Gouernours therein, * * * giuing the gouernment of Iutie (at this present called Ditmarsse) * * * [to] two valiant & warlike Lords, Horuendile and Fengon, sonnes to Geruendile, who likewise had beene Gouernour of that Prouince. Now the greatest honor that men of noble birth could at that time win and obtaine, was in exercising the art of Piracie vpon the seas; assayling their neighbours, & the countries bordering vpon them: and how much the more they vsed to rob, pill, and spoyle other Prouinces, and Ilands farre adiacent, so much the more their honours and reputation increased and augmented: wherein Horuendile obtained the highest place in his time, beeing the most renouned Pirate that in those dayes scoured the seas, & hauens of the North parts: whose great fame, so mooued the heart of Collere king of Norway, that he was much grieued to heare that Horuendile surmounting him in feates of armes, thereby obscuring the glorie by him alreadie obtained vpon the seas * * * This valiant and hardy king, hauing chalenged Horuendile to fight with him body to body, the combate was by him accepted, with conditions, that hee which should be vanquished, should loose all the riches he had in his ship, and that the vanquisher should cause the body of the vanquished (that should bee slaine

1. Translated anonymously from *Le Cinquiesme Tome des Histoires Tragiques* of F. de Belleforest (Paris, 1582), and published in London in 1608. The following extracts are taken from the unique copy of the translation preserved in the Library of Trinity College, Cambridge, and are reproduced here by kind permission of the Master and Fellows of Trinity College. The punctuation of the original has been slightly modified. The spelling of the original has been preserved. In the French text, the hero's name is Amleth.

in the combate) to be honourably buried, death being the prise
and reward of him that should loose the battaile: and to conclude, Collere king of Norway (although a valiant, hardy and
couragious prince) was in the end vanquished and slaine by
Horuendile: who presently caused a Tombe to be erected, and
therein (with all honorable obseques fit for a prince) buried the
body of king Collere, according to their auncient manner, and
superstitions in those dayes, and the conditions of the combate,
bereauing the Kings shippes of all their riches, and hauing slaine
the kings sister, a very braue and valiant warriour, and ouer runne
all the coast of Norway, and the Northren Ilands, returned home
againe layden with much treasure, sending the most part thereof
to his soueraigne king Rodericke, thereby to procure his good lik-
ing, and so to be accounted one of the greatest fauorites about his
maiestie.

The King allured by those presents, and esteeming himselfe
happy to haue so valiant a subiect, sought by a great fauour and
courtesie, to make him become bounden vnto him perpetually,
giuing him Geruth his daughter to his wife, of whom he knew
Horuendile to bee already much inamored: and the more to honor
him, determined himselfe in person to conduct her into Iutie,
where the marriage was celebrated according to the ancient manner: and to be briefe, of this marriage proceeded Hamblet, of
whom I intend to speake, and for his cause haue chosen to renew
this present Hystorie.

Fengon, brother to this Prince Horuendile, who onely fretting
and despighting in his heart at the great honor and reputation
wonne by his brother in warlike affaires, but solicited and pro-
uoked (by a foolish ielousie) to see him honored with royall ali-
ance, and fearing thereby to bee deposed from his part of the
gouernment: or rather desiring to be onely Gouernour: thereby
to obscure the memorie of the victories and conquests of his
brother Horuendile; determined (whatsoeuer happened) to kill
him, which hee effected in such sort, that no man once so much
as suspected him, euery man esteeming that from such and so
firme a knot of alliance and consanguinitie, there could proceed
no other issue then the full effects of vertue and courtesie * * *
Was not this a craftie and subtile Counsellor: but he might haue
thought that the mother, knowing her husbands case, would not
cast her sonne into the danger of death. But Fengon hauing secretly assembled certain men, & perceiuing himself strong enough
to execute his interprise, Horuendile his brother being at a ban-
quet with his friends, sodainely set vpon him, where he slewe him

as traiterously, as cunningly he purged himselfe of so detestable a murther to his subiects: for that before he had any violent or bloody handes, or once committed parricide vpon his brother, hee had incestuously abused his wife, whose honour he ought as well to haue sought and procured, as traiterously he pursued and effected his destruction: and it is most certaine, that the man that abandoneth himselfe to any notorious and wicked action, whereby he becommeth a great sinner, hee careth not to commit much more haynous and abhominable offences, & couered his boldnesse and wicked practise with so great subtiltie and policie, and vnder a vaile of meere simplicitie, that beeing fauoured for the honest loue that he bare to his sister in lawe, for whose sake hee affirmed, hee had in that sort murthered his brother, that his sinne found excuse among the common people, & of the Nobilitie was esteemed for iustice: for that Geruth being as courteous a Princesse, as any then liuing in the North parts, and one that had neuer once so much as offended any of her subiects, either commons, or Courtyers; this adulterer and infamous murtherer, slaundered his dead brother, that hee would haue slaine his wife, and that hee by chance finding him vpon the point ready to doe it, in defence of the Lady had slaine him, bearing off the blows which as then hee strooke at the innocent Princesse, without any other cause of malice whatsoeuer: wherein hee wanted no false witnesses to approoue his act, which deposed in like sort, as the wicked calumniator himselfe protested, being the same persons that had born him company, & were participants of his treason, so that instead of pursuing him as a parricide, & an incestuous person, al the Courtyers admired and flattered him in his good fortune: making more account of false witnesses and detestable wicked reporters, and more honouring the callumniators, then they esteemed of those that seeking to call the matter in question, and admiring the vertues of the murthered Prince would haue punished the massacrers and bereauers of his life. Which was the cause that Fengon, boldned and incouraged by such impunitie, durst venture to couple himselfe in marriage with her, whom hee vsed as his Concubine, during good Horuendiles life, in that sort spotting his name with a double vice, and charging his conscience with abhominable guilt, and twofold impietie, as incestuous adulterie, and parricide murther: and that the vnfortunate and wicked woman, that had receaued the honour to bee the wife of one of the valiantest and wisest Princes in the North, imbased her selfe in such vile sort, as to falsifie her faith vnto him, and which is worse, to marrie him, that had bin the tyranous murtherer of her lawfull husband:

which made diuers men thinke, that she had been the causer of the murther, thereby to liue in her adultery without controle. * * *

Chapter II. How Hamblet counterfeited the mad man, to escape the tyrannie of his vncle, and how he was tempted by a woman (through his vncles procurement) who thereby thought to vnderminde the Prince, and by that meanes to finde out whether he counterfeited madnesse or not: and how Hamblet would by no meanes bee brought to consent vnto her; and what followed.

Geruth hauing (as I sayd before) so much forgotten herselfe, the prince Hamblet perceiuing himselfe to bee in danger of his life, as beeing abandoned of his owne mother, and forsaken of all men; and assuring himselfe that Fengon would not detract[2] the time, to send him the same way his father Horuendile was gone: to begiule the tyrant in his subtilties (that esteemed him to bee of such a minde, that if he once attained to mans estate, he wold not long delay the time to reuenge the death of his father) counterfeiting the mad man with such craft & subtill practises, that hee made shewe as if hee had vtterly lost his wittes: and vnder that vayle hee couered his pretence, and defended his life from the treasons and practises of the tyrant his vncle. * * *

Hamblet in this sorte counterfeiting the madde man, many times did diuers actions of great and deepe consideration, and often made such and so fitte answeres, that a wise man would soone haue iudged from what spirite so fine an inuention mighte proceede, for that standing by the fire and sharpning sticks like poynards and prickes, one in smiling manner asked him wherefore he made those little staues so sharpe at the points, I prepare (saith he) piersing dartes, and sharpe arrowes, to reuenge my fathers death, fooles as I said before, esteemed those his words as nothing, but men of quicke spirits, and such as hadde a deeper reache began to suspect somewhat, esteeming that vnder that kinde of folly there lay hidden a greate & rare subtilty, such as one day might bee preiudiciall to their prince, saying that vnder colour of such rudenes he shadowed a crafty pollicy, and by his deuised simplicitye, he concealed a sharp and pregnant spirit, for which cause they counselled the king to try, & know if it were possible, how to discouer the intent & meaning of the young prince, & they could find no better, nor more fit inuention to intrap him then to set some faire, and beawtifull woman in a secret place, that with flattering speeches and all the craftiest meanes she could vse, should purposely seek to allure his mind to haue his pleasure of

2. Delay.

her. * * * To this end certaine courtiers were appointed to leade
Hamblet into a solitary place within the woods, whether they
brought the woman, inciting him to take their pleasures together,
and to imbrace one another * * * and surely the poore prince
at this assault had bin in great danger, if a gentleman (that in
Horuendiles time had bin nourished with him) had not showne
himselfe more affectioned to the bringing vp he had receiued with
Hamblet, then desirous to please the Tirant, who by all meanes
sought to intangle the sonne in the same nets wherein the father
had ended his dayes. This Gentleman bare the courtiers (appointed
as aforesaide of this treason) company, more desiring to giue
the prince instructions what he should do, then to intrap him
making full account that the least showe of perfect sence and
wisdome that Hamblet should make, would be sufficient to cause
him to loose his life: and therefore by certain signes, he gaue
Hamblet intelligence, in what danger hee was like to fall if by any
meanes hee seemed to obaye, or once like the wanton toyes, &
vicious prouocations of the gentlewoman, sent thither by his
Uncle: which much abashed the prince, as then wholy beeing in
affection to the Lady, but by her he was likewise informed of the
treason, as being one that from her infancy loued and fauoured
him, and would haue been exceeding sorrowfull for his misfortune,
and much more to leaue his companie without inioying the pleasure of his body, whome shee loued more than her selfe. The
Prince in this sort hauing both deceiued the courtiers, and the
Ladyes expectation, that affirmed and swoore that hee neuer once
offered to haue his pleasure of the woman, although in subtilty
hee affirmed the contrary: euery man there vpon assured themselues that without all doubt hee was distraught of his sences, that
his braynes were as then wholly void of force and incapable of
reasonable apprehension so that as then Fengons practise took no
effect: but for al that he left not off: still seeking by al meanes
to finde out Hamblets subtilty: as in the next chapter you shall
perceiue.

*Chapter III. How Fengon Vncle to Hamblet a second time to
intrap him in his pollitick madnes: caused one of his counsellors
to be secretly hidden in the Queenes chamber: behind the arras, to
heare what speeches past betweene Hamblet and the Queen and
how Hamblet killed him, and escaped that danger and what followed.*

Among the friends of Fengon, ther was one that aboue al the
rest, doubted of Hamblets practises, in counterfeiting the madman, who for that cause said, that it was impossible that so craftie

a gallant as Hamblet that counterfeited the foole, should be discouered with so common & vnskilfull practises, which might easily
bee perceiued, and that to finde out his politique pretence it were
necessary to inuent some subtill and craftie meanes, more atrac-
tiue: wherby the gallant might not haue the leysure to vse his accustomed dissimulation, which to effect he said he knewe a fit
waie and a most conuenient meane to effect the kings desire, and
thereby to intrap Hamblet in his subtilties, and cause him of his
owne accord to fall into the net prepared for him, and thereby
euidently shewe his secret meaning: his deuise was thus, that King
Fengon should make as though he were to goe some long voyage,
concerning affayres of great importance and that in the meane
time Hamblet should be shut vp alone in a chamber with his
mother, wherein some other should secretly be hidden behind
the hangings, vnknowne either to him or his mother, there to
stand and heere their speeches, and the complots by them to bee
taken, concerning the accomplishments of the dissembling fooles
pretence, assuring the king that if there were any point of wisedome and perfect sence in the gallants spirit that without all
doubte he would easily discouer it to his mother as being deuoid
of all feare that she would vtter or make knowne his secret intent,
beeing the woman that had borne him in her bodie, and nourished
him so carefully, and withall offered himselfe to be the man, that
should stand to harken, and beare witnesse of Hamblets speeches
with his mother, that hee might not be esteemed a counsellor in such
a case, wherein he refused to be the executioner, for the behoofe and
seruice of his prince. This inuention pleased the King exceeding
well, esteeming it as the onelie, and soueraigne remedie to heale
the prince of his lunacie, and to that ende making a long voyage
issued out of his pallace, and road to hunt in the forrest, meane
time the counsellor entred secretly into the Queenes chamber,
and there hid himselfe behind the arras,[3] not long before the
Queen and Hamblet came thither, who beeing craftie and pol-
litique, as soone as hee was within the chamber doubting some
treason, and fearing if he should speake seuerely and wisely to his
mother touching his secret practises he would be vnderstood, and
by that meanes intercepted, vsed his ordinary manner of dissimulation, and began to come like a cocke beating with his armes, in

3. Here, and in what follows, Shakespeare's play has obviously influenced
the translation. There is no mention
of "hangings" or of an arras in the
original. Israel Gollancz, in *The
Sources of Hamlet* (Oxford, 1926, pp.
319–20), notes: "In Belleforest (as
in Saxo) the counsellor hides under a
quilt (F. *loudier, lodier;* L. *stramen-*
tum): Hamlet jumps on this quilt
(*sauta sur ce lodier*); in *The Hystorie*
the quilt becomes a curtain or tapestry
—'hangings' and 'arras,' from Shakespeare. And, further, the English translator adds what is not found in
Belleforest or Saxo, the very words of
the play, 'A rat! a rat!'"

such manner as cockes vse to strike with their wings, vpon the hangings of the chamber, whereby feeling something stirring vnder them, hee cried a rat a rat, and presently drawing his sworde thrust it into the hangings, which done, pulled the counsellour (halfe dead) out by the heeles, made an end of killing him, and beeing slaine, cut his bodie in peeces, which he caused to be boyled and then cast it into an open vaulte or priuie, that so it mighte serue for foode to the hogges, by which meanes hauing discouered the ambushe, and giuen the inuenter thereof his iust rewarde, hee came againe to his mother, who in the meane time wepte and tormented her selfe, to see all her hopes frustrate, for that what fault soeuer she had committed, yet was shee sore grieued, to see her onely child made a meere mockery, euery man reproaching her with his folly, one point whereof she had as then seene before her eyes, which was no small pricke to her conscience, esteeming that the Gods sent her that punishment, for ioyning incestuously in marriage with the tyrannous murtherer of her husband * * * and while in this sort she sate tormenting her selfe, Hamlet entred into the chamber, who hauing once againe searched euery corner of the same, distrusting his mother as well as the rest, and perceiuing himselfe to bee alone, began in sober and discreet manner to speak vnto her saying.

What treason is this, O most infamous woman! of all that euer prostrated themselues to the will of an abhominable whoremonger who vnder the vail of a dissembling creature couereth the most wicked and detestable crime that man could euer imagine, or was committed. How may I be assured to trust you, that like a vile wanton adulteresse, altogether impudent & giuen ouer to her pleasure, runnes spreading forth her armes ioyfully to imbrace the trayterous villanous tyrant, that murthered my father, and most incestuously receiuest the villain into the lawfull bed of your loyall spouse, impudently entertaining him in steede of the deare father of your miserable and discomforted sonne, if the gods graunt him not the grace speedilie to escape from a captiuity so vnworthie the degree he holdeth, and the race & noble familie of his ancestors. Is this the part of a queene, and daughter to a king? to liue like a bruite beast, (and like a mare that yeeldeth her bodie to the horse that hath beaten hir companion awaye,) to followe the pleasure of an abhominable king, that hath murthered a farre more honester and better man than himself in massacring Horuendile, the honor, and glory of the Danes, who are now esteemed of no force nor valour at all, since the shining splendure of knighthood, was brought to an end by the most wickedest, and cruellest villaine liuing vpon earth: I for my part will neuer account him for my kinsman, nor once knowe him for mine vncle, nor you my deer mother for not hauing respect to the blud that ought to haue vnited vs so straightly together & who neither with your honor nor without suspition of consent to the death of your husband could euer haue agreed to haue marryed with his cruell enemie: O Queene Geruthe, it is the part of a bitch, to couple with many, and desire acquaintance of diuers mastiffes: it is licentiousnes only that hath made you deface out of your minde the memory of the valor & vertues of the good King your husband and my father: it was an vnbrideled desire that guided the daughter of Roderick to imbrace the Tirant Fengon, & not to remember Horuendile (vnworthy of so strange intertainment), neither that he killed his brother traiterously, and that shee being his fathers wife betrayed him, although he so well fauoured and loued her, that for her sake he vtterly bereaued Norway of her riches and valiant souldiers, to augment the treasures of Roderick, and make Geruthe wife to the hardyest prince in Europe. It is not the parte of a woman, much lesse of a princesse, in whome all modesty, curtesie, compassion and loue ought to abound, thus to leaue her deare child to fortune in the bloody & murtherous hands of a villain and traytor, bruite beasts do not so: for Lyons, Tygers, ounces, and leopards fight for the safety and defence of their whelpes, and birds that haue beakes, claws and wings, resist such as would rauish them of their yong ones, but you to the contrary expose and deliuer mee to death, whereas ye should defend me. Is not this as much as if you should betray me, when you knowing the peruersenes of the tyrant and his intents, ful of deadly counsell as touching the race & image of his brother, haue not once sought nor desired to finde the meanes to saue your child (& only son) by sending him into Swethland, Norway or England, rather then to leaue him as a pray to youre infamous adulterer? bee not offended I praye you Madame, if transported with dolour and griefe I speake so boldely vnto you, and that I respect you lesse then duetie requireth, for you hauing forgotten mee, and wholy reiected the memorye of the deceased K. my father, must not bee abashed if I also surpasse the bounds and limits of due consideration. Beholde into what distresse I am now fallen, and to what mischiefe my fortune and your ouer greate lightnesse, and want of wisedome haue induced mee, that I am constrained to playe the madde man to saue my life in steed of vsing and practising armes, following aduentures, and seeking all meanes to make my selfe knowne to bee the true and vndoubted heire of the valiant and vertuous King Horuendile, it was not without cause, and iuste occasion, that my gestures, countenances and words seeme all to proceed from a madman, and that I desire to haue all men esteeme me wholy depriued of sence and reasonable vnderstanding, by cause I am well assured, that he that hath made no conscience to kill his owne brother, (accustomed to murthers, & allured with desire of gouernement without controll in his treasons) will not spare to saue himselfe with the like crueltie, in the blood, & flesh of the loyns of his brother, by him massacred: & therefore it is better for me to fayne madnesse then to vse my right sences as nature hath bestowed them vpon me. The bright shining clearnes therof I am forced to hide vnder this shadow of dissimulation, as the sun doth hir beams vnder some great cloud, when the wether in sommertime ouercasteth: the face of a mad man, serueth to couer my gallant countenance, & the gestures of a fool are fit for me, to the end that guiding my self wisely therein I may preserue my life for the Danes & the memory of my late deceased father, for that the desire of reuenging his death is so ingrauen in my heart that if I dye not shortly, I hope to take such and so great vengeance, that these Countryes shall foreuer speake thereof. Neuerthelesse I must stay the time, meanes, and occasion, lest by making ouer great hast, I be now the cause of mine owne sodaine ruine and ouerthrow, and by that meanes, end, before I beginne to effect my hearts desire: hee that hath to doe with a wicked, disloyall, cruell, and discourteous man, must vse craft, and politike inuentions, such as a fine witte can best imagine, not to discouer his interprise: for seeing that by force I cannot effect my desire, reason alloweth me by dissimulation, subtiltie, and secret practises to proceed therein. To conclude, weepe not (Madame) to see my folly, but rather sigh and lament your owne offence, tormenting your conscience in regard of the infamie that hath so defiled the ancient renowne and glorie that (in times past) honoured Queene Geruth: for wee are not to sorrowe and grieue at other mens vices, but for our owne misdeedes, and great follyes. Desiring you, for the surplus of my proceedings, aboue all things (as you loue your owne life and welfare) that neither the king, nor any other may by any meanes know mine intent, and let me alone with the rest, for I hope in the ende to bring my purpose to effect. Although the Queene perceiued herselfe neerly touched, and that Hamlet mooued her to the quicke, where she felt herselfe interested: neuertheless shee forgot all disdaine & wrath, which thereby she might as then haue had, hearing herselfe so sharply chiden & reprooued, for the joy she then conceaued, to behold the gallant spirit of her sonne, and to thinke what she might hope, & the easier expect of his so great policie and wisdome. But on the one side she durst not lift vp her eyes to behold him, remembring her offence, & on the other side she would gladly haue imbraced her son, in regard of the wise admonitions by him giuen vnto her, which as then quenched the flames of vnbridled desire, and before had moued her to affect K. Fengon: to ingraff in her heart the vertuous actions of her lawfull spouse, whom inwardly she much lamented, when she beheld the liuely image and portraiture of his vertue & great wisedome in her childe, representing his fathers haughtie and valiant heart: and so ouercome and vanquished with this honest passion, and weeping most bitterly, hauing long time fixed her eyes vpon Hamlet, as beeing rauished into some great and deepe contemplation, & as it were wholy amazed; at the last imbracing him in her armes (with the like loue that a vertuous mother may or can vse, to kisse and entertaine her owne childe) shee spake vnto him in this manner.

I know well (my Sonne) that I haue done thee great wrong in marrying with Fengon, the cruell tyrant and murtherer of thy father, and my loyal spouse: but when thou shalt consider the small meanes of resistance, and the treason of the Palace, with the little cause of confidence we are to expect or hope for of the Courtiers, all wrought to his will: as also the power hee made ready, if I should haue refused to like of him, thou wouldest rather excuse, then accuse me of lasciuiousnes or inconstancy, much lesse offer me that wrong, to suspect that euer thy mother Geruthe once consented to the death & murther of her husband: swearing vnto thee (by the maiestie of the Gods) that if it had layne in my power to haue resisted the Tyrant, although it had beene with the losse of my blood, yea and of my life, I would surely haue saued the life of my Lord and husband, with as good a will & desire, as since that time, I haue often beene a meanes to hinder and impeach the shortning of thy life, which being taken away, I will no longer liue here vpon earth: for seeing that thy sences are whole and sound, I am in hope to see an easie meanes inuented, for the reuenging of thy fathers death. Neuerthelesse, mine owne sweet sonne, if thou hast pittie of thyselfe, or care of the memorie of thy father (although thou wilt do nothing for her, that deserueth not the name of a mother in this respect) I pray thee carie thine affayres wisely, bee not hastie, nor ouer furious in thy interprises, neither yet aduance thyselfe more then reason shall mooue thee to effect thy purpose. Thou seest there is not almost any man wherein thou mayest put thy trust, nor any woman to whom I dare vtter the least part of my secrets, that would not presently report it to thine aduersarie, who although in outward shew he dissembleth to loue thee, the better to inioy his pleasures of me, yet hee distrusteth and feareth mee for thy sake, and is not so simple to be easily perswaded, that thou art a foole or mad, so that if thou chance to doe any thing that seemeth to proceed of wisedome or policie (how secretly soeuer it be done) he will presently be informed thereof, and I am greatly afraide that the deuils haue shewed him, what hath past at this present betweene vs: (Fortune so much pursueth and contrarieth our ease and welfare) or that this murther that now thou hast committed, be not the cause of both our destructions, which I by no meanes will seeme to know, but will keepe secret both thy wisedone & hardy interprise. Beseeching the Gods (my good sonne) that they guiding thy heart, directing thy counsels and prospering thy interprise, I may see thee possesse and inioy that which is thy right, and weare the crowne of Denmarke, by the Tyrant taken from thee: that I may reioyce in thy prosperitie, and therewith content my self, seeing with what courage and boldnesse thou shalt take vengeance vpon the murtherer of thy father, as also vpon all those that haue assisted and fauoured him, in his murtherous and bloody enterprise.

Madame (sayd Hamlet) I will put my trust in you, and from hencefoorth meane not to meddle further with your affayres, beseeching you (as you loue your owne flesh and blood) that you will from hence foorth no more esteeme of the adulterer mine enemie, whom I will surely kill, or cause to be put to death, in despite of all the deuils in hel: and haue he neuer so manie flattering courtezans to defend him yet will I bring him to his death, & they themselues also shall beare him company therein: as they haue bin his peruerse counsellors in the action of killing my father, and his companions in his treason, massacre, and cruell enterprise. And reason requireth, that euen as trayterously they then caused their prince to bee put to death, that with the like (nay well much more) iustice they should pay the interest of their fellonious actions. * * *

After this Fengon (as if hee had beene out some long iourney) came to the Court againe, and asked for him that had receiued the charge to play the intillegencer, to entrap Hamlet, in his dissembled wisedome, was abashed to heare neither newes nor tydings of him, and for that cause asked Hamlet what was become of him: naming the man. The Prince that neuer vsed lying, and who in all the answers that euer he made (during his counterfeit madnesse) neuer strayed from the trueth (as a generous minde is a mortal enemie to vntruth) answered and sayd, that the counsellor he sought for, was gone downe through the priuie, where beeing choaked by the filthynesse of the place, the Hogs meeting him had filled their bellyes.[4]

---

4. What follows in Belleforest—the account of Hamlet's voyage to England, his sojourn there, his return to Denmark and the manner of his revenge—parallels in all important details the narration of those events as given in Saxo.

Essays in
Criticism

JOHN DENNIS

From An Essay on the Genius and Writings of Shakespeare†

* * * But indeed Shakespeare has been wanting in the exact distribution of poetical justice not only in his *Coriolanus*, but in most of his best tragedies, in which the guilty and the innocent perish promiscuously; as Duncan and Banquo in *Macbeth*, as likewise Lady Macduff and her children; Desdemona in *Othello*; Cordelia, Kent, and King Lear, in the tragedy that bears his name; Brutus and Portia in *Julius Caesar*, and young Hamlet in the *Tragedy of Hamlet*. For though it may be said in defense of the last, that Hamlet had a design to kill his uncle who then reigned; yet this is justified by no less than a call from heaven, and raising up one from the dead to urge him to it. The good and the bad then perishing promiscuously in the best of Shakespeare's tragedies, there can be either none or very weak instruction in them: for such promiscuous events call the government of providence into question, and by sceptics and libertines are resolved into chance.

ANONYMOUS

From Some Remarks on the Tragedy of Hamlet Prince of Denmark‡

Now I am come to mention Hamlet's madness, I must speak my opinion of our poet's conduct in this particular. To conform to the ground-work of his plot, Shakespeare makes the young prince feign himself mad. I cannot but think this to be injudicious; for so far from securing himself from any violence which he feared from the usurper, which was his design in so doing, it seems to have been the most likely way of getting himself confined, and consequently, debarred from an opportunity of revenging his

† London, 1712; pp. 9–10.
‡ London, 1736. This has often been attributed to Sir Thomas Hanmer, but the attribution has been challenged. For the argument against it, see Clar- ence D. Thorpe, "Thomas Hanmer and the Anonymous Essay on *Hamlet*," *Modern Language Notes*, XLIX (1934), 493–98. This extract is from pp. 33–34.

father's death, which now seemed to be his only aim; and accordingly it was the occasion of his being sent away to England. Which design, had it taken effect upon his life, he never could have revenged his father's murder. To speak truth, our poet, by keeping too close to the ground-work of his plot, has fallen into an absurdity; for there appears no reason at all in nature, why the young prince did not put the usurper to death as soon as possible, especially as Hamlet is represented as a youth so brave, and so careless of his own life.

The case indeed is this: Had Hamlet gone naturally to work, as we could suppose such a prince to do in parallel circumstances, there would have been an end of our play. The poet therefore was obliged to delay his hero's revenge; but then he should have contrived some good reason for it.

SAMUEL JOHNSON

[The Praise of Variety]†

If the dramas of Shakespeare were to be characterized, each by the particular excellence which distinguishes it from the rest, we must allow to the tragedy of *Hamlet* the praise of variety. The incidents are so numerous, that the argument of the play would make a long tale. The scenes are interchangeably diversified with merriment and solemnity; with merriment that includes judicious and instructive observations, and solemnity, not strained by poetical violence above the natural sentiments of man. New characters appear from time to time in continual succession, exhibiting various forms of life and particular modes of conversation. The pretended madness of Hamlet causes much mirth, the mournful distraction of Ophelia fills the heart with tenderness, and every personage produces the effect intended, from the apparition that in the first act chills the blood with horror, to the fop in the last, that exposes affectation to just contempt.

The conduct is perhaps not wholly secure against objections. The action is indeed for the most part in continual progression, but there are some scenes which neither forward nor retard it. Of the feigned madness of Hamlet there appears no adequate cause, for he does nothing which he might not have done with the reputation of sanity. He plays the madman most, when he treats Ophelia

† From *The Plays of William Shakespeare* (London, 1765), VIII, 311.

with so much rudeness, which seems to be useless and wanton cruelty.

Hamlet is, through the whole play, rather an instrument than an agent. After he has, by the stratagem of the play, convicted the King, he makes no attempt to punish him, and his death is at last effected by an incident which Hamlet has no part in producing.

The catastrophe is not very happily produced; the exchange of weapons is rather an expedient of necessity, than a stroke of art. A scheme might easily have been formed, to kill Hamlet with the dagger, and Laertes with the bowl.

The poet is accused of having shown little regard to poetical justice, and may be charged with equal neglect of poetical probability. The apparition left the regions of the dead to little purpose; the revenge which he demands is not obtained but by the death of him that was required to take it; and the gratification which would arise from the destruction of an usurper and a murderer, is abated by the untimely death of Ophelia, the young, the beautiful, the harmless, and the pious.

WILLIAM RICHARDSON

The Character of Hamlet†

* * * The death of his father was a natural evil, and as such he endures it. That he is excluded from succeeding immediately to the royalty that belongs to him, seems to affect him slightly; for to vehement and vain ambition he appears superior. He is moved by finer principles, by an exquisite sense of virtue, of moral beauty and turpitude. The impropriety of Gertrude's behavior, her ingratitude to the memory of her former husband, and the depravity she discovers in the choice of a successor, afflict his soul, and cast him into utter agony. Here then is the principle and spring of all his actions. * * *

The man whose sense of moral excellence is uncommonly exquisite, will find it a source of pleasure and of pain in his commerce with mankind. Susceptible of every moral impression, the display of virtuous actions will yield him delight, and the contrary excite uneasiness. * * * The triumph and inward joy of a son, on account of the fame and the high desert of a parent, is of a nature

† From *A Philosophical Analysis and Illustration of some of Shakespeare's* Remarkable Characters (London, 1774), pp. 97–98, 100–104.

very sublime and tender. His sorrow is no less acute and overwhelming, if those, united to him by a connection so intimate, have acted unbecomingly, and have incurred disgrace. Such is the condition of Hamlet. Exquisitely sensible of moral beauty and deformity, he discerns turpitude in a parent. Surprise, on a discovery so painful and unexpected, adds bitterness to his sorrow; and led, by the same moral principle to admire and glory in the high desert of his father, even this admiration contributes to his uneasiness. Aversion to his uncle, arising from the same origin, has a similar tendency, and augments his anguish. All these feelings and emotions uniting together, are rendered still more violent, exasperated by his recent interview with the Queen, struggling for utterance, but restrained. Agitated and overwhelmed with afflicting images, no soothing, no exhilarating affection can have admission into his heart. His imagination is visited by no vision of happiness; and he wishes for deliverance from his afflictions, by being delivered from a painful existence.

HENRY MACKENZIE

Criticism on the Character and Tragedy of Hamlet†

* * *

Of all the characters of Shakspeare, that of Hamlet has been generally thought the most difficult to be reduced to any fixed or settled principle. With the strongest purposes of revenge, he is irresolute and inactive; amidst the gloom of the deepest melancholy, he is gay and jocular; and while he is described as a passionate lover, he seems indifferent about the object of his affections. It may be worth while to inquire whether any leading idea can be found, upon which these apparent contradictions may be reconciled, and a character so pleasing in the closet, and so much applauded on the stage, rendered as unambiguous in the general as it is striking in detail. I will venture to lay before my readers some observations on this subject, though with the diffidence due to a question of which the public has doubted, and much abler critics have already written.

The basis of Hamlet's character seems to be an extreme sensibil-

† From *The Mirror*, No. 99, April 18, 1770. Reprinted in *Memorials of* *Shakespeare*, edited by Nathan Drake (London, 1828), pp. 371–78.

ity of mind, apt to be strongly impressed by its situation, and overpowered by the feelings which that situation excites. Naturally of the most virtuous and most amiable dispositions, the circumstances in which he was placed unhinged those principles of action, which, in another situation, would have delighted mankind, and made himself happy. That kind of distress which he suffered was, beyond all others, calculated to produce this effect. His misfortunes were not the misfortunes of accident, which, though they may overwhelm at first, the mind will soon call up reflections to alleviate, and hopes to cheer: they were such as reflection only serves to irritate, such as rankle in the soul's tenderest part, her sense of virtue, and feelings of natural affection; they arose from an uncle's villainy, a mother's guilt, a father's murder!—Yet amidst the gloom of melancholy, and the agitation of passion, in which his calamities involve him, there are occasional breakings-out of a mind richly endowed by nature, and cultivated by education. We perceive gentleness in his demeanour, wit in his conversation, taste in his amusements, and wisdom in his reflections.

That Hamlet's character, thus formed by nature, and thus modelled by situation, is often variable and uncertain, I am not disposed to deny. I will content myself with the supposition that this is the very character which Shakspeare meant to allot him. Finding such a character in real life, of a person endowed with feelings so delicate as to border on weakness, with sensibility too exquisite to allow of determined action, he has placed it where it could be best exhibited, in scenes of wonder, of terror, and of indignation, where its varying emotions might be most strongly marked amidst the workings of imagination, and the war of the passions.

This is the very management of the character by which, above all others, we could be interested in its behalf. Had Shakspeare made Hamlet pursue his vengeance with a steady determined purpose, had he led him through difficulties arising from accidental causes, and not from the doubts and hesitation of his own mind, the anxiety of the spectator might have been highly raised; but it would have been anxiety for the event, not for the person. As it is, we feel not only the virtues, but the weaknesses of Hamlet, as our own; we see a man who, in other circumstances, would have exercised all the moral and social virtues, one whom nature had formed to be

> Th' expectancy and rose of the fair state,
> The glass of fashion, and the mould of form,
> Th' observ'd of all observers,

placed in a situation in which even the amiable qualities of his mind serve but to aggravate his distress, and to perplex his conduct. Our compassion for the first, and our anxiety for the latter, are excited in the strongest manner; and hence arises that indescribable charm in Hamlet, which attracts every reader and every spectator, which the more perfect characters of other tragedies never dispose us to feel.

The Orestes of the Greek poet, who, at his first appearance, lays down a plan of vengeance which he resolutely pursues, interests us for the accomplishment of his purpose; but of him we think only as the instrument of that justice which we wish to overtake the murderers of Agamemnon. We feel with Orestes, (or rather with Sophocles, for in such passages we always hear the poet in his hero,) that 'it is fit that such gross infringements of the moral law should be punished with death, in order to render wickedness less frequent;' but when Horatio exclaims on the death of his friend,

> Now crack'd a noble heart!

we forget the murder of the king, the villainy of Claudius, the guilt of Gertrude; our recollection dwells only on the memory of that 'sweet prince,' the delicacy of whose feelings a milder planet should have ruled, whose gentle virtues should have bloomed through a life of felicity and usefulness.

Hamlet, from the very opening of the piece, is delineated as one under the dominion of melancholy, whose spirits were overborne by his feelings. Grief for his father's death, and displeasure at his mother's marriage, prey on his mind; and he seems, with the weakness natural to such a disposition, to yield to their controul. He does not attempt to resist or combat these impressions, but is willing to fly from the contest, though it were into the grave.

> Oh! that this too too solid flesh would melt, &c.

Even after his father's ghost has informed him of his murder, and commissioned him to avenge it, we find him complaining of that situation in which his fate had placed him:

> The time is out of joint; oh! cursed spight,
> That ever I was born to set it right!

And afterwards, in the perplexity of his condition, meditating on the expediency of suicide:

> To be, or not to be, that is the question.

The account he gives of his own feelings to Rosencrantz and Guildenstern, which is evidently spoken in earnest, though somewhat covered with the mist of his affected distraction, is exactly descriptive of a mind full of that weariness of life which is characteristic of low spirits: 'This goodly frame, the earth, seems to me a sterile promontory,' &c. And, indeed, he expressly delineates his own character as of the kind above-mentioned, when, hesitating on the evidence of his uncle's villainy, he says,

> The spirit that I have seen
> May be the devil, and the devil hath power
> T' assume a pleasing shape; yea, and perhaps,
> *Out of my weakness and my melancholy,*
> Abuses me to damn me.

This doubt of the grounds on which our purpose is founded, is as often the effect as the cause of irresolution, which first hesitates, and then seeks out an excuse for its hesitation.

It may, perhaps, be doing Shakspeare no injustice to suppose that he sometimes began a play without having fixed in his mind, in any determined manner, the plan or conduct of his piece. The character of some principal person of the drama might strike his imagination strongly in the opening scenes; as he went on, this character would continue to impress itself on the conduct as well as the discourse of that person, and, it is possible, might affect the situations and incidents, especially in those romantic or legendary subjects, where history did not confine him to certain unchangeable events. In the story of Amleth, the son of Horwondil, told by Saxo-Grammaticus, from which the tragedy of Hamlet is taken, the young prince, who is to revenge the death of his father, murdered by his uncle Fengo, counterfeits madness, that he may be allowed to remain about the court in safety and without suspicion. He never forgets his purposed vengeance, and acts with much more cunning towards its accomplishment than the Hamlet of Shakspeare. But Shakspeare, wishing to elevate the hero of his tragedy, and at the same time to interest the audience in his behalf, throws around him, from the beginning, the majesty of melancholy, along with that sort of weakness and irresolution which frequently attends it. The incident of the Ghost, which is entirely the poet's own, and not to be found in the Danish legend, not only produces the happiest stage effect, but is also of the greatest advantage in unfolding that character which is stamped on the young prince at the opening of the play. In the communications of such a visionary being, there is an uncertain kind of belief, and a dark unlimited horror, which are aptly suited to display the wavering purpose and varied emotions of a mind endowed with a delicacy of feeling that often shakes its fortitude, with sensibility that overpowers its strength.

JOHANN WOLFGANG VON GOETHE

[A Soul Unfit]†

* * * "Conceive a prince such as I have painted him, and that his father suddenly dies. Ambition and the love of rule are not the passions that inspire him. As a king's son, he would have been contented; but now he is first constrained to consider the difference which separates a sovereign from a subject. The crown was not hereditary; yet a longer possession of it by his father would have strengthened the pretensions of an only son, and secured his hopes of the succession. In place of this, he now beholds himself excluded by his uncle, in spite of specious promises, most probably forever. He is now poor in goods and favor, and a stranger in the scene which from youth he had looked upon as his inheritance. His temper here assumes its first mournful tinge. He feels that now he is not more, that he is less, than a private nobleman; he offers himself as the servant of every one; he is not courteous and condescending, he is needy and degraded.

"His past condition he remembers as a vanished dream. It is in vain that his uncle strives to cheer him, to present his situation in another point of view. The feeling of his nothingness will not leave him.

"The second stroke that came upon him wounded deeper, bowed still more. It was the marriage of his mother. The faithful tender son had yet a mother, when his father passed away. He hoped, in the company of his surviving noble-minded parent, to reverence the heroic form of the departed; but his mother too he loses, and it is something worse than death that robs him of her. The trustful image, which a good child loves to form of its parents, is gone. With the dead there is no help, on the living no hold. She also is a woman, and her name is Frailty, like that of all her sex.

"Now first does he feel himself completely bent and orphaned; and no happiness of life can repay what he has lost. Not reflective or sorrowful by nature, reflection and sorrow have become for him a heavy obligation. It is thus that we see him first enter on the scene. * * *

"Figure to yourselves this youth, * * * this son of princes; conceive him vividly, bring his state before your eyes, and then ob-

† From *Wilhelm Meister's Apprenticeship* (1795), translated by Thomas Carlyle. This selection is drawn from Book IV, Chapter 13.

serve him when he learns that his father's spirit walks; stand by him in the terrors of the night, when the venerable ghost itself appears before him. A horrid shudder passes over him; he speaks to the mysterious form; he sees it beckon him; he follows it, and hears. The fearful accusation of his uncle rings in his ears; the summons to revenge, and the piercing oft-repeated prayer, Remember me!

"And when the ghost has vanished, who is it that stands before us? A young hero panting for vengeance? A prince by birth, rejoicing to be called to punish the usurper of his crown? No! trouble and astonishment take hold of the solitary young man: he grows bitter against smiling villains, swears that he will not forget the spirit, and concludes with the significant ejaculation:—

> 'The time is out of joint: O cursed spite,
> That ever I was born to set it right!'

"In these words, I imagine, will be found the key to Hamlet's whole procedure. To me it is clear that Shakespeare meant, in the present case, to represent the effects of a great action laid upon a soul unfit for the performance of it. In this view the whole piece seems to me to be composed. There is an oak-tree planted in a costly jar, which should have borne only pleasant flowers in its bosom; the roots expand, the jar is shivered.

"A lovely, pure, noble, and most moral nature, without the strength of nerve which forms a hero, sinks beneath a burden which it cannot bear and must not cast away. All duties are holy for him; the present is too hard. Impossibilities have been required of him; not in themselves impossibilities, but such for him. He winds, and turns, and torments himself; he advances and recoils; is ever put in mind, ever puts himself in mind; at last does all but lose his purpose from his thoughts; yet still without recovering his peace of mind."

* * *

AUGUSTUS WILLIAM SCHLEGEL

Criticisms on Shakspeare's Tragedies: Hamlet†

* * * *Hamlet* is singular in its kind: a tragedy of thought inspired by continual and never-satisfied meditation on human

† From *Lectures on Dramatic Art and Literature* (1808), translated by John Black (London, 1846), pp. 404–6.

destiny and the dark perplexity of the events of this world, and calculated to call forth the very same meditation in the minds of the spectators. This enigmatical work resembles those irrational equations in which a fraction of unknown magnitude always remains, that will in no way admit of solution. Much has been said, much written, on this piece, and yet no thinking head who anew expresses himself on it, will (in his view of the connexion and the signification of all the parts) entirely coincide with his predecessors. What naturally most astonishes us, is the fact that with such hidden purposes, with a foundation laid in such unfathomable depth, the whole should, at a first view, exhibit an extremely popular appearance. The dread appearance of the Ghost takes possession of the mind and the imagination almost at the very commencement; then the play within the play, in which, as in a glass, we see reflected the crime, whose fruitlessly attempted punishment constitutes the subject-matter of the piece; the alarm with which it fills the King; Hamlet's pretended and Ophelia's real madness; her death and burial; the meeting of Hamlet and Laertes at her grave; their combat, and the grand determination; lastly, the appearance of the young hero Fortinbras, who, with warlike pomp, pays the last honours to an extinct family of kings; the interspersion of comic characteristic scenes with Polonius, the courtiers, and the grave-diggers, which have all of them their signification,—all this fills the stage with an animated and varied movement. The only circumstance from which this piece might be judged to be less theatrical than other tragedies of Shakspeare is, that in the last scenes the main action either stands still or appears to retrograde. This, however, was inevitable, and lay in the nature of the subject. The whole is intended to show that a calculating consideration, which exhausts all the relations and possible consequences of a deed, must cripple the power of acting; as Hamlet himself expresses it:—

> And thus the native hue of resolution
> Is sicklied o'er with the pale cast of thought;
> And enterprises of great pith and moment,
> With this regard, their currents turn awry,
> And lose the name of action.

With respect to Hamlet's character: I cannot, as I understand the poet's views, pronounce altogether so favourable a sentence upon it as Goethe does. He is, it is true, of a highly cultivated mind, a prince of royal manners, endowed with the finest sense of propriety, susceptible of noble ambition, and open in the highest degree to an enthusiastic admiration of that excellence in others of which he himself is deficient. He acts the part of madness with unrivalled power, convincing the persons who are sent to examine into his supposed loss of reason, merely by telling them unwelcome truths, and rallying them with the most caustic wit. But in the resolutions which he so often embraces and always leaves unexecuted, his weakness is too apparent: he does himself only justice when he implies that there is no greater dissimilarity than between himself and Hercules. He is not solely impelled by necessity to artifice and dissimulation, he has a natural inclination for crooked ways; he is a hypocrite towards himself; his far-fetched scruples are often mere pretexts to cover his want of determination: thoughts, as he says on a different occasion, which have

> —— but one part wisdom
> And ever three parts coward. ——

He has been chiefly condemned both for his harshness in repulsing the love of Ophelia, which he himself had cherished, and for his insensibility at her death. But he is too much overwhelmed with his own sorrow to have any compassion to spare for others; besides his outward indifference gives us by no means the measure of his internal perturbation. On the other hand, we evidently perceive in him a malicious joy, when he has succeeded in getting rid of his enemies, more through necessity and accident, which alone are able to impel him to quick and decisive measures, than by the merit of his own courage, as he himself confesses after the murder of Polonius, and with respect to Rosencrantz and Guildenstern. Hamlet has no firm belief either in himself or in anything else: from expressions of religious confidence he passes over to sceptical doubts; he believes in the Ghost of his father as long as he sees it, but as soon as it has disappeared, it appears to him almost in the light of a deception.[1] He has even gone so far as to say, "there is nothing either good or bad, but thinking makes it so;" with him the poet loses himself here in labyrinths of thought, in which neither end nor beginning is discoverable. The stars themselves, from the course of events, afford no answer to the question so urgently proposed to them. A voice from another world, commissioned it would appear, by heaven, demands vengeance for a monstrous enormity, and the demand remains without effect; the criminals are at last punished, but, as it were, by an accidental blow, and not in the solemn way requisite to convey to the world a

---

1. It has been censured as a contradiction, that Hamlet in the soliloquy on self-murder should say,
The undiscover'd country, from whose bourn
No traveller returns—— —
For was not the Ghost a returned traveller? Shakspeare, however, purposely wished to show, that Hamlet could not fix himself in any conviction of any kind whatever.

warning example of justice; irresolute foresight, cunning treachery, and impetuous rage, hurry on to a common destruction; the less guilty and the innocent are equally involved in the general ruin. The destiny of humanity is there exhibited as a gigantic Sphinx, which threatens to precipitate into the abyss of scepticism all who are unable to solve her dreadful enigmas.

* * *

SAMUEL TAYLOR COLERIDGE

Notes on the Tragedies: *Hamlet*†

* * * The preparation *informative* of the audience [is] just as much as was precisely necessary: how gradual first, and with the uncertainty appertaining to a question—

What, has *this thing* appeared *again* to-night.

Even the word "again" has its *credibilizing* effect. Then the representative of the ignorance of the audience, Horatio (not himself but [quoted by] Marcellus to Bernardo) anticipates the common solution, " 'tis but our phantasy." But Marcellus rises secondly into "[this] dreaded sight." Then this "thing" becomes at once an "apparition," and that too an intelligent spirit that is to be *spoken* to.

Tush, tush! 'twill not appear.

Then the shivery feeling, at such a time, with two eye-witnesses, of sitting down to hear a story of a ghost, and this, too, a ghost that had appeared two nights before [at] about this very time. The effort of the narrator to master his own imaginative terrors; the consequent elevation of the style, itself a continuation of this effort; the turning off to an *outward* object, "yon same star." O heaven! words are wasted to those that feel and to those who do not feel the exquisite judgement of Shakespeare. * * *

[I. i. 70–72.
   Mar. Good now, sit down, and tell me, he that knows,
Why this same strict and most observant watch
So nightly toils the subject of the land.]

† From *Coleridge's Shakespearean Criticism*, edited by Thomas M. Raysor (Cambridge: Harvard University Press), pp. 20–37. Copyright © 1930 by the President and Fellows of Harvard College, 1958 by Thomas M. Raysor. Reprinted by permission of the editor. The footnotes are Raysor's.

The exquisitely natural transit into the narration retrospective. [When the Ghost re-appears, note] Horatio's increased courage from having translated the late individual spectre into thought and past experience, and Marcellus' and Bernardo's sympathy with it [Horatio's courage] in daring to strike, while yet the former feeling returns in

> We do it wrong [being so majestical,
> To offer it the show of violence.]

* * *

[I. i. 169–71.
Let us impart what we have seen to-night
Unto young Hamlet; for, upon my life,
This spirit, dumb to us, will speak to him.]

The unobtrusive and yet fully adequate mode of introducing the main character, *young* Hamlet, upon whom transfers itself all the interest excited for the acts and concerns of the king, his father.

[I. ii.] Relief by change of scene to the royal court. This [relief is desirable] on any occasion; but how judicious that Hamlet should not have to take up the leavings of exhaustion. The set, pedantically antithetic form of the king's speech —tho' in the concerns that galled the heels of conscience, rhetorical below a king, yet in what follows, not without majesty. Was he not a royal brother?

* * *

[I. iii.] This scene must be regarded as one of Shakespeare's lyric movements in the play, and the skill with which it is interwoven with the dramatic parts is peculiarly an excellence of our poet. You experience the sensation of a pause without the sense of a stop. You will observe in Ophelia's short and general answer to the long speech of Laertes the natural carelessness of innocence, which cannot think such a code of cautions and prudences necessary to its own preservation.

* * *

[I. iv.] In addition to the other excellencies of Hamlet's speech concerning the wassail music, so finely revealing the predominant idealism, the ratiocinative meditativeness of his character, it has the advantage of giving nature and probability to the impassioned continuity of the speech instantly directed to the Ghost. The momentum had been given to his mental activity, the full current of the thoughts and words had set in, and the very forgetfulness, in the fervor of his argumentation, of the purpose for which he was there, aided in preventing the appearance from benumbing the mind. Consequently, it acted as a new impulse, a sudden stroke which increased the velocity of the body already in motion, while it altered the direction. The co-presence of Horatio, Marcellus, and Bernardo is most judiciously contrived, for it renders the courage of Hamlet and his impetuous eloquence perfectly intelligible. The knowledge, the *unthought* of consciousness, the *sensation*, of human auditors, of flesh and blood sympathists, acts as a support, a stimulation *a tergo*, while the *front* of the mind, the whole consciousness of the speaker, is filled by the solemn apparition. Add, too, that the apparition itself has by its frequent previous appearances been brought nearer to a thing of this world. This accrescence of objectivity in a ghost that yet retains all its ghostly attributes and fearful subjectivity, is truly wonderful.

[I. v. 92–112. The speech of Hamlet as the Ghost vanishes.
Ham. O all you host of heaven! O earth! what else?
And shall I couple hell? O, fie! Hold, hold, my heart; etc.]

I remember nothing equal to this burst unless it be the first speech of Prometheus,[1] after the exit of Vulcan and the two Afrites, in Aeschylus. But Shakespeare alone could have produced the vow of Hamlet to make his memory a blank of all maxims and generalized truths that "observation had copied there," followed by the immediate noting down the generalized fact,

That one may smile, and smile, and be a villain.

[II. i. Polonius and Reynaldo. Polonius and Ophelia.]
In all things dependent on, or rather made up of, fine address, the *manner* is no more or otherwise rememberable than the light motions, steps, and gestures of youth and health. But this is almost everything; no wonder, therefore, if that which can be *put down by rule* in the memory should appear mere poring, maudlin-eyed cunning, slyness blinking thro' the watery eye of superannuation. So in this admirable scene, Polonius, who is throughout the skeleton of his own former skill and statecraft, hunts the trail of policy at a dead scent, supplied by the weak fever-smell in his own nostrils.

* * *

1. *Prometheus Bound*, 88–127. The following reference to the 'two Afrites' seems curious, for Afrites are evil demons of Mohammedan mythology; but it is clear that Coleridge refers to the two attendants of Vulcan, Power and Force (βία and Κράτος).

[II. ii. 172–73.
Pol. Do you know me, my lord?
Ham. Excellent well; you are a fishmonger.]

["Fishmonger";] *i.e.* you are sent to *fish* out the secret. This is Hamlet's meaning. The purposely obscure lines—

For if the sun [breed maggots in a dead dog, being a god kissing carrion—Have you a daughter?]

I rather think refer to some thought in Hamlet's mind contrasting the lovely daughter with such a tedious old fool, her father, as *he* represents Polonius to himself. "Why, fool as he is, he is some degrees in rank above a dead dog's carcase; and if the sun, being a god that kisses carrion, can raise life out of a dead dog, why may [not] good fortune, that favors fools, have raised a lovely girl out of this dead-alive old fool."

* * *

[II. ii. 423–89.
'The rugged Pyrrhus, he whose sable arms,' etc.]

This admirable substitution of the epic for the dramatic, giving such a *reality* to the impassioned dramatic diction of Shakespeare's own dialogue,[2] and authorized too by the actual style of the tragedies before Shakespeare (*Porrex and Ferrex*, *Titus Andronicus*, etc.) is worthy of notice. The fancy that a burlesque was intended, sinks below criticism. The lines, as *epic* narrative, are superb.

* * *

[III. i. 103.
Ham. Ha, ha! are you honest?]

Here it is evident that the penetrating Hamlet perceived, from the strange and forced manner of Ophelia, that the sweet girl was not acting a part of her own—in short, saw into the stratagem— and his after speeches are not directed to Ophelia, but to the listeners and spies.

Hamlet here discovers that he is watched, and Ophelia a decoy. Even this in a mood so anxious and irritable accounts for a certain harshness in him; and yet a wild upworking of love, sporting with

2. For this fine observation Coleridge is indebted to Schlegel, though with alterations. Schlegel's excellent treatment of this problem is worth reading in its entirety, but space forbids quotation of more than two sentences which Coleridge used. "They [Shakespeare's commentators] have not considered that this speech must not be judged by itself but in the place where it stands. That which is meant to appear as dramatic invention in the play itself, must contrast with the play's dignified poetry in the same degree as theatrical elevation with simple nature." *Werke*, vi. 251.

opposites with a wilful self-tormenting irony, is perceptible throughout: *ex. gr.* "I did love you" [3] and [his reference to] the faults of the sex from which Ophelia is so characteristically free that the freedom therefrom constitutes her character. Here again Shakespeare's charm of constituting female character by absence of characters, [of] outjuttings.[4]

[III. i. 143–45, Hamlet to Ophelia.
. . . . I say, we will have no more marriages: those that are married already, all but one, shall live; the rest shall keep as they are.]

The dallying with the inward purpose that of one who had not brought his mind to the steady acting point, would fain *sting* the uncle's mind,—but to stab the body!

The soliloquy of Ophelia is the perfection of love—so exquisitely unselfish!

[III. ii. The dialogue of Hamlet with the players.]

One and among the happiest [instances] of Shakespeare's power of diversifying the scene while he is carrying on the plot.

[III. ii. 93–95.
Pol. I did enact Julius Caesar: I was killed i' the Capitol; Brutus killed me.
Ham. It was a brute part of him to kill so capital a calf there.]

In any direct form to have kept Hamlet's love for Ophelia before the audience, would have made a breach in the unity of the interest; but yet to the thoughtful reader it is suggested by his spite to poor Polonius, whom he cannot let rest.

[III. ii. The play.]

As in the first interview with the players by *epic* verse, so here [the style of the play performed before the court is distinguished] by rhyme.

* * *

[III. ii. 358–60. Hamlet's soliloquy.
. . . . now could I drink hot blood,
And do such bitter business as the day
Would quake to look on.]

The utmost Hamlet arrives to is a disposition, a mood, to do *something*. *What* is still left undecided, while every word he utters tends to betray his disguise.

---

3. "I did love you once."   4. Cf. i. 133, 233; ii. 353–54.

The perfect equal to any call of the moment is Hamlet, let it only not be for a future.

* * *

[III. iii. 27–29.
Pol. My lord, he's going to his mother's closet:
Behind the arras I'll convey myself,
To hear the process.]

Polonius's volunteer obtrusion of himself into this business, while it is appropriate to his character, still letching after former importance, removes all likelihood that Hamlet should suspect his presence, and prevents us from making his death injure Hamlet in our opinion.

[III. iii. 36–72. The king's remorse.
O, my offence is rank, it smells to heaven.]

The king's speech well marks the difference between crime and guilt of habit. The conscience is still admitted to audience. Nay, even as an audible soliloquy, it is far less improbable than is supposed by such as have watched men only in the beaten road of their feelings. But it deserves to be dwelt on, that final "All may be well"; a degree of merit [is] attributed by the self-flattering soul to its own struggle, tho' baffled, and to the indefinite half-promise, half-command, to persevere in religious duties. The divine medium of the Christian doctrine of expiation [is] in this: not what you have done, but what you *are*, must determine. Metanoia.[5]

* * *

[III. iv. 29–31.
Ham. A bloody deed! almost as bad, good mother,
As kill a king, and marry with his brother.
Queen. As kill a king!]

I confess that Shakespeare has left the character of the queen in an unpleasant perplexity. Was she or was she not conscious of the fratricide?

[IV. ii. 12–14.
Ros. Take you me for a sponge, my lord?
Ham. Ay, sir; that soaks up the king's countenance, his rewards, his authorities.]

Hamlet's madness is made to consist in the full utterance of all the thoughts that had past thro' his mind before—in telling home truths.

5. Μετάνοια, repentance.

[IV. v. Ophelia's singing.] The conjunction here of these two thoughts that had never subsisted in disjunction, the love for Hamlet and her filial love, and the guileless floating on the surface of her pure imagination of the cautions so lately expressed and the fears not too delicately avowed by her father and brother concerning the danger to which her honor lay exposed.

> Thought and affliction, passion, murder[6] itself,
> She turns to favor and to prettiness.
>
> [IV. v. 181–82.]

This play of association is sweetly instanced in the close—

> . . . . My brother shall know of it: and [so] I thank you for your good *counsel.*   [IV. v. 69–70.]

* * *

[IV. vi. Hamlet's capture by the pirates, as explained in his letter.]

Almost the only play of Shakespeare, in which mere accidents, independent of all will, form an essential part of the plot; but here how judiciously in keeping with the character of the over-meditative Hamlet, ever at last determined by accident or by a fit of passion.

[IV. vii. 81–106. The king] first awakens Laertes' vanity by the praises of the report[er], then gratifies it by the report itself, and then [comes to the point—

> . . . . Sir, this report of his]
> Did Hamlet so envenom with his envy
> [That he could nothing do but wish and beg
> Your sudden coming o'er, to play with him.]

And that Laertes might be excused in some degree for not cooling, the act concludes with the affecting death of Ophelia. Who does not see [her], like a little projection of land into a lake or stream, covered with spring-flowers, lying quietly reflected in the great waters, but at length [being] undermined and loosened, becomes a floating faery isle, and after a brief vagrancy sinks almost without an eddy!

* * *

[V. i.] The contrast between the clowns and Hamlet as two extremes—the [clowns'] mockery of logic, the traditional wit valued like truth for its antiquity, and treasured up, like a tune, for use.

6. Read *'hell.'*

The Character of Hamlet.

1. Shakespeare's mode of conceiving characters out of his own intellectual and moral faculties, by conceiving any one intellectual or moral faculty in morbid excess and then placing himself, thus mutilated and diseased, under given circumstances. This we shall have repeated occasion to re-state and enforce. In Hamlet I conceive him to have wished to exemplify the moral necessity of a due balance between our attention to outward objects and our meditation on inward thoughts—a due balance between the real and the imaginary world. In Hamlet this balance does not exist—his thoughts, images, and fancy [being] far more vivid than his perceptions, and his very perceptions instantly passing thro' the medium of his contemplations, and acquiring as they pass a form and color not naturally their own. Hence great, enormous, intellectual activity, and a consequent proportionate aversion to real action, with all its symptoms and accompanying qualities.

Action is transitory, a step, a blow,[7] etc.

WILLIAM HAZLITT

Characters of Shakespear's Plays: Hamlet†

This is that Hamlet the Dane, whom we read of in our youth, and whom we may be said almost to remember in our after-years; he who made that famous soliloquy on life, who gave the advice to the players, who thought 'this goodly frame, the earth, a steril promontory, and this brave o'er-hanging firmament, the air, this majestical roof fretted with golden fire, a foul and pestilent congregation of vapours'; whom 'man delighted not, nor woman neither'; he who talked with the grave-diggers, and moralised on Yorick's skull; the school-fellow of Rosencraus and Guildenstern at Wittenberg; the friend of Horatio; the lover of Ophelia; he that was mad and sent to England; the slow avenger of his father's death; who lived at the court of Horwendillus five hundred years before we were born, but all whose thoughts we seem to know as

7. "Action is transitory—a step, a blow,
. . . . . .
Suffering is permanent, obscure and

dark,
And shares the nature of infinity."
Wordsworth, *The Borderers*, III.v.
† From *Characters of Shakespear's Plays* (1817).

well as we do our own, because we have read them in Shakespear.

Hamlet is a name; his speeches and sayings but the idle coinage of the poet's brain. What then, are they not real? They are as real as our own thoughts. Their reality is in the reader's mind. It is *we* who are Hamlet. This play has a prophetic truth, which is above that of history. Whoever has become thoughtful and melancholy through his own mishaps or those of others; whoever has borne about with him the clouded brow of reflection, and thought himself 'too much i' th' sun'; whoever has seen the golden lamp of day dimmed by envious mists rising in his own breast, and could find in the world before him only a dull blank with nothing left remarkable in it; whoever has known 'the pangs of despised love, the insolence of office, or the spurns which patient merit of the unworthy takes'; he who has felt his mind sink within him, and sadness cling to his heart like a malady, who has had his hopes blighted and his youth staggered by the apparitions of strange things; who cannot be well at ease, while he sees evil hovering near him like a spectre; whose powers of action have been eaten up by thought, he to whom the universe seems infinite, and himself nothing; whose bitterness of soul makes him careless of consequences, and who goes to a play as his best resource to shove off, to a second remove, the evils of life by a mock representation of them—this is the true Hamlet.

We have been so used to this tragedy that we hardly know how to criticise it any more than we should know how to describe our own faces. But we must make such observations as we can. It is the one of Shakespear's plays that we think of the oftenest, because it abounds most in striking reflections on human life, and because the distresses of Hamlet are transferred, by the turn of his mind, to the general account of humanity. Whatever happens to him we apply to ourselves, because he applies it so himself as a means of general reasoning. He is a great moraliser; and what makes him worth attending to is, that he moralises on his own feelings and experience. He is not a common-place pedant. If *Lear* is distinguished by the greatest depth of passion, HAMLET is the most remarkable for the ingenuity, originality, and unstudied development of character. Shakespear had more magnanimity than any other poet, and he has shewn more of it in this play than in any other. There is no attempt to force an interest: every thing is left for time and circumstances to unfold. The attention is excited without effort, the incidents succeed each other as matters of course, the characters think and speak and act just as they might do, if left entirely to themselves. There is no set purpose, no straining at a point. The observations are suggested by the passing scene—

the gusts of passion come and go like sounds of music borne on the wind. The whole play is an exact transcript of what might be supposed to have taken place at the court of Denmark, at the remote period of time fixed upon, before the modern refinements in morals and manners were heard of. It would have been interesting enough to have been admitted as a by-stander in such a scene, at such a time, to have heard and witnessed something of what was going on. But here we are more than spectators. We have not only 'the outward pageants and the signs of grief'; but 'we have that within which passes shew.' We read the thoughts of the heart, we catch the passions living as they rise. Other dramatic writers give us very fine versions and paraphrases of nature; but Shakespear, together with his own comments, gives us the original text, that we may judge for ourselves. This is a very great advantage.

The character of Hamlet stands quite by itself. It is not a character marked by strength of will or even of passion, but by refinement of thought and sentiment. Hamlet is as little of the hero as a man can well be: but he is a young and princely novice, full of high enthusiasm and quick sensibility—the sport of circumstances, questioning with fortune and refining on his own feelings, and forced from the natural bias of his disposition by the strangeness of his situation. He seems incapable of deliberate action, and is only hurried into extremities on the spur of the occasion, when he has no time to reflect, as in the scene where he kills Polonius, and again, where he alters the letters which Rosencraus and Guildenstern are taking with them to England, purporting his death. At other times, when he is most bound to act, he remains puzzled, undecided, and sceptical, dallies with his purposes, till the occasion is lost, and finds out some pretence to relapse into indolence and thoughtfulness again. For this reason he refuses to kill the King when he is at his prayers, and by a refinement in malice, which is in truth only an excuse for his own want of resolution, defers his revenge to a more fatal opportunity, when he shall be engaged in some act 'that has no relish of salvation in it.'

> 'He kneels and prays,
> And now I'll do't, and so he goes to heaven,
> And so am I reveng'd: *that would be scann'd.*
> He kill'd my father, and for that,
> I, his sole son, send him to heaven.
> Why this is reward, not revenge.
> Up sword and know thou a more horrid time,
>   When he is drunk, asleep, or in a rage.'

He is the prince of philosophical speculators; and because he cannot have his revenge perfect, according to the most refined idea his wish can form, he declines it altogether. So he scruples to trust the suggestions of the ghost, contrives the scene of the play to have surer proof of his uncle's guilt, and then rests satisfied with this confirmation of his suspicions, and the success of his experiment, instead of acting upon it. Yet he is sensible of his own weakness, taxes himself with it, and tries to reason himself out of it.

> 'How all occasions do inform against me,
> And spur my dull revenge! What is a man,
> If his chief good and market of his time
> Be but to sleep and feed? A beast; no more.
> Sure he that made us with such large discourse,
> Looking before and after, gave us not
> That capability and god-like reason
> To rust in us unus'd. Now whether it be
> Bestial oblivion, or some craven scruple
> Of thinking too precisely on th' event,—
> A thought which quarter'd, hath but one part wisdom,
> And ever three parts coward;—I do not know
> Why yet I live to say, this thing's to do;
> Sith I have cause, and will, and strength, and means
> To do it. Examples gross as earth exhort me:
> Witness this army of such mass and charge,
> Led by a delicate and tender prince,
> Whose spirit with divine ambition puff'd,
> Makes mouths at the invisible event,
> Exposing what is mortal and unsure
> To all that fortune, death, and danger dare,
> Even for an egg-shell. 'Tis not to be great
> Never to stir without great argument;
> But greatly to find quarrel in a straw,
> When honour's at the stake. How stand I then,
> That have a father kill'd, a mother stain'd,
> Excitements of my reason and my blood,
> And let all sleep, while to my shame I see
> The imminent death of twenty thousand men,
> That for a fantasy and trick of fame,
> Go to their graves like beds, fight for a plot
> Whereon the numbers cannot try the cause,
> Which is not tomb enough and continent
> To hide the slain?—O, from this time forth,
> My thoughts be bloody or be nothing worth.'

Still he does nothing; and this very speculation on his own infirmity only affords him another occasion for indulging it. It is not from any want of attachment to his father or of abhorrence of his murder that Hamlet is thus dilatory, but it is more to his taste to indulge his imagination in reflecting upon the enormity of the crime and refining on his schemes of vengeance, than to put them into immediate practice. His ruling passion is to think, not to act: and any vague pretext that flatters this propensity instantly diverts him from his previous purposes.

The moral perfection of this character has been called in question, we think, by those who did not understand it. It is more interesting than according to rules; amiable, though not faultless. The ethical delineations of 'that noble and liberal casuist' (as Shakespear has been well called) do not exhibit the drab-coloured quakerism of morality. His plays are not copied either from The Whole Duty of Man, or from The Academy of Compliments! We confess we are a little shocked at the want of refinement in those who are shocked at the want of refinement in Hamlet. The neglect of punctilious exactness in his behaviour either partakes of the 'licence of the time,' or else belongs to the very excess of intellectual refinement in the character, which makes the common rules of life, as well as his own purpose, sit loose upon him. He may be said to be amenable only to the tribunal of his own thoughts, and is too much taken up with the airy world of contemplation to lay as much stress as he ought on the practical consequences of things. His habitual principles of action are unhinged and out of joint with the time. His conduct to Ophelia is quite natural in his circumstances. It is that of assumed severity only. It is the effect of disappointed hope, of bitter regrets, of affection suspended, not obliterated, by the distractions of the scene around him! Amidst the natural and preternatural horrors of his situation, he might be excused in delicacy from carrying on a regular courtship. When 'his father's spirit was in arms,' it was not a time for the son to make love in. He could neither marry Ophelia, nor wound her mind by explaining the cause of his alienation, which he durst hardly trust himself to think of. It would have taken him years to have come to a direct explanation on the point. In the harassed state of his mind, he could not have done much otherwise than he did. His conduct does not contradict what he says when he sees her funeral,

> 'I loved Ophelia: forty thousand brothers
> Could not with all their quantity of love
> Make up my sum.'

Nothing can be more affecting or beautiful than the Queen's apostrophe to Ophelia on throwing the flowers into the grave.

> —'Sweets to the sweet, farewell.
> I hop'd thou should'st have been my Hamlet's wife:
> I thought thy bride-bed to have deck'd, sweet maid,
> And not have strew'd thy grave.'

Shakespear was thoroughly a master of the mixed motives of human character, and he here shews us the Queen, who was so criminal in some respects, not without sensibility and affection in other relations of life.—Ophelia is a character almost too exquisitely touching to be dwelt upon. Oh rose of May, oh flower too soon faded! Her love, her madness, her death, are described with the truest touches of tenderness and pathos. It is a character which nobody but Shakespear could have drawn in the way that he has done, and to the conception of which there is not even the smallest approach, except in some of the old romantic ballads.[1] Her brother, Laertes, is a character we do not like so well: he is too hot and choleric, and somewhat rhodomontade. Polonius is a perfect character in its kind; nor is there any foundation for the objections which have been made to the consistency of this part. It is said that he acts very foolishly and talks very sensibly. There is no inconsistency in that. Again, that he talks wisely at one time and foolishly at another; that his advice to Laertes is very excellent, and his advice to the King and Queen on the subject of Hamlet's madness very ridiculous. But he gives the one as a father, and is sincere in it; he gives the other as a mere courtier, a busy-body, and is accordingly officious, garrulous, and impertinent. In short, Shakespear has been accused of inconsistency in this and other characters, only because he has kept up the distinction which there is in nature, between the understandings and the moral habits of men, between the absurdity of their ideas and the absurdity of their motives. Polonius is not a fool, but he makes himself so. His folly, whether in his actions or speeches, comes under the head of impropriety of intention.

We do not like to see our author's plays acted, and least of all, HAMLET. There is no play that suffers so much in being transferred to the stage. Hamlet himself seems hardly capable of being acted. Mr. Kemble[2] unavoidably fails in this character from a want of ease and variety. The character of Hamlet is made up of undulating lines; it has the yielding flexibility of 'a wave o' th' sea.' Mr. Kemble plays it like a man in armour, with a determined inveteracy of purpose, in one undeviating straight line, which is as remote from the natural grace and refined susceptibility of the character, as the sharp angles and abrupt starts which Mr. Kean[3] introduces into the part. Mr. Kean's Hamlet is as much too splenetic and rash as

1. In the account of her death, a friend has pointed out an instance of the poet's exact observation of nature:—
'There is a willow growing o'er a brook.
   That shews its hoary leaves i' th'
      glassy stream.'
The inside of the leaves of the willow,
next the water, is of a whitish colour, and the reflection would therefore be 'hoary.'
2. John Philip Kemble, English actor (1757–1823) [Editor].
3. Edmund Kean, English actor (1787–1833) [Editor].

Mr. Kemble's is too deliberate and formal. His manner is too strong and pointed. He throws a severity, approaching to virulence, into the common observations and answers. There is nothing of this in Hamlet. He is, as it were, wrapped up in his reflections, and only *thinks aloud*. There should therefore be no attempt to impress what he says upon others by a studied exaggeration of emphasis or manner; no *talking at* his hearers. There should be as much of the gentleman and scholar as possible infused into the part, and as little of the actor. A pensive air of sadness should sit reluctantly upon his brow, but no appearance of fixed and sullen gloom. He is full of weakness and melancholy, but there is no harshness in his nature. He is the most amiable of misanthropes.

A. C. BRADLEY

[What Actually Happens in the Play]†

* * * Turn to the first words Hamlet utters when he is alone; turn, that is to say, to the place where the author is likely to indicate his meaning most plainly. What do you hear?

> *O, that this too too solid flesh would melt,*
> *Thaw and resolve itself into a dew!*
> *Or that the Everlasting had not fix'd*
> *His canon 'gainst self-slaughter! O God! God!*
> *How weary, stale, flat and unprofitable,*
> *Seem to me all the uses of this world!*
> *Fie on't! ah fie! 'tis an unweeded garden,*
> *That grows to seed; things rank and gross in nature*
> *Possess it merely.*

Here are a sickness of life, and even a longing for death, so intense that nothing stands between Hamlet and suicide except religious awe. And what has caused them? The rest of the soliloquy so thrusts the answer upon us that it might seem impossible to miss it. It was not his father's death; that doubtless brought deep grief, but mere grief for some one loved and lost does not make a noble spirit loathe the world as a place full only of things rank and gross. It was not the vague suspicion that we know Hamlet felt. Still less was it the loss of the crown; for though the subserviency of the electors might well disgust him, there is not a reference to the subject in the soliloquy, nor

† From *Shakespearean Tragedy* (London, 1903). Bradley's footnotes have been omitted.

any sign elsewhere that it greatly occupied his mind. It was the moral shock of the sudden ghastly disclosure of his mother's true nature, falling on him when his heart was aching with love, and his body doubtless was weakened by sorrow. And it is essential, however disagreeable, to realise the nature of this shock. It matters little here whether Hamlet's age was twenty or thirty: in either case his mother was a matron of mature years. All his life he had believed in her, we may be sure, as such a son would. He had seen her not merely devoted to his father, but hanging on him like a newly-wedded bride, hanging on him

> As if increase of appetite had grown
> By what it fed on.

He had seen her following his body 'like Niobe, all tears.' And then within a month—'O God! a beast would have mourned longer'—she married again, and married Hamlet's uncle, a man utterly contemptible and loathsome in his eyes; married him in what to Hamlet was incestuous wedlock; married him not for any reason of state, nor even out of old family affection, but in such a way that her son was forced to see in her action not only an astounding shallowness of feeling but an eruption of coarse sensuality, 'rank and gross,' speeding post-haste to its horrible delight. Is it possible to conceive an experience more desolating to a man such as we have seen Hamlet to be; and is its result anything but perfectly natural? It brings bewildered horror, then loathing, then despair of human nature. His whole mind is poisoned. He can never see Ophelia in the same light again: she is a woman, and his mother is a woman: if she mentions the word 'brief' to him, the answer drops from his lips like venom, 'as woman's love.' The last words of the soliloquy, which is *wholly* concerned with this subject, are,

> But break, my heart, for I must hold my tongue!

He can do nothing. He must lock in his heart, not any suspicion of his uncle that moves obscurely there, but that horror and loathing; and if his heart ever found relief, it was when those feelings, mingled with the love that never died out in him, poured themselves forth in a flood as he stood in his mother's chamber beside his father's marriage-bed.

If we still wonder, and ask why the effect of this shock should be so tremendous, let us observe that *now* the conditions have arisen under which Hamlet's highest endowments, his moral sensibility and his genius, become his enemies. A nature morally blunter would have felt even so dreadful a revelation less keenly. A slower and more limited and positive mind might not have extended so widely through its world the disgust and disbelief that have entered it. But Hamlet has the imagination which, for evil as well as good, feels and sees all things in one. Thought is the element of his life, and his thought is infected. He cannot prevent himself from probing and lacerating the wound in his soul. One idea, full of peril, holds him fast, and he cries out in agony at it, but is impotent to free himself ('Must I remember?' 'Let me not think on't'). And when, with the fading of his passion, the vividness of this idea abates, it does so only to leave behind a boundless weariness and a sick longing for death.

And this is the time which his fate chooses. In this hour of uttermost weakness, this sinking of his whole being towards annihilation, there comes on him, bursting the bounds of the natural world with a shock of astonishment and terror, the revelation of his mother's adultery and his father's murder, and, with this, the demand on him, in the name of everything dearest and most sacred, to arise and act. And for a moment, though his brain reels and totters, his soul leaps up in passion to answer this demand. But it comes too late. It does not strike home the last rivet in the melancholy which holds him bound.

> *The time is out of joint! O cursed spite*
> *That ever I was born to set it right,—*

so he mutters within an hour of the moment when he vowed to give his life to the duty of revenge; and the rest of the story exhibits his vain efforts to fulfil this duty, his unconscious self-excuses and unavailing self-reproaches, and the tragic results of his delay.

'Melancholy,' I said, not dejection, nor yet insanity. That Hamlet was not far from insanity is very probable. His adoption of the pretence of madness may well have been due in part to fear of the reality; to an instinct of self-preservation, a forefeeling that the pretence would enable him to give some utterance to the load that pressed on his heart and brain, and a fear that he would be unable altogether to repress such utterance. And if the pathologist calls his state melancholia, and even proceeds to determine its species, I see nothing to object to in that; I am grateful to him for emphasising the fact that Hamlet's melancholy was no mere common depression of spirits; and I have no doubt that many readers of the play would understand it better if they read an account of melancholia in a work on mental diseases. If we like to use the word 'disease' loosely, Hamlet's condition may truly be called disease. No exertion of will could have dispelled it. Even if he had been able at once to do the bidding of the Ghost he would doubtless have still remained for some time under the cloud. It would be absurdly unjust to call *Hamlet* a study of melancholy, but it contains such a study.

But this melancholy is something very different from insanity, in anything like the usual meaning of that word. No doubt it might develop into insanity. The longing for death might become an irresistible impulse to self-destruction; the disorder of feeling and will might extend to sense and intellect; delusions might arise; and the man might become, as we say, incapable and irresponsible. But Hamlet's melancholy is some way from this condition. It is a totally different thing from the madness which he feigns; and he never, when alone or in company with Horatio alone, exhibits the signs of that madness. Nor is the dramatic use of this melancholy, again, open to the objections which would justly be made to the portrayal of an insanity which brought the hero to a tragic end. The man who suffers as Hamlet suffers—and thousands go about their business suffering thus in greater or less degree—is considered irresponsible neither by other people nor by himself: he is only too keenly conscious of his responsibility. He is therefore, so far, quite capable of being a tragic agent, which an insane person, at any rate according to Shakespeare's practice, is not. And, finally, Hamlet's state is not one which a healthy mind is unable sufficiently to imagine. It is probably not further from average experience, nor more difficult to realise, than the great tragic passions of Othello, Antony or Macbeth.

Let me try to show now, briefly, how much this melancholy accounts for.

It accounts for the main fact, Hamlet's inaction. For the *immediate* cause of that is simply that his habitual feeling is one of disgust at life and everything in it, himself included,—a disgust which varies in intensity, rising at times into a longing for death, sinking often into weary apathy, but is never dispelled for more than brief intervals. Such a state of feeling is inevitably adverse to *any* kind of decided action; the body is inert, the mind indifferent or worse; its response is, 'it does not matter,' 'it is not worth while,' 'it is no good.' And the action required of Hamlet is very exceptional. It is violent, dangerous, difficult to accomplish perfectly, on one side repulsive to a man of honour and sensitive feeling, on another side involved in a certain mystery (here come in thus, in their subordinate place, various causes of inaction assigned by various theories). These obstacles would not suffice to prevent

Hamlet from acting, if his state were normal; and against them there operate, even in his morbid state, healthy and positive feelings, love of his father, loathing of his uncle, desire of revenge, desire to do duty. But the retarding motives acquire an unnatural strength because they have an ally in something far stronger than themselves, the melancholic disgust and apathy; while the healthy motives, emerging with difficulty from the central mass of diseased feeling, rapidly sink back into it and 'lose the name of action.' We *see* them doing so; and sometimes the process is quite simple, no analytical reflection on the deed intervening between the outburst of passion and the relapse into melancholy. But this melancholy is perfectly consistent also with that incessant dissection of the task assigned, of which the Schlegel-Coleridge theory makes so much. For those endless questions (as we may imagine them), 'Was I deceived by the Ghost? How am I to do the deed? When? Where? What will be the consequence of attempting it—success, my death, utter misunderstanding, mere mischief to the State? Can it be right to do it, or noble to kill a defenceless man? What is the good of doing it in such a world as this?'—all this, and whatever else passed in a sickening round through Hamlet's mind, was not the healthy and right deliberation of a man with such a task, but otiose thinking hardly deserving the name of thought, an unconscious weaving of pretexts for inaction, aimless tossings on a sick bed, symptoms of melancholy which only increased it by deepening self-contempt.

Again, (*a*) this state accounts for Hamlet's energy as well as for his lassitude, those quick decided actions of his being the outcome of a nature normally far from passive, now suddenly stimulated, and producing healthy impulses which work themselves out before they have time to subside. (*b*) It accounts for the evidently keen satisfaction which some of these actions give to him. He arranges the play-scene with lively interest, and exults in its success, not really because it brings him nearer to his goal, but partly because it has hurt his enemy and partly because it has demonstrated his own skill (III. ii. 252–270). He looks forward almost with glee to countermining the King's designs in sending him away (III. iv. 209–213), and looks back with obvious satisfaction, even with pride, to the address and vigour he displayed on the voyage (v. ii. 1–55). These were not *the* action on which his morbid self-feeling had centred; he feels in them his old force, and escapes in them from his disgust. (*c*) It accounts for the pleasure with which he meets old acquaintances, like his 'school-fellows' or the actors. The former observed (and we can observe) in him a 'kind of joy' at first, though it is followed by 'much forcing of his disposition' as he attempts to keep this joy and his courtesy alive in spite of the misery which so soon returns upon him and the suspicion he is forced to feel. (d) It accounts no less for the painful features of his character as seen in the play, his almost savage irritability on the one hand, and on the other his self-absorption, his callousness, his insensibility to the fates of those whom he despises, and to the feelings even of those whom he loves. These are frequent symptoms of such melancholy, and (e) they sometimes alternate, as they do in Hamlet, with bursts of transitory, almost hysterical, and quite fruitless emotion. It is to these last (of which a part of the soliloquy, 'O what a rogue,' gives a good example) that Hamlet alludes when, to the Ghost, he speaks of himself as 'lapsed in *passion*,' and it is doubtless partly his conscious weakness in regard to them that inspires his praise of Horatio as a man who is not 'passion's slave.'

Finally, Hamlet's melancholy accounts for two things which seem to be explained by nothing else. The first of these is his apathy or 'lethargy.' We are bound to consider the evidence which the text supplies of this, though it is usual to ignore it. When Hamlet mentions, as one possible cause of his inaction, his 'thinking too precisely on the event,' he mentions another, 'bestial oblivion'; and the thing against which he inveighs in the greater part of that soliloquy (IV. iv.) is not the excess or the misuse of reason (which for him here and always is god-like), but this *bestial* oblivion or '*dullness*,' this 'letting all *sleep*,' this allowing of heaven-sent reason to 'fust unused':

> *What is a man,*
> *If his chief good and market of his time*
> *Be but to sleep and feed? a beast, no more.*

So, in the soliloquy in II. ii. he accuses himself of being 'a *dull* and muddy-mettled rascal,' who 'peaks [mopes] like John-a-dreams, unpregnant of his cause,' dully indifferent to his cause. So, when the Ghost appears to him the second time, he accuses himself of being tardy and lapsed in *time*; and the Ghost speaks of his purpose being almost *blunted*, and bids him not to *forget* (cf. 'oblivion'). And so, what is emphasized in those undramatic but significant speeches of the player-king and of Claudius [III. ii. 170 ff., IV. vii. 108 ff.] is the mere dying away of purpose or of love. Surely what all this points to is not a condition of excessive but useless mental activity (indeed there is, in reality, curiously little about that in the text), but rather one of dull, apathetic, brooding gloom, in which Hamlet, so far from analysing his duty, is not thinking of it at all, but for the time literally *forgets* it. It seems to me we are driven to think of Hamlet *chiefly* thus during the long time which elapsed between the appearance of the Ghost and the events presented in the Second Act. The Ghost, in fact, had more reason than we suppose at first for leaving with Hamlet as his parting injunction the command, 'Remember me,' and for greeting him, on reappearing, with the command, 'Do not forget.' These little things in Shakespeare are not accidents.

The second trait which is fully explained only by Hamlet's melancholy is his own inability to understand why he delays. This emerges in a marked degree when an occasion like the player's emotion or the sight of Fortinbras's army stings Hamlet into shame at his inaction. 'Why,' he asks himself in genuine bewilderment, 'do I linger? Can the cause be cowardice? Can it be sloth? Can it be thinking too precisely of the event? And does *that* again mean cowardice? What is it that makes me sit idle when I feel it is shameful to do so, and when I have *cause, and will, and strength, and means,* to act?' A man irresolute merely because he was considering a proposed action too minutely would not feel this bewilderment. A man might feel it whose conscience secretly condemned the act which his explicit consciousness approved; but we have seen that there is no sufficient evidence to justify us in conceiving Hamlet thus. These are the questions of a man stimulated for the moment to shake off the weight of his melancholy, and, because for the moment he is free from it, unable to understand the paralysing pressure which it exerts at other times.

I have dwelt thus at length on Hamlet's melancholy because, from the psychological point of view, it is the centre of the tragedy, and to omit it from consideration or to underrate its intensity is to make Shakespeare's story unintelligible. But the psychological point of view is not equivalent to the tragic; and, having once given its due weight to the fact of Hamlet's melancholy, we may freely admit, or rather may be anxious to insist, that this pathological condition would excite but little, if any, tragic interest if it were not the condition of a nature distinguished by that speculative genius on which the Schlegel-Coleridge type of theory lays stress. Such theories misinterpret the connection between that genius and Hamlet's failure, but still it is this connection which gives to his story its peculiar fascination and makes it appear (if the phrase may be allowed) as the symbol of a tragic mystery inherent in human nature. Wherever this mystery touches us, wherever we are forced to feel the wonder and awe of man's godlike 'apprehension' and his 'thoughts that wander through eternity,' and at the same time are forced to see him powerless in his petty sphere of action, and powerless (it would appear) from the very divinity of his thought, we remember Hamlet. And this is the reason why, in the great ideal movement which began towards the close of the eighteenth century, this tragedy acquired a position unique among Shakespeare's dramas, and shared only by Goethe's *Faust*. It was not that *Hamlet* is Shakespeare's greatest tragedy or most perfect work of art; it was that *Hamlet* most brings home to us at once the sense of the soul's infinity, and the sense of the doom which not only circumscribes that infinity but appears to be its offspring.

T. S. ELIOT

Hamlet and His Problems†

Few critics have ever admitted that *Hamlet* the play is the primary problem, and Hamlet the character only secondary. And Hamlet the character has had an especial temptation for that most dangerous type of critic: the critic with a mind which is naturally of the creative order, but which through some weakness in creative power exercises itself in criticism instead. These minds often find in Hamlet a vicarious existence for their own artistic realization. Such a mind had Goethe, who made of Hamlet a Werther; and such had Coleridge, who made of Hamlet a Coleridge; and probably neither of these men in writing about Hamlet remembered that his first business was to study a work of art. The kind of criticism that Goethe and Coleridge produced, in writing of Hamlet, is the most misleading kind possible. For they both possessed unquestionable critical insight, and both make their critical aberrations the more plausible by the substitution—of their own Hamlet for Shakespeare's—which their creative gift effects. We should be thankful that Walter Pater did not fix his attention on this play.

Two writers of our time, Mr. J. M. Robertson and Professor Stoll of the University of Minnesota, have issued small books which can be praised for moving in the other direction. Mr. Stoll performs a service in recalling to our attention the labours of the critics of the seventeenth and eighteenth centuries,[1] observing that they knew less about psychology than more recent Hamlet critics, but they were nearer in spirit to Shakespeare's art; and as they in-

† From *Selected Essays of T. S. Eliot*, New Edition, copyright 1932, 1936, 1950, by Harcourt, Brace & World, Inc.; copyright © 1960 by T. S. Eliot, pp. 46–50. Reprinted by permission of Harcourt, Brace & World, Inc., and Faber and Faber, Ltd.
1. I have never, by the way, seen a cogent refutation of Thomas Rymer's objections to *Othello*.

sisted on the importance of the effect of the whole rather than on the importance of the leading character, they were nearer, in their old-fashioned way, to the secret of dramatic art in general.

Qua work of art, the work of art cannot be interpreted; there is nothing to interpret; we can only criticise it according to standards, in comparison to other works of art; and for "interpretation" the chief task is the presentation of relevant historical facts which the reader is not assumed to know. Mr. Robertson points out, very pertinently, how critics have failed in their "interpretation" of *Hamlet* by ignoring what ought to be very obvious: that *Hamlet* is a stratification, that it represents the efforts of a series of men, each making what he could out of the work of his predecessors. The *Hamlet* of Shakespeare will appear to us very differently if, instead of treating the whole action of the play as due to Shakespeare's design, we perceive his *Hamlet* to be superposed upon much cruder material which persists even in the final form.

We know that there was an older play by Thomas Kyd, that extraordinary dramatic (if not poetic) genius who was in all probability the author of two plays so dissimilar as *The Spanish Tragedy* and *Arden of Feversham*; and what this play was like we can guess from three clues: from *The Spanish Tragedy* itself, from the tale of Belleforest upon which Kyd's *Hamlet* must have been based, and from a version acted in Germany in Shakespeare's lifetime which bears strong evidence of having been adapted from the earlier, not from the later, play. From these three sources it is clear that in the earlier play the motive was a revenge-motive simply; that the action or delay is caused, as in *The Spanish Tragedy*, solely by the difficulty of assassinating a monarch surrounded by guards; and that the "madness" of Hamlet was feigned in order to escape suspicion, and successfully. In the final play of Shakespeare, on the other hand, there is a motive which is more important than that of revenge, and which explicitly "blunts" the latter; the delay in revenge is unexplained on grounds of necessity or expediency; and the effect of the "madness" is not to lull but to arouse the king's suspicion. The alteration is not complete enough, however, to be convincing. Furthermore, there are verbal parallels so close to *The Spanish Tragedy* as to leave no doubt that in places Shakespeare was merely *revising* the text of Kyd. And finally there are unexplained scenes—the Polonius-Laertes and the Polonius-Reynaldo scenes—for which there is little excuse; these scenes are not in the verse style of Kyd, and not beyond doubt in the style of Shakespeare. These Mr. Robertson believes to be scenes in the original play of Kyd reworked by a third hand, perhaps Chapman, before Shakespeare touched the play. And he concludes, with very strong show of reason, that the original play of Kyd was, like certain other revenge plays, in two parts of five acts each. The upshot of Mr. Robertson's examination is, we believe, irrefragable: that Shakespeare's *Hamlet*, so far as it is Shakespeare's, is a play dealing with the effect of a mother's guilt upon her son, and that Shakespeare was unable to impose this motive successfully upon the "intractable" material of the old play.

Of the intractability there can be no doubt. So far from being Shakespeare's masterpiece, the play is most certainly an artistic failure. In several ways the play is puzzling, and disquieting as is none of the others. Of all the plays it is the longest and is possibly the one on which Shakespeare spent most pains; and yet he has left in it superfluous and inconsistent scenes which even hasty revision should have noticed. The versification is variable. Lines like

> Look, the morn, in russet mantle clad,
> Walks o'er the dew of yon high eastern hill,

are of the Shakespeare of *Romeo and Juliet*. The lines in Act V, sc. ii,

> Sir, in my heart there was a kind of fighting
> That would not let me sleep . . .
> Up from my cabin,
> My sea-gown scarf'd about me, in the dark
> Grop'd I to find out them: had my desire;
> Finger'd their packet;

are of his quite mature. Both workmanship and thought are in an unstable position. We are surely justified in attributing the play, with that other profoundly interesting play of "intractable" material and astonishing versification, *Measure for Measure*, to a period of crisis, after which follow the tragic successes which culminate in *Coriolanus*. *Coriolanus* may be not as "interesting" as *Hamlet*, but it is, with *Antony and Cleopatra*, Shakespeare's most assured artistic success. And probably more people have thought *Hamlet* a work of art because they found it interesting, than have found it interesting because it is a work of art. It is the "Mona Lisa" of literature.

The grounds of *Hamlet's* failure are not immediately obvious. Mr. Robertson is undoubtedly correct in concluding that the essential emotion of the play is the feeling of a son towards a guilty mother:

[Hamlet's] tone is that of one who has suffered tortures on the score of his mother's degradation. . . . The guilt of a mother is an almost intolerable motive for drama, but it had to be maintained and emphasized to supply a psychological solution, or rather a hint of one.

This, however, is by no means the whole story. It is not merely the "guilt of a mother" that cannot be handled as Shakespeare handled the suspicion of Othello, the infatuation of Antony, or the pride of Coriolanus. The subject might conceivably have expanded into a tragedy like these, intelligible, self-complete, in the sunlight. *Hamlet,* like the sonnets, is full of some stuff that the writer could not drag to light, contemplate, or manipulate into art. And when we search for this feeling, we find it, as in the sonnets, very difficult to localize. You cannot point to it in the speeches; indeed, if you examine the two famous soliloquies you see the versification of Shakespeare, but a content which might be claimed by another, perhaps by the author of *The Revenge of Bussy d'Ambois,* Act V, sc. i. We find Shakespeare's *Hamlet* not in the action, not in any quotations that we might select, so much as in an unmistakable tone which is unmistakably not in the earlier play.

The only way of expressing emotion in the form of art is by finding an "objective correlative"; in other words, a set of objects, a situation, a chain of events which shall be the formula of that *particular* emotion; such that when the external facts, which must terminate in sensory experience, are given, the emotion is immediately evoked. If you examine any of Shakespeare's more successful tragedies, you will find this exact equivalence; you will find that the state of mind of Lady Macbeth walking in her sleep has been communicated to you by a skilful accumulation of imagined sensory impressions; the words of Macbeth on hearing of his wife's death strike us as if, given the sequence of events, these words were automatically released by the last event in the series. The artistic "inevitability" lies in this complete adequacy of the external to the emotion; and this is precisely what is deficient in *Hamlet.* Hamlet (the man) is dominated by an emotion which is inexpressible, because it is in *excess* of the facts as they appear. And the supposed identity of Hamlet with his author is genuine to this point: that Hamlet's bafflement at the absence of objective equivalent to his feelings is a prolongation of the bafflement of his creator in the face of his artistic problem. Hamlet is up against the difficulty that his disgust is occasioned by his mother, but that his mother is not an adequate equivalent for it; his disgust envelops and exceeds her. It is thus a feeling which he cannot understand; he cannot objectify it, and it therefore remains to poison life and obstruct action. None of the possible actions can satisfy it; and nothing that Shakespeare can do with the plot can express Hamlet for him. And it must be noticed that the very nature of the *données* of the problem precludes objective equivalence. To have heightened the criminality of Gertrude would have been to provide the formula for a totally different emotion in Hamlet; it is just *because* her character is so negative and insignificant that she arouses in Hamlet the feeling which she is incapable of representing.

The "madness" of Hamlet lay to Shakespeare's hand; in the earlier play a simple ruse, and to the end, we may presume, understood as a ruse by the audience. For Shakespeare it is less than madness and more than feigned. The levity of Hamlet, his repetition of phrase, his puns, are not part of a deliberate plan of dissimulation, but a form of emotional relief. In the character Hamlet it is the buffoonery of an emotion which can find no outlet in action; in the dramatist it is the buffoonery of an emotion which he cannot express in art. The intense feeling, ecstatic or terrible, without an object or exceeding its object, is something which every person of sensibility has known; it is doubtless a subject of study for pathologists. It often occurs in adolescence: the ordinary person puts these feelings to sleep, or trims down his feelings to fit the business world; the artist keeps them alive by his ability to intensify the world to his emotions. The Hamlet of Laforgue is an adolescent; the Hamlet of Shakespeare is not, he has not that explanation and excuse. We must simply admit that here Shakespeare tackled a problem which proved too much for him. Why he attempted it at all is an insoluble puzzle; under compulsion of what experience he attempted to express the inexpressibly horrible, we cannot ever know. We need a great many facts in his biography; and we should like to know whether, and when, and after or at the same time as what personal experience, he read Montaigne, II. xii, *Apologie de Raimond Sebond*. We should have, finally, to know something which is by hypothesis unknowable, for we assume it to be an experience which, in the manner indicated, exceeded the facts. We should have to understand things which Shakespeare did not understand himself.

* * *

ELMER EDGAR STOLL

Hamlet's Fault†

In the soliloquies, to be sure, Hamlet also roundly abuses himself. In the soliloquy at the end of the second act—"O what a rogue and peasant slave am I"—he contrasts his own sluggishness with the Player's passion, and dubs himself a rogue, a dull and muddy-mettled rascal, a peaking John-a-dreams, an ass, a coward. "Am I a coward?" he cries, catching himself, or his manhood rebounding, as it were, against the charge:

> Who calls me villain, breaks my pate across,
> Plucks off my beard and blows it in my face,
> Tweaks me by the nose, gives me the lie i' the throat
> As deep as to the lungs, who does me this?

Echo answers, Who? and he rouses himself, and shakes off the slanders he has been showering upon himself, like the true and sensible man that he is. In another soliloquy, his last, he complains of himself again as he enviously admires the energy and valor of Fortinbras:

> Now, whether it be
> Bestial oblivion, or some craven scruple
> Of thinking too precisely on the event,—
> A thought which, quarter'd, hath but one part wisdom
> And ever three parts coward,—I do not know
> Why yet I live to say, "This thing's to do,"
> Sith I have cause and will and strength and means
> To do't.

But here again the charge is unmade in the making. Here, though there is more analysis, Hamlet himself accepts none of the alternatives that offer. He "does not know"; he has "will and strength and means to do it";—these are the last words, and it is they that stick in our minds. Shakespeare will not suffer him, after all, to testify against himself. What he does is to let Hamlet pull himself together.[1]

---

† From "Hamlet": An Historical and Comparative Study (Minneapolis; University of Minnesota Press, 1919), pp. 20–25.
[1]. As it seems to me, this is the plain and natural interpretation, and for that reason, if for no other to be accepted.

Here is no pessimism, no despair, no doubt of himself. "What's wrong with me?" he says, as any of us might do. "I haven't been myself of late." Certainly there is no mystery-mongering on the part of the poet. The emphasis is not on "I do not know" but on the

Several times I have had occasion, in my essays on Elizabethan subjects, to show that soliloquies are to pass current at their face value; and are the truth itself, not to be gainsaid, like the comment of prologue or chorus or of modern or ancient *raisonneur*. And this is no exception: that Hamlet should not give the audience a handle against himself the dramatist has taken good care.

* * *

Confessions in soliloquy, moreover, are generally confirmed,— are, in Shakespeare's tragedy at least, never contradicted by the comment of other characters in a position to know, or by the confidences imparted to them by the character himself. Hamlet eventually tells Horatio of his uncle's guilt and his own purpose, but not of his difficulties or failures in carrying it out. To Horatio (or to himself, indeed) he never complains of any specific dereliction of duty such as sparing the King at prayer. Nor to any one is he known to have a defect. No one ever ventures to speak of him slightingly or critically. Why does not the King, Laertes, or Fortinbras despise him for a scholar and dreamer, at least, instead of taking him as they all do for the worthy son of his warrior sire? Why does not the Queen once sigh, or Horatio sadly shake his head? He is a courtier, soldier, scholar, the expectancy and rose of the fair state, cries Ophelia, and there is no suggestion that she is saying it as one who does not know. It is the accepted opinion. The King fears him, and shrinks from bringing him to account for Polonius' death, he says, because of the great love the general gender bear him. The sinful Queen quails under his rebuke, and yet loves him too well to betray his confidence. And, as often in Shakespeare's tragedies, at the end of the play judgment to the same effect is pronounced on his character by a disinterested party,

final clause; and there can be no mystery if he has "strength and means and will to do it." Never before or after is a mystery hinted at. To be sure, Hamlet does not know why he delays, either here or in his former soliloquy of self-reproach; but that is because there is no reason why; and Shakespeare simply avails himself of the familiar fact that now and then the most practical person in the world will say: "I don't know why I haven't done that." Save for this, it would be strange indeed if Hamlet should not "know why," seeing that whenever any other character of Shakespeare's concerns himself about his motives he knows them, even with a startling exactness. The good know how good theirs are; the wicked, how wicked. And Hamlet is the keenest-witted, the most introspective of the lot. All this, to be sure, runs counter to the common interpretation, that, unlike most characters, Hamlet is a real person, and that it is the authentic sign of his reality that we cannot explain him—that he cannot explain himself. See Professor E. H. Wright's article "Inconsistency in Characterization," in Columbia *Shakespearean Studies* (1916), especially pp. 390, 392. Like many others, but unlike the poet, Mr. Wright makes much of the mystery here, identifying it with the inscrutable mystery of the living soul; —but that I complain of him rather than of his predecessors is due to the fact that he is nearest at hand, and is not only a scholar but, in this book, has the company and countenance of scholars.

like the chorus of the Greeks. The closing funeral orations, observes Professor Schick, are always spoken by the dramatist himself "Let four captains," cries Fortinbras,

> Bear Hamlet, like a soldier, to the stage,
> For he was likely, had he been put on,
> To have proved most royally; and, for his passage,
> The soldiers' music and the rites of war
> Speak loudly for him.
> Take up the bodies. Such a sight as this
> Becomes the field, but here shows much amiss.
> Go, bid the soldiers shoot.

A royal salute is given. For no one else in death has Shakespeare let the trumpets blare and cannon thunder; but this youth, says the man whom Hamlet himself had emulated, would have made a kingly king. It is like the judgment pronounced at the end by Cassio on Othello; like that pronounced by Antony on Brutus; and like that pronounced by Octavius on Antony himself and his queen. But in none of these cases is the praise so unmingled with blame, as if (were the poet to have his way) the villain, fate, and false fortune, not the hero himself, must bear the whole heavy burden. Critics there are who have thought that Fortinbras said it all in irony, but not those who are most in sympathy with Shakespeare's art. So the words could not have been understood; or even if they had been, they would have disturbed that note of calm and reconciliation which Shakespeare in his great tragedies always reaches at the close. No respectable person in his dramas, for that matter, consciously or unconsciously speaks lightly of the dead. The poet's own personal humor, it would seem, did not sally across the confines of the frivolous or profane.

Here, or somewhere, one would have expected comment on Hamlet's shortcomings, his weakness or tragic fault. Instead, there is only praise from his friends, fear and hatred from his enemies. How is it possible, then, that a tragic fault or weakness could have been intended? Not only do Shakespeare's heroes know their faults, like Lear at the beginning, or Othello at the end, as Hamlet says he does not (and would seem to have none to know), but their friends and enemies know them too. The Fool and Kent know Lear's, Lady Macbeth her husband's, Enobarbus Antony's, Cassius Brutus', and Iago Othello's; but Horatio, Ophelia, Gertrude, Laertes, Fortinbras, who at the end avers that as a king he would have proved right royally, even Claudius himself, find in Hamlet no weakness at all! Only Horatio, of course, who alone is in the secret of the murder, could know of the procrastination or suspect it. He does not even hint at it. But Laertes might at least have belittled his swordsmanship, Polonius his statesmanship, and Claudius at times might have questioned his formidableness as a foe. Indeed, who so likely to know his own fault as Hamlet himself? At every other point (and at this as well!) he, like other Shakespearean characters, knows himself even as he is known.[2]

* * *

The charges, then, which Hamlet brings against himself are not, though they might well be, confirmed or substantiated. Instead, the evidence points the other way. In addition to what we have already considered, there is the fact that the two soliloquies of self-reproach are so contrived as to end each in a definite resolve, and that a resolve which is kept. "The play's the thing," in the one case; "From this time forth my thoughts be bloody or be nothing worth," in the other. Both times Hamlet, upon consideration, mends his ways: he turns from his sin of inaction, and his repentance is unto life. But the action he resolves on, you say, is not to the point—not revenge. You say this, however, because you are a critic, or a psychologist; or because you have read others' criticisms of the play; or because you have read the play more than you have seen it. In both cases it is action, not collapse; in both cases it is action which has to do with the King and with thwarting him; what is more, in both cases it is action which wholly satisfies the speaker himself. After the second soliloquy he complains of himself, questions himself, no more. And that the audience will observe, and are meant to observe, much more readily than the circumstance that the action is not the supreme one of killing the King. So the dramatist is enabled to content his audience, shield his hero, and still prolong his play.

* * *

2. A friend calls my attention to the fact that in thus interpreting Hamlet's reproaches, as well as in the general conception of Hamlet as not irresolute, I am following Swinburne, in his *Study of Shakespeare* (1895), pp. 161–69. I had not read this particular passage for some years:
"That Hamlet should seem at times to accept for himself, and even to enforce by reiteration of argument upon his conscience and his reason, some such conviction or suspicion as to his own character, tells much rather in disfavour than in favour of its truth. A man whose natural temptation was to swerve, whose inborn inclination was to shrink and skulk aside from duty and from action, would hardly be the first and last person to suspect his own weakness, the one only unbiassed judge and witness of sufficiently sharp-sighted candour and accuracy to estimate aright his poverty of nature and the malformation of his mind."

The only point at which I am constrained to dissent from the great poet's judgment is where, having recognized that "the signal characteristic of Hamlet's inmost nature is by no means irresolution or hesitation or any form of weakness," he adds, "but rather the strong conflux of contending forces." But he lets it go at that, and in the discussion as a whole he is as remarkable for his clearness of perception as his readers (*quorum pars!*) have been for their dulness. He wrote in 1879; how many have gone on writing since! * * *

G. WILSON KNIGHT

The Embassy of Death: An Essay on *Hamlet*†

* * *

It is usual in Shakespeare's plays for the main theme to be reflected in subsidiary incidents, persons, and detailed suggestion
throughout. Now the theme of *Hamlet* is death. Life that is bound
for the disintegration of the grave, love that does not survive the
loved one's life—both, in their insistence on death as the primary
fact of nature, are branded on the mind of Hamlet, burned into
it, searing it with agony. The bereavement of Hamlet and his
consequent mental agony bordering on madness is mirrored in the
bereavement of Ophelia and her madness. The death of the
Queen's love is reflected in the swift passing of the love of the
Player-Queen, in the 'Murder of Gonzago.' Death is over the whole
play. Polonius and Ophelia die during the action, and Ophelia is
buried before our eyes. Hamlet arranges the deaths of Rosencrantz
and Guildenstern. The plot is set in motion by the murder of
Hamlet's father, and the play opens with the apparition of the
Ghost:

> What may this mean,
> That thou, dead corse, again in complete steel
> Revisit'st thus the glimpses of the moon,
> Making night hideous; and we fools of nature
> So horridly to shake our dispositions
> With thoughts beyond the reaches of our souls?   (I. iv. 51)

Those first scenes strike the note of the play—death. We hear of
terrors beyond the grave, from the Ghost (I. v.) and from the
meditations of Hamlet (III. i.). We hear of horrors in the grave
from Hamlet whose mind is obsessed with hideous thoughts of
the body's decay. Hamlet's dialogue with the King about the dead
Polonius (IV. iii. 16) is painful; and the graveyard meditations,
though often beautiful, are remorselessly realistic. Hamlet holds
Yorick's skull:

> *Hamlet.* . . . Now, get you to my lady's chamber and tell her,
>   let her paint an inch thick, to this favour she must come;
>   make her laugh at that. Prithee, Horatio, tell me one thing.

† From *The Wheel of Fire*, by G.
Wilson Knight (London: Methuen &
Co., Ltd., 1930), Copyright © 1930
by Methuen & Co., Ltd. Reprinted by
permission.

Horatio. What's that, my lord?
Hamlet. Dost thou think Alexander looked o' this fashion i' the
earth?
Horatio. E'en so.
Hamlet. And smelt so? pah!   (v. i. 170)

The general thought of death, intimately related to the predomi-
nating human theme, the pain in Hamlet's mind, is thus suf-
fused through the whole play. And yet the play, as a whole, scarcely
gives us that sense of blackness and the abysms of spiritual evil
which we find in *Macbeth;* nor is there the universal gloom of *King
Lear.* This is due partly to the difference in the technique of *Hamlet* from that of *Macbeth* or *King Lear.* Macbeth, the protagonist
and heroic victim of evil, rises gigantic from the murk of an evil
universe; Lear, the king of suffering, towers over a universe that
itself toils in pain. Thus in *Macbeth* and *King Lear* the predomi-
nating imaginative atmospheres are used not to contrast with the
mental universe of the hero, but to aid and support it, as it were,
with similarity, to render realistic the extravagant and daring effects of volcanic passion to which the poet allows his protagonist to
give voice. We are forced by the attendant personification, the
verbal colour, the symbolism and events of the play as a whole,
to feel the hero's suffering, to see with his eyes. But in *Hamlet*
this is not so. We need not see through Hamlet's eyes. Though
the idea of death is recurrent through the play, it is not implanted
in the minds of other persons as is the consciousness of evil
throughout *Macbeth* and the consciousness of suffering throughout
King Lear. Except for the original murder of Hamlet's father, the
Hamlet universe is one of healthy and robust life, good-nature,
humour, romantic strength, and welfare: against this background
is the figure of Hamlet pale with the consciousness of death. He is
the ambassador of death walking amid life. The effect is at first
primarily one of separation. But it is to be noted that the consciousness of death, and consequent bitterness, cruelty, and inaction, in
Hamlet not only grows in his own mind disintegrating it as we
watch, but also spreads its effects outward among the other persons like a blighting disease, and, as the play progresses, by its
very passivity and negation of purpose, insidiously undermines the
health of the state, and adds victim to victim until at the end the
stage is filled with corpses. It is, as it were, a nihilistic birth in the
consciousness of Hamlet that spreads its deadly venom around.
That Hamlet is originally blameless, that the King is originally
guilty, may well be granted. But, if we refuse to be diverted from
a clear vision by questions of praise and blame, responsibility and
causality, and watch only the actions and reactions of the persons

as they appear, we shall observe a striking reversal of the usual commentary.

If we are to attain a true interpretation of Shakespeare we must work from a centre of consciousness near that of the creative instinct of the poet. We must think less in terms of causality and more in terms of imaginative impact. Now Claudius is not drawn as wholly evil—far from it. We see the government of Denmark working smoothly. Claudius shows every sign of being an excellent diplomatist and king. He is troubled by young Fortinbras, and dispatches ambassadors to the sick King of Norway demanding that he suppress the raids of his nephew. His speech to the ambassadors bears the stamp of clear and exact thought and an efficient and confident control of affairs:

> . . . and we here dispatch
> You, good Cornelius, and you, Voltimand,
> For bearers of this greeting to old Norway;
> Giving to you no further personal power
> To business with the king, more than the scope
> Of these delated articles allow.
> Farewell, and let your haste commend your duty.   (I. ii. 33)

The ambassadors soon return successful. Claudius listens to their reply, receives the King of Norway's letter, and hears that young Fortinbras desires a free pass through Denmark to lead his soldiers against the Poles. Claudius answers:

> It likes us well;
> And at our more consider'd time we'll read,
> Answer, and think upon this business.
> Meantime we thank you for your well-took labour:
> Go to your rest; at night we'll feast together:
> Most welcome home!   (II. ii. 80)

Tact has found an easy settlement where arms and opposition might have wasted the strength of Denmark. Notice his reservation of detailed attention when once he knows the main issues are clear; the courteous yet dignified attitude to his subordinates and the true leader's consideration for their comfort; and the invitation to the feast. The impression given by these speeches is one of quick efficiency—the efficiency of the man who can dispose of business without unnecessary circumstance, and so leaves himself time for enjoying the good things of life: a man kindly, confident, and fond of pleasure.

Throughout the first half of the play Claudius is the typical kindly uncle, besides being a good king. His advice to Hamlet about his exaggerated mourning for his father's death is admirable common sense:

> Fie! 'Tis a fault to Heaven,
> A fault against the dead, a fault to nature,
> To reason most absurd; whose common theme
> Is death of fathers, and who still hath cried,
> From the first corse, till he that died to-day,
> 'This must be so.' (i. ii. 101)

It is the advice of worldly common sense opposed to the extreme misery of a sensitive nature paralysed by the facts of death and unfaithfulness. This contrast points the relative significance of the King and his court to Hamlet. They are of the world—with their crimes, their follies, their shallownesses, their pomp and glitter; they are of humanity, with all its failings, it is true, but yet of humanity. They assert the importance of human life, they believe in it, in themselves. Whereas Hamlet is inhuman, since he has seen through the tinsel of life and love, he believes in nothing, not even himself, except the memory of a ghost, and his black-robed presence is a reminder to everyone of the fact of death. There is no question but that Hamlet is right. The King's smiles hide murder, his mother's love for her new consort is unfaithfulness to Hamlet's father, Ophelia has deserted Hamlet at the hour of his need. Hamlet's philosophy may be inevitable, blameless, and irrefutable. But it is the negation of life. It is death. Hence Hamlet is a continual fear to Claudius, a reminder of his crime. It is a mistake to consider Claudius as a hardened criminal. When Polonius remarks on the hypocrisy of mankind, he murmurs to himself:

> O, 'tis too true!
> How smart a lash that speech doth give my conscience!
> The harlot's cheek, beautied with plastering art,
> Is not more ugly to the thing that helps it
> Than is my deed to my most painted word:
> O heavy burthen! (iii. i. 49)

Again, Hamlet's play wrenches his soul with remorse—primarily not fear of Hamlet, as one might expect, but a genuine remorse—and gives us that most beautiful prayer of a stricken soul beginning, 'O, my offence is rank, it smells to Heaven' (iii. iii. 43):

> . . . What if this cursed hand
> Were thicker than itself with brother's blood,
> Is there not rain enough in the sweet heavens
> To wash it white as snow? Whereto serves mercy
> But to confront the visage of offence?

He fears that his prayer is worthless. He is still trammelled by the enjoyment of the fruits of his crime. 'My fault is past,' he cries. But what does that avail, since he has his crown and his queen still, the prizes of murder? His dilemma is profound and raises the problem I am pointing in this essay. Claudius, as he appears in the play, is not a criminal. He is—strange as it may seem—a good and gentle king, enmeshed by the chain of causality linking him with his crime. And this chain he might, perhaps, have broken except for Hamlet, and all would have been well. But, granted the presence of Hamlet—which Claudius at first genuinely desired, persuading him not to return to Wittenberg as he wished—and granted the fact of his original crime which cannot now be altered, Claudius can hardly be blamed for his later actions. They are forced on him. As King, he could scarcely be expected to do otherwise. Hamlet is a danger to the state, even apart from his knowledge of Claudius' guilt. He is an inhuman—or superhuman—presence, whose consciousness—somewhat like Dostoievsky's Stavrogin—is centred on death. Like Stavrogin, he is feared by those around him. They are always trying in vain to find out what is wrong with him. They cannot understand him. He is a creature of another world. As King of Denmark he would have been a thousand times more dangerous than Claudius. The end of Claudius' prayer is pathetic:

> What then? What rests?
> Try what repentance can: what can it not?
> Yet what can it when one can not repent?
> O wretched state! O bosom black as death!
> O limed soul, that, struggling to be free,
> Art more engaged! Help, angels! make assay!
> Bow stubborn knees; and, heart with strings of steel,
> Be soft as sinews of the new-born babe!
> All may be well. (III. iii. 64)

Set against this lovely prayer—the fine flower of a human soul in anguish—is the entrance of Hamlet, the late joy of torturing the King's conscience still written on his face, his eye a-glitter with the intoxication of conquest, vengeance in his mind; his purpose altered only by the devilish hope of finding a more damning moment in which to slaughter the King, next hastening to his mother to wring her soul too. Which then, at this moment in the play, is nearer the Kingdom of Heaven? Whose words would be more acceptable of Jesus' God? Which is the embodiment of spiritual good, which of evil? The question of the relative morality of Hamlet and Claudius reflects the ultimate problem of this play.

* * *

I have concentrated on Claudius' virtues. They are manifest. So are his faults—his original crime, his skill in the less admirable kind of policy, treachery, and intrigue. But I would point clearly that, in the movement of the play, his faults are forced on him, and he is distinguished by creative and wise action, a sense of purpose, benevolence, a faith in himself and those around him, by love of his Queen:

> . . . and for myself—
> My virtue or my plague, be it either which—
> She's so conjunctive to my life and soul,
> That as the star moves not but in his sphere,
> I could not but by her.   (IV. vii. 12)

In short he is very human. Now these are the very qualities Hamlet lacks. Hamlet is inhuman. He has seen through humanity. And this inhuman cynicism, however justifiable in this case on the plane of causality and individual responsibility, is a deadly and venomous thing. Instinctively the creatures of earth, Laertes, Polonius, Ophelia, Rosencrantz and Guildenstern, league themselves with Claudius: they are of his kind. They sever themselves from Hamlet. Laertes sternly warns Ophelia against her intimacy with Hamlet, so does Polonius. They are, in fact, all leagued against him, they are puzzled by him or fear him: he has no friend except Horatio, and Horatio, after the Ghost scenes, becomes a queer shadowy character who rarely gets beyond 'E'en so, my lord', 'My lord——', and such-like phrases. The other persons are firmly drawn, in the round, creatures of flesh and blood. But Hamlet is not of flesh and blood, he is a spirit of penetrating intellect and cynicism and misery, without faith in himself or anyone else, murdering his love of Ophelia, on the brink of insanity, taking delight in cruelty, torturing Claudius, wringing his mother's heart, a poison in the midst of the healthy bustle of the court. He is a superman among men. And he is a superman because he has walked and held converse with death, and his consciousness works in terms of death and the negation of cynicism. He has seen the truth, not alone of Denmark, but of humanity, of the universe: and the truth is evil. Thus Hamlet is an element of evil in the state of Denmark. The poison of his mental existence spreads outwards among things of flesh and blood, like acid eating into metal. They are helpless before his very inactivity and fall one after the other, like victims of an infectious disease. They are strong with the strength of health—but the demon of Hamlet's mind is a stronger thing than they. Futilely they try to get him out of their country; anything to get rid of him, he is not safe. But he goes with a cynical smile, and is no sooner gone than he is back again in their midst, meditating in graveyards, at home with death. Not till it has slain all, is the demon that grips Hamlet satisfied. And last it slays Hamlet himself:

> The spirit that I have seen
> May be the Devil . . .   (II. ii. 565)

It was.

It was the devil of the knowledge of death, which possesses Hamlet and drives him from misery and pain to increasing bitterness, cynicism, murder, and madness. He has indeed bought converse with his father's spirit at the price of enduring and spreading Hell on earth. But however much we may sympathize with Ophelia, with Polonius, Rosencrantz, Guildenstern, the Queen, and Claudius, there is one reservation to be made. It is Hamlet who is right. What he says and thinks of them is true, and there is no fault in his logic. His own mother is indeed faithless, and the prettiness of Ophelia does in truth enclose a spirit as fragile and untrustworthy as her earthly beauty; Polonius is 'a foolish prating knave'; Rosencrantz and Guildenstern are time-servers and flatterers; Claudius, whose benevolence hides the guilt of murder, is, by virtue of that fact, 'a damned smiling villain'. In the same way the demon of cynicism which is in the mind of the poet and expresses itself in the figures of this play, has always this characteristic: it is right. One cannot argue with the cynic. It is unwise to offer him battle. For in the warfare of logic it will be found that he has all the guns.

* * *

Thus Hamlet spends a great part of his time watching, analysing, and probing others. He unhesitatingly lances each in turn in his weakest spot. He is usually quite merciless. But all he actually accomplishes is to torment them all, terrorize them. They are dreadfully afraid of him. Hamlet is so powerful. He is, as it were, the channel of a mysterious force, a force which derives largely from his having seen through them all. In contact with him they know their own faults: neither they nor we should know them otherwise. He exposes faults everywhere. But he is not tragic in the usual Shakespearian sense; there is no surge and swell of passion pressing onward through the play to leave us, as in *King Lear*, with the mightly crash and backwash of a tragic peace. There is not this direct rhythm in Hamlet—there is no straight course. Instead of being dynamic, the force of Hamlet is, paradoxically, static. Its poison is the poison of negation, nothingness, threatening a world of positive assertion. But even this element is not the whole of Hamlet. He can speak lovingly to his mother at one moment, and the next, in an excess of revulsion, torment her with a withering and brutal sarcasm. One moment he can cry:

> I loved Ophelia: forty thousand brothers
> Could not, with all their quantity of love,
> Make up my sum. (v. i. 247)

Shortly after he scorns himself for his outbreak. His mind reflects swift changes. He may for a moment or two see with the eyes of humour, gentleness, love—then suddenly the whole universe is blackened, goes out, leaves utter vacancy. This is, indeed, the secret of the play's fascination and its lack of unified and concise poetic statement. Hamlet is a dualized personality, wavering, oscillating between grace and the hell of cynicism. The plot reflects this see-saw motion; it lacks direction, pivoting on Hamlet's incertitude, and analysis holds the fascination of giddiness. Nor can Hamlet feel anything passionately for long, since passion implies purpose, and he has no one purpose for any length of time. One element in Hamlet, and that a very important one, is the negation of any passion whatsoever. His disease—or vision—is primarily one of negation, of death. Hamlet is a living death in the midst of life; that is why the play sounds the note of death so strong and sombre at the start. The Ghost was conceived throughout as a portent not kind but sinister. That sepulchral cataclysm at the beginning is the key to the whole play. *Hamlet* begins with an explosion in the first act; the rest of the play is the reverberation thereof. From the first act onwards Hamlet is, as it were, blackened, scorched by that shattering revelation. The usual process is reversed and the climax is at the start. Hamlet, already in despair, converses early with death. * * * Finally 'this fell sergeant, death' (v. ii. 321) arrests him too. This is his mysterious strength, ghost-begotten, before which the rest succumb. That is why this play is so rich in death—why its meaning is analysed by Hamlet in soliloquy, why Hamlet is so fascinated by the skulls the Grave-digger unearths; why so many 'casual slaughters' and 'deaths put on by cunning and forced cause' (v. ii. 367) disrupt the action, till we are propelled to the last holocaust of mortality and Fortinbras' comment:

> This quarry cries on havoc. O proud death,
> What feast is toward in thine eternal cell,
> That thou so many princes at a shot
> So bloodily hast struck? (v. ii. 349)

The Ghost may or may not have been a 'goblin damned'; it certainly was no 'spirit of health' (I. iv. 40). The play ends with a dead march. The action grows out of eternity, closes in it. The ominous discharge of ordnance thus reverberates three times: once, before Hamlet sees the Ghost, and twice in Act v. The eternity of death falls as an abyss at either end, and Hamlet crosses the stage of life aureoled in its ghostly luminance.

JOHN DOVER WILSON

Hamlet and Ophelia†

The attitude of Hamlet towards Ophelia is without doubt the greatest of all the puzzles in the play, greater even than that of the delay itself, a fact which should long ago have created suspicion that in the course of three centuries Shakespeare's original intentions have somehow been obscured. The difficulty is not that, having once loved Ophelia, Hamlet ceases to do so. This is explained, as most critics have agreed, by his mother's conduct which has put him quite out of love with Love and has poisoned his whole imagination. The exclamation "Frailty thy name is woman!" in the first soliloquy, we come to feel later, embraces Ophelia as well as Gertrude, while in the bedroom scene he as good as taxes his mother with destroying his capacity for affection, when he accuses her of

> such an act
> That blurs the grace and blush of modesty,
> Calls virtue hypocrite, *takes off the rose*
> *From the fair forehead of an innocent love*
> And sets a blister there.

Moreover, it is clear that in the tirades of the nunnery scene he is thinking almost as much of his mother as of Ophelia.

The word "blister" in the passage just quoted introduces us to the real problem; for it refers to the branding of a harlot. Why brand "an *innocent* love" thus? Gertrude had played the harlot with Claudius; why pour abuse which might be appropriate to her upon the unoffending head of Ophelia? * * *

For, whatever weakness we may be expected to find in Hamlet's

† From *What Happens in Hamlet*, by John Dover Wilson (New York; Cambridge University Press, 1959), pp. 101–8. Copyright © 1959 by Cambridge University Press. Reprinted by permission. Wilson's footnotes are here omitted.

character, however severely Shakespeare judges him and asks us to
judge him also, it is vital to his purpose that we should retain our
interest in him and admiration for him right up to the end. Rob
us of our respect for the hero and *Hamlet* ceases to be a tragedy;
yet that is just what his unexplained behaviour to Ophelia threatens to do. There is a savage side to Hamlet, which comes out in
his ruthlessness towards Rosencrantz and Guildenstern, and in the
speech as the King kneels in prayer, a speech that Dr Johnson found
"too horrible to be read or to be uttered". Yet this savagery, dis-
cordant as it is with our scale of values, does not detract from our
general sense of the nobility and greatness of the man. But savagery towards a gentle and inoffensive child, one whom he had
loved and whose worst crime towards him is lack of understanding
and inability to disobey her father's commands, is a very different
matter. It is, in fact, irreconcilable with everything else we are told
about him.

Hamlet treats Ophelia like a prostitute; and the only possible
defence for him is to show that he had grounds for so doing.
What can they have been? The answer came to me, late in this
inquiry, when after trying many solutions of the Hamlet-Ophelia
tangle I had given the whole thing up and had ceased thinking
about it. I was making the first draft of my Notes for *Hamlet* in
the edition recently published by the Cambridge University Press,
and asking questions, as an editor must, about the meaning of
word and situation at each step I took. Presently I arrived at the
point, early in 2.2, at which Polonius and Claudius devise the
plot of listening to Hamlet and Ophelia behind the arras, when
my attention was arrested by this line in the speech of Polonius:

> At such a time I'll loose my daughter to him.

The expression was not new to me. I had met it before in *The
Tempest* at 2.1.124, where the cynical Sebastian sneers at Alonso
because he would not marry his daughter to a European prince,

> But rather loose her to an African;

and in *The Merry Wives* at 2.1.163, where the confident Master
Page declares of Falstaff that "if he should intend this voyage towards my wife, I would turn her loose to him; and what he gets
more of her than sharp words, let it lie on my head". I had met
it also, listening to present-day farmers in the north of England
discussing the breeding of horses and cattle; and that this was the
meaning intended, a meaning that would assuredly not escape an
Elizabethan audience, was confirmed to my mind by Polonius

speaking of "a farm and carters" five lines later, in accordance with Shakespeare's habit of sustained imagery.

But to understand the point of it and its connection with what follows, we must have the whole context before us. I quote from the Second Quarto text:

King. How may we try it further?
Pol. You know sometimes he walks foure houres together   160
Heere in the Lobby.
Quee. So he dooes indeede.
Pol. At such a time, Ile loose my daughter to him,
Be you and I behind an Arras then,
Marke the encounter, if he loue her not,
And be not from his reason falne thereon
Let me be no assistant for a state
But keepe a farme and carters.
King. We will try it.

Enter Hamlet.

Quee. But looke where sadly the poore wretch comes reading.
Pol. Away, I doe beseech you both away, *Exit King and Queene.*
Ile bord him presently, oh giue me leaue,   170
How dooes my good Lord Hamlet?
Ham. Well, God a mercy.
Pol. Doe you knowe me my Lord?
Ham. Excellent well, you are a Fishmonger.
Pol. Not I my Lord.   175
Ham. Then I would you were so honest a man.
Pol. Honest my Lord.
Ham. I sir to be honest as this world goes,
Is to be one man pickt out of tenne thousand.
Pol. That's very true my Lord.   180
Ham. For if the sunne breede maggots in a dead dogge, being a good kissing carrion. Haue you a daughter?
Pol. I haue my Lord.
Ham. Let her not walke i'th Sunne, conception is a blessing, But as your daughter may conceaue, friend looke to't.

Everything that Hamlet here says is capable of an equivocal interpretation reflecting upon Polonius and Ophelia. "Fishmonger", as many commentators have noted, means a pandar or procurer; "carrion" was a common expression at that time for "flesh" in the carnal sense; while the quibble in "conception" needs no explaining. And when I asked myself why Hamlet should suddenly call Polonius a bawd and his daughter a prostitute—for that is what it all amounts to—I could discover but one possible answer to my question, namely that "Fishmonger" and the rest follows immediately upon "loose my daughter to him". Nor was this the end of the matter. For what might Hamlet mean by his sarcastic advice to the father not to let the daughter "walke i'th Sunne", or by the reference to the sun breeding in the "carrion" exposed to it? Bearing in mind Hamlet's punning retort "I am too much in the 'son' ", in answer to Claudius's unctuous question at 1.2.64,

> And now my cousin Hamlet, and my son,
> How is it that the clouds still hang on you?—

and recalling Falstaff's apostrophe to Prince Hal: "Shall the blessed sun of heaven prove a micher and eat blackberries? a question not to be asked. Shall the son of England prove a thief and take purses? a question to be asked", [1 *Henry IV*, 2.4.449–53] is it not obvious that Hamlet here means by "Sunne" the sun or son of Denmark, the heir apparent, in other words himself? And if so, "let her not walke i'th Sunne" is to be paraphrased "take care that you do not loose your daughter to me!"

What then? *Hamlet must have overheard what Polonius said to the King.* The context allows no escape from this conclusion, inasmuch as what Hamlet says to Polonius is only intelligible if the conclusion be allowed. It remains to examine the text in order to discover, if possible, what Shakespeare's intentions, clearly impaired in some way by corruption, may have been. We are left, of course, to conjecture, but even so we are not entirely without clues. Says Polonius:

> You know sometimes he walks four hours together
> Here in the lobby;

and as he speaks we may imagine him jerking a thumb over his shoulder towards the inner-stage before which the three plotters stand, their faces to the audience. Words and the action are a direct invitation to the spectators to look in that direction; and, as they do so, Hamlet enters the inner-stage from the door at the back, his eyes upon his book, quite unconscious at first that his uncle, his mother and Polonius are on the outer-stage, which stands for the audience-chamber of the castle. In short, "Here in the lobby" is equivalent to a stage-direction, and marks with practical certainty the moment at which Hamlet comes in and the place of his entry. And it is the right moment; for the entry should seem unquestionably accidental, lest the audience should suspect him of deliberate spying. It would never do, for example, to let him linger in his place of concealment. Between the King's question "How may we try it further?" and his resolve "We will try it" there lie eight lines of dialogue. They just give Hamlet time to enter the lobby, grow conscious of voices in the larger chamber beyond, pause for a moment beside the entrance thereto, compose his features, and come forward. But brief as the period is, it is long enough for him to take in the whole eavesdropping plot and to implicate Ophelia beyond possibility of doubt in his ears as one of his uncle's minions.

Nor does the textual aspect of the matter present any insuperable difficulties. If things are as I contend, there must have been two entries for Hamlet in Shakespeare's manuscript at this point: one for the inner-stage at l. 159 or l. 161 and the other for the outer-stage at l. 167 where it now stands. Such a double-entry would have been puzzling to a compositor or a transcriber, and it is not at all surprising to find the first one absent in both the Second Quarto and First Folio texts, seeing that it might easily have been mistaken as a prompt entry,[1] while the Queen's words "But look where sadly the poor wretch comes reading" would be accepted as showing which was the entry intended by the author. The omission is rendered all the more probable by the fact that both texts tend to omit important stage-directions, and that on more than one occasion such omissions occur at the same place in both editions.

Hamlet's accidental discovery of the intention to spy upon him has a bearing much wider than his attitude towards Ophelia. Indeed, the manner in which it eases the general working of the plot is strong testimony in its favour. As we shall find, it constitutes the mainspring of the events that follow in acts 2 and 3; it renders the nunnery scene playable and intelligible as never before; it adds all kinds of fresh light and shade to the play scene. In a word, its recovery means the restoration of a highly important piece of the dramatic structure. * * *

1. In preparing manuscript play books for performance prompters occasionally repeated entries in the margin a little in advance of those in the original with the intention of bringing "the characters on at the back of the stage a few moments earlier in order that they may be able to enter into the dialogue at the correct point". Cf. W. W. Greg, *Elizabethan Dramatic Documents*, p. 217.

HARLEY GRANVILLE-BARKER

The Five Acts of the Editors†

The long-accepted division of the play into five acts is not, of course, authentic. Here, as with other plays, the editors of the Folio were bent upon giving their author this classic dignity; and it may be, besides, that by 1623 theatrical practice had itself imposed this division upon such of his plays as were still being acted. In the private theaters it had commonly been the custom to divide plays into acts and to provide music for intervals. The practice of the public theaters is a matter of dispute. If they did observe act divisions—four of them—they are hardly likely to have done so more than formally unless or until they also had some entertaining means of filling the gaps.[1] It is possible that their practice changed, and this during Shakespeare's own lifetime. He certainly did not (except for one instance) think out his plays in five-act form; whatever the exigencies of its performance are to be, the play itself is an indivisible whole. It was the telling of a story; its shape would be dictated by the nature of the story and the need to make this dramatically effective. And that meant, among other things, that if there were to be breaks in its progress, one generally did better to minimize than to accentuate them; for the attention of an audience, once captured, must be held.

In the dividing-up of *Hamlet* the Folio editors for some reason get no further than *Actus Secundus;*[2] and not till the "Players' Quarto" of 1676, do we find an end made of their Act II, and a III, IV and V. That almost certainly represents the theatrical practice of the Restoration; but quite possibly it has an earlier origin in the performance of the play in private theaters about the date of the printing of the Folio. Rowe (who, for text, picks and chooses between Q2 and F1) adopts it, and later editors follow him.[3]

† From *Preface to Hamlet,* by Harley Granville-Barker (New York: Hill & Wang, 1957), pp. 34–40. Copyright © 1957 by Hill & Wang. Reprinted by permission.
1. Or unless the strain upon the audience became too great. That might entail a definite pause or so for recovery; but hardly four pauses. The Elizabethans, moreover, could apparently support sieges from which their modern descendants shrink. Their sermons ran notably to length. While the plays could be acted through in two hours or a little longer, there would be no physical need for a pause.
2. To be quite accurate, they mark it *Scaena Secunda* and stop there. But scene-division is another matter. This is implicit in the text; for it depends, customarily, upon the incidence of a cleared stage.
3. It the more certainly represents Restoration theatrical practice that this

But, whatever its origin, it illustrates no consistent dramatic purpose on Shakespeare's part. It cannot but to some extent thwart his technique; and at one point—in the contriving of the end of a third act and a beginning for a fourth—the offense is patent and the cobbling of the clumsiest.[4]

A unit of dramatic action for a first act—if there had to be one —was not hard to find; for the story, as Shakespeare tells it, carries us at a sustained stretch and upon a plainly indicated time-scheme to the Ghost's revelation and Hamlet's heartsick acceptance of his task. So definite an "act" is this, on both counts, that an editor is tempted to set down as definitely at the end of it: *Some weeks pass.* Now Shakespeare certainly suggests in the next scene that time has been passing; a remark of Ophelia's several scenes later makes it, in fact, a calculable two months. But, to realize this, we should need, as the line is spoken, to connect it mentally with another line spoken by Hamlet almost as long before, and do a small sum in subtraction—which we certainly shall not do at that moment. No such exact impression, therefore, is meant to be made on us.

The divider ends his second act upon Hamlet's resolution to put Claudius to the test of the play. This is an important milestone in the story; the scene is sure to gain applause; and in the following scene, if we are listening carefully, we shall gather that between the two a night has passed. So here, for the act-divider, are excuses enough for a few minutes' halt. Hamlet will have wrought us to share in his excitement; we shall relieve our feelings by applauding; we shall be given time to adjust our recollection of what has passed and prepare for what is promised. It may well be that Shakespeare's own actors found they had to give their audience an occasional rest from the strain of attention to such a play as *Hamlet*; it would be a greater mental-plus-emotional strain than any earlier play had exacted. It may even be that, Shakespeare consenting, they picked on this juncture as the likeliest for the purpose hereabouts; he might even pick on it himself. Nevertheless, since he did not so plan the play, the halt and the pause betray

---

Quarto (of Davenant's editing, presumably) marks passages "to be omitted in representation," which are not included in the Folio's abbreviation of Q2. It will still be a homage to classical tradition; but there is no doubt, I think, that, whatever had been done earlier, the Restoration theater did observe the five-act division, either by formal or appreciable pauses in the performance.

4. Dr. Johnson comments severely on it, and other editors may note its ineptitude. But Dowden (for instance) only says in the introduction to the *Hamlet* volume of the Arden Shakespeare that "the received division between III. and IV. is unfortunate," taking for granted, apparently, that for some sort of five-act form Shakespeare himself was responsible. And while he records the pertinent variants in his *apparatus criticus*, he leaves them without comment. Of so little importance did this aspect of Shakespeare's stagecraft seem even to him.

his stagecraft. He is not apt to check the impulse of his action at an emotional crisis which only anticipates a sharper crisis still, but rather to find means to relax the tension, yet without so loosening it as to lose hold on his audience. And his dramatic intention here is plain. It is to carry us straight from the deadly intent of Hamlet's

> The play's the thing
> Wherein I'll catch the conscience of the King.

to the sight of the puzzled King and Queen questioning the still equally puzzled Rosencrantz and Guildenstern, but learning with relief—that the harmless pastime of a play is in hand!

> it doth much content me
> To hear him so inclin'd.
> Good gentlemen, give him a further edge,
> And drive his purpose on to these delights.

says the unsuspecting Claudius. With the loss of the quick sequence of the scenes, the irony of this will be largely lost.

Further, not five minutes should elapse (there are fifty-five lines to speak) between that passionate soliloquy with its ringing and resolute end (the sound of it will be still in our ears) and the pessimism of

> To be or not to be . . .

This is one of a series of such contrasts, a capital feature in the presenting of the character. Here, too, the full effect will be lost if the continuity of the action is broken.

As to the passing of a night between the scenes; at a guess, Shakespeare did not think about the matter at all till he came to write the sentence in the second scene indicating that a night has passed. (Nor, even so, is this a certain sign that it has; the performance may have been impatiently hurried forward.) It was natural in the earlier scene for Hamlet to set the play for "tomorrow night," since he had to write the "speech of some dozen or sixteen lines" to be inserted in it. But after the passionate

> O, what a rogue and peasant slave am I! . . .

what concerns Shakespeare is to see that the unavoidable anti-climax is at least given some antidote. Rosencrantz's reply to the Queen, that

> certain players
> . . . have already order
> *This night* to play before him.

The Five Acts of the Editors · 201

provides this. It restimulates our interest. The exciting event we are expecting is already nearer. That is the dramatic worth of the statement; the chronology is incidental to it.

For a halt and a pause at the end of what is known as the closet-scene there can, as we said, be no excuse whatever. By a very usual turn of Elizabethan technique one scene simply evolves into another when the characters pass from the inner stage (the closet) to the outer (some antechamber or lobby).[5] And a change in the Folio—made by whatever hand—does but better Shakespeare's main intention, which plainly is to carry forward the action here with as little slackening as possible. It is the King who is driving it ahead; for his purpose is to rid himself of his enemy without delay. And the pulse of the play has never been more feverish, nor Hamlet more beside himself; and he knows he "must to England." If somehow or other hereabouts this now lengthy third act must be brought to an end, the act-divider has but to let pass another hundred and fifty lines. Hamlet by then will be gone, and Claudius gain a breathing-space, and we can be allowed one too.

To complete the customary tale one has now only to find an end for the fourth and as likely a beginning for a fifth act. Our act-divider could hardly have done much better than he does. We hear of Ophelia's death; there is finality in that. The ensnaring of Hamlet has been prepared against his promised return, so that the pause intervening will be an expectant one. And—since the last act is to begin with the Gravediggers—it will give the stage carpenters a good chance to open the grave-trap and make all ready. But, once again, Shakespeare's intentions (though here they may not be grossly thwarted) are falsified. The suspense between the news of Hamlet's return (brought first to Horatio, then to the King) and his actual appearance is fully provided for by the scenes which intervene. And a break in the action here can only weaken the effect of the apposition of the tragic fantasy of Ophelia's madness, the warped cunning of the King's plotting with Laertes, the lyric beauty of the tale of the girl's death on the one hand, and on the other the wholesome prose humor of the Clowns. Hamlet, when he arrives, is, by that colloquy in the graveyard, to point this contrast for us. The simple and the clever, the innocent and the guilty alike all come to the grave—to the plain prose of the grave.

5. "Hamlet in madness hath Polonius slain, / And from his mother's closet hath he dragged him. . . ."—the King tells Rosencrantz and Guildenstern; *i.e.*, from some place other than this in which he now stands speaking. The Elizabethan imagination will have responded the more readily to this changing of place by passing from inner stage to outer since it answered to the disposition of the Elizabethan house, in which one passed, as a rule, directly from room to room, not by a corridor. * * *

But how much more effective the pointing will be if we have also let Shakespeare realize the contrast for us, as he has planned to!

For our own convenience we may make pauses in the performance of the plays. Shakespeare himself had doubtless sometimes to show his audiences that consideration. If he did not at first, the growing length of his maturer work will surely have compelled him to. It would be both a sturdy and a spellbound crowd, indeed, that could—literally, as to about half of them—stand up to an uninterrupted performance of *Hamlet, King Lear* or *Antony and Cleopatra.* But he never ceased to conceive a play as a single organic whole, nor its action as a continuous progress—which a never-halted performance of the shorter *Comedy of Errors, Love's Labour's Lost* or *The Merchant of Venice* could quite well show it to be.[6] And to learn how to minimize our dramatic loss, if we must interrupt a performance here and there, the Procrustean editors should first be forgotten; then the play's natural structure will appear, and divisions can at least be made to conform, as far as possible, to that.[7]

6. I believe this to be essentially true, but subject—as with so much else to be said about his work—to qualification and exception. Among the earlier plays, the exceptional length of *Richard III* is puzzling; among the later, one seems to detect a positive effort to keep *Measure for Measure* and *Othello* within bounds. *Henry V* is definitely divided into acts. *Romeo and Juliet* shows some rudiments of a division by choruses. *A Winter's Tale* is dramatically divided into two parts. It may be hazarded, perhaps, that Shakespeare was indifferent to external form, though as willing to experiment in it—as he was to take a popular subject for the making of a play, or to pay a passing compliment to Elizabeth or James. But he did most eagerly experiment in the expression of the dramatic *ideas* which possessed him.

Another point. In estimating the acting-time of a play one must always consider the nature of the subject and the method of the writing; mere line measurement can be deceptive. *A Comedy of Errors* and *Love's Labour's Lost* will move far more swiftly than *As You Like It* or *Twelfth Night.* *Hamlet* moves at very varying speeds; averaged out, the pace both of *Measure for Measure* and *Coriolanus* will probably be slower. It is likely, again, that any play would then have been acted at a quicker pace than it commonly is today. The verse, and even the prose, would be spoken quicker; first, because the art of speaking was the actor's primary achievement; secondly, because in that age of little reading and much public discourse audiences would be better listeners too.

Yet another. The quickest shifting of the simplest scenes will add, say, half an hour to a quite straightforward "platform" performance of *Antony and Cleopatra.*

7. It is hard to wipe the five-act division clean from one's consciousness. Most modern editions insist on retaining it, with a bare reference, if that, to its unauthenticity. Dover Wilson, in the new Cambridge Shakespeare, relegates it to the margin. That is a gain; and it is no doubt hard to go further, since some system of reference from text to notes and from one edition to another is needed, and this is on all counts the most convenient. The thing is to remember, when one is considering the play aesthetically, that these acts—and sometimes the scenes—have no true existence. The student must constantly have this in mind, or he will find himself still thinking of the play in acts and scenes—and thinking wrong. And it is for this reason that I have—with some difficulty for myself; I hope less for my readers—avoided all reference to acts and numbered scenes in this Preface.

THEODORE SPENCER

Hamlet and the Nature of Reality†

* * *

It is a commonplace of Shakespeare criticism that beginning with *Hamlet* and extending through the great tragedies, we are aware of an increase in scope, an enlargement of dimension, which marks a new stage in Shakespeare's dramatic career. What I should like to do in the present paper is to suggest, by an analysis of *Hamlet*, that this sense of enlargement and depth is partly brought about through an awareness of how the difference between appearance and reality could be used in the creation of dramatic character and situation. But before we come to the play itself, it will be necessary to make an apparent digression.

The average Elizabethan lived in a world very different from ours; a world in which the fundamental assumption was that of hierarchical order. There was a cosmological hierarchy, a political and social hierarchy, and a psychological hierarchy, and each was a reflection of the others. The governing of the state could be seen as an image of the order of the stars, and the order of the stars was reflected in the order of the faculties of man. The Ptolemaic heavens revolved around the earth; and as the sun was the largest and most resplendent of the planets, so the king was the center of the state. Similarly, as the earth was the center of the universe, so justice was the immovable center of political virtue. The cosmological and political orders were reflected in the order of nature: Aristotle had described it in the *De Anima* and elsewhere, and though there might be different interpretations of details, the essentials of the scheme were unhesitatingly accepted. The scale rose from inanimate matter, through the vegetative soul of plants, the sensible soul of animals, the rational soul operating through the body of man, the pure intelligence of angels, up to the pure actuality of God. Man was an essential link in the chain—the necessary mixture of body and soul to complete the order. If man did not exist, it would have been necessary—in fact it *had* been necessary—to invent him. And man was more than this: he was the end for which the rest of the universe had been created. "There

† From the *Journal of English Literary History*, V (December, 1938), 255–71. Copyright © 1938 by the *Journal of* *English Literary History*. Reprinted by permission. This selection is from sections 2 and 3 of the essay.

is nothing," says Raymonde de Sabonde, "in this world which does not work day and night for man's benefit, the universe exists for him, because of him, and was planned and arranged in its marvellous structure for his good."[1] "This heavenly creature whom we call man," writes the English translator of Romei's *Courtier's Academie* (1598), "was compounded of soule and body, the whiche body, having to be the harbour of a most fayre and immortale soule, was created . . . most exquisite, with his eyes toward heaven, and (man) was placed in the midst of the world, to the end that as in an ample theatre, hee might behold and contemplate the workes of the great God, and the beauty of the whole world . . . and therefore man was worthily called a little world, seeing the body of man is no other but a little modell of the sensible world, and his soule an image of the world intelligible."[2] Microcosm and macrocosm alike reflected the glory of the divine architect who had planned so admirable a structure, and it was the chief business of man on earth to study the two books—the book of nature, and the book of the scriptures—which God had given him, so that by knowing the truth, he could know himself, and hence reach some knowledge of the God who had made him.

* * *

So described, the system appears, as indeed it was, not only orderly but optimistic. Yet underneath this tripartite order, of which man was the center, there were, in the sixteenth century, certain disturbing conceptions which painted the scene in different colors. In the first place, the earth could be seen, according to the Ptolomaic system, not only as the center and most important part of the universe, but as exactly the opposite. It could be regarded, to use Professor Lovejoy's words, as "the place farthest removed from the Empyrean, the bottom of the creation, to which its dregs and baser elements sank."[3] Or, as Marston put it, in more Elizabethan language: "This earth is the only grave and Golgotha wherein all things that live must rot; 'tis but the draught wherein the heavenly bodies discharge their corruption; the very muckhill on which the sublunary orbs cast their excrements."[4] In the second place, man, the chief inhabitant of this tiny and remote globe, could be regarded as equally unworthy and corrupt, for since the fall of Adam he had only a faint glimmering of its original gift of

1. I translate from Montaigne's translation of the *Natural Theology*, Chapter 97.
2. Translated by I. K., London, 1598, pp. 16–17.
3. A. O. Lovejoy, *The Great Chain of Being*, Cambridge, Massachusetts, 1936, pp. 101–102. In my opinion, Mr. Lovejoy here exaggerates the prevalence of this more pessimistic view. The other was equally common—probably more so.
4. *The Malcontent*, 4.2.

natural reason, and hence, through his own fault, he was the only creature who had disrupted the system. The miseries of man, as a consequence of this fact, were very heavily emphasized in the sixteenth century by moralists and satirists alike. * * *

Thus, in the inherited, the universally accepted, Christian view of man and his universe there was an implicit conflict between man's dignity and wretchedness * * * This particular conflict, however, no matter how deep it went and no matter how many aspects it presented, could after all be solved; the doctrines of grace and redemption existed for the purpose. But there was another conflict, more particular to the sixteenth century, and, since it was new, perhaps more emotionally and intellectually disturbing. It consisted in this: that in the sixteenth century each one of the interrelated orders—cosmological, political, and natural—which were the frame, the basic pattern, of all Elizabethan thinking, was being punctured by a doubt. Copernicus had questioned the cosmological order, Machiavelli had questioned the political order, Montaigne had questioned the natural order. The consequences were enormous.

In order to understand what the theory of Copernicus implied, it is necessary to have as vivid a picture as possible of the difference between his system and the Aristotelian or Ptolomaic. Upon the structure of the Ptolomaic system, with the earth in the center, everything had been built; the order of creation, astrology, the theory of the microcosm and the macrocosm, the parallels between the universe and the state. But when the sun was put at the center, and the earth set between Mars and Venus as a mobile and subsidiary planet, the whole elaborate structure, with all its interdependencies, so easy to visualize, so convenient for metaphor and allusion, lost its meaning. "If the celestial spheres," said Hooker, "should forget their wonted motions, and by irregular volubility turn themselves any way . . . what would become of man himself, whom all these things do now serve?"[5]

We must, however, as Miss Marjorie Nicolson and others have shown, be on our guard against over-emphasizing the effects of the Copernican theory on the popular mind. It was confronted at first, considering its implications, with remarkably little opposition. * * * Being simpler than the elaborate Ptolomaic system, it was welcomed by mathematicians as an easier means of making astronomical calculations, but it was not until Galileo perfected the telescope that it was seriously considered to be a true description of reality. Even Galileo at first hesitated to support it, not because he feared it would get him into trouble, but because he

5. Quoted by J. B. Black, *The Reign of Elizabeth*, Oxford, 1936, p. 261.

feared it might make him ridiculous. Nothing could show more clearly how strongly the Ptolomaic view was entrenched.

And naturally so. For the whole inherited order depended on it, as Donne was one of the first people to realize. He saw—the lines from the *First Anniversary* are almost too familiar to quote—that the new astronomy not only set the inherited cosmology awry, so that the sun and the earth were lost, it also affected the state, the order of society, and the individual:

> Prince, subject, father, son, are things forgot
> For every man alone thinks he hath got
> To be a phoenix, and that then can be
> None of that kind of which he is, but he.

It broke down the order which Ulysses, in Shakespeare's *Troilus and Cressida* (1, 2) had so admirably expounded, and which so intimately related to each other the planets, the government of states, and the government of the individual. * * *

The ideas of Machiavelli had a different reception from those of Copernicus. Though for about half a generation after *The Prince* was published its views attracted no very remarkable degree of attention, once they were seriously considered the storm broke with what now seems an extraordinary violence. * * *

The reasons for Machiavelli's reputation can perhaps best be realized by comparing *The Prince* with the *De Officiis* of Cicero, just as the effect of the Copernican system can best be seen by comparing it with the Ptolomaic. For the *De Officiis*, as much as the *Politics* of Aristotle, from which it was partly derived, represents the official sixteenth century doctrine. Prudence, justice, liberality, greatness of soul, these and other virtues characterized the public man; the life of reason, in public as in private, implied the pursuit of virtue. All medieval thought said the same thing; it was the basis of political theory, and like the inherited Elizabethan psychology, it was fundamentally optimistic, and it was intimately concerned with morality. But Machiavelli, in the words of J. W. Allen, "thought of the state as a morally isolated thing."[6] He was fundamentally practical. He regarded human history divorced from revelation, and human nature divorced from grace; he looked at man, as Bacon said, not as he should be, but as he is, and he found that man was naturally evil and that the best way to govern him for his own good was by fear and by force. The view may have been sound, but it was outrageous to Elizabethan sensibilities. Was this the truth, underneath the idealistic appearance, about

6. J. W. Allen, *History of Political Thought in the Sixteenth Century*, New York, 1928, p. 477.

man as a political animal? The Elizabethans refused to believe it:
the violence of their feeling on the subject may be taken as an
indication that, below the surface, they realized—with a half-
horrified fascination—that the ideas of Machiavelli, which they
received in so distorted a form, might after all be true.

Montaigne's position is less easy to summarize. But the implication of his ideas, at least those in the *Apology for Raymond
Sebonde*, could be just as devastating to the inherited view of
man's place in the natural sphere as the ideas of Copernicus and
Machiavelli might be to man's place in the spheres of cosmology
and politics. Again this is brought out most clearly by contrast, and
this time we need go no further than the work which Montaigne
was apparently setting out to defend. I know of no book which
more optimistically and thoroughly describes the inherited view of
the order of nature than Sabonde's *Natural Theology*. Its optimism
is, in fact, almost heretical. All the ranks of nature, he says, lead
up to man: his reason sets him apart from all the other animals,
and by a proper use of it he can come to a full knowledge of himself, the external world, and God.

But these are just the assumptions that Montaigne, in his
Apology, sets out to deny. Man can know nothing by himself, says
Montaigne; he cannot know God, he cannot know his soul, he cannot know nature. His senses are hopelessly unreliable, there are no
satisfactory standards of beauty or of anything else, everything is
in a flux, and the only way man can rise from his ignorant and
ignominious position is by divine assistance. His purpose in writing
the essay, says Montaigne, is to make people "sensible of the in-
anity, the vanity, and insignificance of man; to wrest out of their
fists the miserable weapon of their reason; to make them bow
the head and bite the dust under the authority and reverence of
the divine majesty."[7]

Of course all this, though extreme, is neither entirely unorthodox
nor necessarily disturbing. * * * But there was one point—and
it was this that bothered the authorities in Rome (from their point
of view quite rightly), when they examined the *Essais* in 1582—
which was *not* orthodox and which *was* disturbing. Montaigne gave
the appearance of saying that there was no fundamental difference
between the faculties of man and those of animals. His remarks, to
be sure, are highly ambiguous, probably on purpose, but he suggests that animals have the capacity, hitherto and for obvious reasons attributed to man alone, of abstracting from sensible phe-
nomena their essential characteristics, and of making them conform, to use his own words, to the soul's "immortal and spiritual

7. *Essays*, 2, 12, translated by E. J. Trechmann, Oxford, 1927, 1, 439–440.

condition."[8] Such a statement has wide implications; it implies, as Montaigne's whole argument, of which this passage is the climax, tends to imply, that there are no true distinctions between the psychology of man and the psychology of animals; that reason amounts to nothing, and that in consequence the whole hierarchy of nature, at a crucial point, is destroyed.

I hope I have made it clear, through these introductory remarks, that the idea of man which lay behind Shakespearean tragedy was, in the first place, inextricably interwoven with the ideas of the state and the world as a whole to a degree which it is difficult for us to realize, and, in the second place, that this interwoven pattern was threatened by an implicit and an explicit conflict. At the time when Shakespeare wrote *Hamlet* there were available for emotional contemplation and for dramatic representation two views of man's nature, two views of the world, two views of the state. Drama could be not merely the conflict between romantic love and external forces, as in *Romeo and Juliet*; it could represent a conflict far more complicated and far more profound.

* * * The creation of dramatic suspense by an internal conflict in a mind aware of the evil reality under the good appearance is the core of the greatness, the originality of *Hamlet*.

We may best begin our discussion by observing what sort of man Hamlet was before his mother's second marriage. According to Ophelia he had a "noble mind," "the courtier's, soldier's, scholar's, eye, tongue, sword." He was

> The expectancy and rose of the fair state,
> The glass of fashion and the mould of form,

a man with a "noble and most sovereign reason." In other words, he was an ideal Renaissance nobleman, himself an idealist, with —to use Bradley's somewhat romantic expression—"an unbounded delight and faith in everything good and beautiful."

But the discovery of his mother's lust and the fact that the kingdom is in the hands of an unworthy man (Hamlet's—the prince's —feeling that the king is not worthy of his position is a more important part of his state of mind when the play opens than is usually realized)—these facts shatter his picture of the world, the state, and the individual. His sense of the evil in all three spheres is as closely interwoven in his first soliloquy as all three spheres were interwoven in sixteenth century thought. It is characteristic of Shakespeare's conception of Hamlet's universalizing mind that he should make Hamlet think, first, of the general rottenness: to

8. *Essays,* ed. cit. 1, 475.

him all the uses of the world are weary, stale, flat, and unprofitable, and things rank and gross in nature possess it entirely. From this he passes to a consideration of the excellence of his father as king, compared to his satyr-like uncle, and he finally dwells at length on the lustfulness of his mother, who has violated the natural law by the brevity of her grief and the hastiness of her marriage.

> O God! a beast, that wants discourse of reason,
> Would have mourned longer.

In other words, in first presenting Hamlet to his audience, Shakespeare uses an interwoven series of references to the world, the state, and the individual, and one reason this first soliloquy is so broken, its rhythms so panting, is that it reflects Hamlet's disillusionment about all three spheres at once. So closely were they related in contemporary thought that to smash one was to smash the others as well.

This, of course, is not the only place where Hamlet thinks in general terms: one of his most striking habits is to stretch his thought to embrace the world as a whole, to talk of infinite space, to use rhetoric that includes the stars. For example, it is characteristic of him that when he approaches Laertes after Laertes has jumped into Ophelia's grave, he should ask who it is who

> Conjures the wandering stars, and makes them stand
> Like wonder-wounded hearers,

when, as a matter of fact, Laertes had not mentioned the stars at all. It is as if Hamlet were attributing to Laertes a thought that would be natural to him, but not to Laertes. Again, the first thing that Hamlet exclaims after the ghost has given his message is "O all you host of heaven!"; and, in his mother's closet, when he upbraids her with her marriage, he describes it not merely as violating human contracts, but as affecting the world as a whole:

> heaven's face doth glow,
> Yea this solidity and compound mass,
> With tristful visage, as against the doom,
> Is thought-sick at the act.

But the occasion on which Hamlet speaks at greatest length of the heavens is, of course, when he describes his state of mind to Rosencrantz and Guildenstern in the second act. * * * To understand the force of his remarks we should have clearly in our minds the thousand and one sixteenth century repetitions of the old teaching, with which every member of Shakespeare's audience must have been familiar, that the surest way to understand man's place in the world and to realize the magnificence of God's creation, was to contemplate the glory of the superior heavens which surrounded the earth. But what Hamlet says is exactly the opposite.

This most excellent canopy the air, look you, this brave o'erhanging firmament, this majestical roof fretted with golden fire, why, it appeareth nothing to me but a foul and pestilent congregation of vapors.

And from this consideration of the macrocosm he passes at once to the microcosm: the sequence of thought was, in his time, almost inevitable; and again he uses the familiar vocabulary of his age (I follow the punctuation of the second quarto and of Dover Wilson, which alone makes sense in terms of Elizabethan psychology):

What a piece of work is a man, how noble in reason, how infinite in faculties, in form and moving, how express and admirable in action, how like an angel in apprehension, how like a god: the beauty of the world; the paragon of animals; and yet to me, what is this quintessence of dust? Man delights not me.

This use of generalization, which is one of the most attractive and important sides to Hamlet's character, illustrates more than Shakespeare's way of describing a single individual; it also illustrates a dramatic device which Shakespeare frequently used at this period in his career, the device of weaving into the texture of his play a point of view or standard of values which the action is violating, but against which—for the proper understanding of the play—the action must be seen. * * * Hamlet's own remarks about reason, the specific virtue of a human being (which Montaigne had so ingeniously labored to minimize) are a case in point. Horatio speaks (1, 4, 73) of the "sovereignty of reason," as does Ophelia, but Hamlet, as is eminently appropriate in a play where the conflict is so much inside a man, is the one who describes the traditional view most fully (4, 4, 33):

> What is a man,
> If his chief good and market of his time
> Be but to sleep and feed? a beast, no more.
> Sure he that made us with such large discourse,
> Looking before and after, gave us not
> That capability and god-like reason
> To fust in us unus'd.

It is worth observing in what terms Shakespeare speaks of reason in the important passages throughout the play. Reason, the specific function of man in the order of nature, is twice referred to as "noble," an adjective, like "sovereign" (also applied to reason), that has connotations in the political order, and, in the passage I have just quoted, it is described as "god-like," an adjective that, to an Elizabethan would have cosmological connotations as well. It may not be fantastic to see, in this adjectival microcosm, an image of the macrocosm I have been trying to define.

At all events, the standard which Hamlet's soliloquy describes is not only the standard which his own behavior violates; it is also the standard which was violated by Gertrude in mourning so briefly for her first husband, and in unnaturally yielding to her lust, so that her reason, in Hamlet's words, has become a pandar to her will, her fleshly desire. In both cases, the appearance, the accepted natural order of good and of the supremacy of reason, is destroyed by the individual reality of evil, and man has sunk to the level of animals, his specific function gone.

The same dramatic device is just as clearly apparent in relation to kingship as it is to cosmology and psychology. Throughout the play there is an emphasis (a direct reflection of contemporary views) on the importance of the king in relation to the state. In this case it is Rosencrantz and Guildenstern, appropriately external figures, who, in an important scene that is often unnoticed, state the accepted ideal most fully (3, 3, 9 ff.).

> *Guildenstern:* Most holy and religious fear it is
> To keep those many many bodies safe
> That live and feed upon your majesty.

> *Rosencrantz:* The single and peculiar life is bound
> With all the strength and armour of the mind
> To keep itself from noyance; but much more
> That spirit upon whose weal depend and rest
> The lives of many. The cease of majesty
> Dies not alone, but, like a gulf doth draw
> What's near it with it; it is a massy wheel,
> Fix'd on the summit of the highest mount,
> To whose huge spokes ten thousand lesser things
> Are mortis'd and adjoin'd; which when it falls,
> Each small annexment, petty consequence,
> Attends the boisterous ruin. Never alone
> Did the king sigh, but with a general groan.

As we hear these lines, set almost in the middle of the play, they appear like a reflective, chorus-like comment on all that has gone before. Hamlet himself is described by Laertes in the same terms in which Rosencrantz describes Claudius. Laertes (1, 3, 19 ff.) tells Ophelia that Hamlet

> may not, as unvalu'd persons do
> Carve for himself, for on his choice depends

> The safety and the health of the whole state;
> And therefore must his choice be circumscrib'd
> Unto the voice and yielding of that body
> Whereof he is the head.

* * *

This speech of Laertes shows, in addition, how careful Shakespeare is, from the very beginning of the play, to emphasize the political side of the action. Much state business is transacted before the king, in the second scene of the first act, finally turns to the particular problem of Hamlet's melancholy: Shakespeare deliberately puts Hamlet's situation in a political environment. This not only increases the scope of the play, it also emphasizes the dramatic conflict. For from whatever side we regard the action there is something politically wrong. From Claudius' point of view it is bad for the state to have a disaffected heir, particularly since he is so much loved by the multitude. From Hamlet's point of view it is abominable to have an unworthy and lustful king. And the appearance of the ghost emphasizes in more general terms our sense of uneasiness about the condition of the state. It bodes, says Horatio (1, 1, 69), "some strange eruption to our state," Hamlet emphasizes the fact that the ghost is armed (1, 3, 224), and the armour implies that the ghost has more than a private purpose in showing himself. No wonder Marcellus says that there is something rotten in the *state* of Denmark. He, and the king, and the ghost, reinforce Hamlet's feelings about the situation, and the speeches of Rosencrantz and Laertes on kingship apply not only to an immediate necessity but also to the importance of kingship itself, and hence they emphasize the enormity of Claudius' previous action in murdering his kingly brother. Again, it is worth remembering the strength of Hamlet's feeling about his uncle's unworthiness as a king—a feeling that shocks (as Hamlet means it to do) the conventional Guildenstern (4, 2, 24):

> *Hamlet:*   The king is a thing—
> *Gildenstern:* A thing, my lord!

Hamlet's description of the king is much stronger elsewhere: he is the "bloat king"—a "king of shreds and patches"—and Hamlet's tendency to generalization surrounds the notion of kingship as it surrounds all his thoughts—

> Imperious Caesar, dead and turned to clay,
> Might stop a hole to keep the wind away.

A king may go a progress through the guts of a beggar: the illusion of kingly power is not the reality; nothing is but thinking makes it so. What is true of the king, of the queen, is true of all human nature—"to be honest, as this world goes, is to be one man picked out of ten thousand." "I am very proud, revengeful, ambitious; with more offenses at my back than I have thoughts to put them in, imagination to give them shape, or time to act them in. What should such fellows as I do crawling between heaven and earth? We are arrant knaves, all." The discovery of individual evil, and the inevitable generalizations, once granted Shakespeare's conception of Hamlet's character, that follow upon it, almost crack his comprehension: cruelty to the innocent Ophelia, expressed again in generalization, is one of the consequences.

In fact, the way Hamlet treats Ophelia, like the way he treats love in general, is a further striking example of Shakespeare's handling of the contrast between appearance and truth. For here too there is an ideal in the background against which the present reality seems coarse and vile. The relation between Hamlet's mother and father had been perfect: he was as fine a husband as he had been a king, his

> love was of that dignity
> That it went hand in hand even with the vow
> (He) made to her in marriage;

he was, says Hamlet,

> so loving to my mother
> That he might not beteem the winds of heaven
> Visit her face too roughly.

But this ideal, an ideal as deeply imbedded in the sixteenth century mind as the ideals of kingship and human reason, is, of course, violated by Gertrude's marriage to Claudius, and Hamlet throughout the play can think of the relation between the sexes only in the coarsest terms. "What shall I do?" the queen asks Hamlet; and he replies:

> Not this, by no means, that I bid you do:
> Let the bloat king tempt you again to bed;
> Pinch wanton on your cheek; call you his mouse;
> And let him, for a pair of reechy kisses,
> Or paddling in your neck with his damned fingers,
> Make you to ravel all this matter out.

It is in this style that Hamlet talks to Ophelia, torturing them both, and the innocent Ophelia herself, in delirium, sings songs at which her courtly sanity would have blushed.

This sense of the reality of evil—in the cosmos, in the state, and in man,—this enlargement of dramatic dimension by significant generalization, this use (not, of course, entirely conscious) of one of the essential conflicts of the age, is what helps to make *Hamlet* so large an organism, and to give it, as the expression of a universal situation, so profound a set of reverberations. Hamlet's disillusionment is a partial expression of a general predicament; the emotions he gives voice to were shared in his own time and have been shared ever since, by many people less miraculously articulate than himself. His discovery of the difference between appearance and reality, which produced in his mind an effect so disillusioning that it paralyzed the sources of deliberate action, was a symptom that the Renaissance in general had brought with it a new set of problems, had opened new psychological vistas, which the earlier views of man had not explored. * * *

C. S. LEWIS

Hamlet: The Prince or the Poem?†

* * * The Hamlet formula, so to speak, is not 'a man who has to avenge his father' but 'a man who has been given a task by a ghost.' Everything else about him is less important than that. If the play did not begin with the cold and darkness and sickening suspense of the ghost scenes it would be a radically different play. If, on the other hand, only the first act had survived, we should have a very tolerable notion of the play's peculiar quality. * * *

This ghost is different from any other ghost in Elizabethan drama—for, to tell the truth, the Elizabethans in general do their ghosts very vilely. It is permanently ambiguous. Indeed the very word 'ghost,' by putting it into the same class with the 'ghosts' of Kyd and Chapman, nay by classifying it at all, puts us on the wrong track. It is 'this thing,' 'this dreaded sight,' an 'illusion,' a 'spirit of health or goblin dam'nd,' liable at any moment to assume 'some other horrible form' which reason could not survive the vision of. Critics have disputed whether Hamlet is sincere when he doubts whether the apparition is his father's ghost or not. I take him to be perfectly sincere. He believes while the thing is present: he doubts when it is away. Doubt, uncertainty, bewilderment to almost any degree, is what the ghost creates not only in Hamlet's mind but in the minds of the other characters. Shake-

† From *Proceedings of the British Academy* (London: Oxford University Press, 1942), XXVIII, 147–52. Copy-

speare does not take the concept of 'ghost' for granted, as other dramatists had done. In his play the appearance of the spectre means a breaking down of the walls of the world and the germination of thoughts that cannot really be thought: chaos is come again.

* * * I have started with the ghost because the ghost appears at the beginning of the play not only to give Hamlet necessary information but also, and even more, to strike the note. From the platform we pass to the court scene and so to Hamlet's first long speech. There are ten lines of it before we reach what is necessary to the plot: lines about the melting of flesh into a dew and the divine prohibition of self-slaughter. We have a second ghost scene after which the play itself, rather than the hero, goes mad for some minutes. We have a second soliloquy on the theme 'to die . . . to sleep'; and a third on 'the witching time of night, when churchyards yawn.' We have the King's effort to pray and Hamlet's comment on it. We have the ghost's third appearance. Ophelia goes mad and is drowned. Then comes the comic relief, surely the strangest comic relief ever written—comic relief beside an open grave, with a further discussion of suicide, a detailed inquiry into the rate of decomposition, a few clutches of skulls, and then 'Alas, poor Yorick!' On top of this, the hideous fighting in the grave; and then, soon, the catastrophe.

* * * The subject of *Hamlet* is death. I do not mean by this that most of the characters die, nor even that life and death are the stakes they play for; that is true of all tragedies. I do not mean that we rise from the reading of the play with the feeling that we have been in cold, empty places, places 'outside,' *nocte tacentia late*, though that is true. * * *

The sense in which death is the subject of *Hamlet* will become apparent if we compare it with other plays. Macbeth has commerce with Hell, but at the very outset of his career dismisses all thought of the life to come. For Brutus and Othello, suicide in the high tragic manner is escape and climax. For Lear death is deliverance. For Romeo and Antony, poignant loss. For all these, as for their author while he writes and the audience while they watch, death is the end: it is almost the frame of the picture. They think of dying: no one thinks, in these plays, of *being dead*. In *Hamlet* we are kept thinking about it all the time, whether in terms of the soul's destiny or of the body's. Purgatory, Hell, Heaven, the wounded name, the rights—or wrongs—of Ophelia's burial, and the staying-power of a tanner's corpse: and beyond this, beyond all Christian and all Pagan maps of the hereafter, comes a curious groping and tapping of thoughts, about 'what dreams may come.' It is this that gives to the whole play its quality of darkness and of misgiving. Of course there is much else in the play: but nearly always, the same groping. The characters are all watching one another, forming theories about one another, listening, contriving, full of anxiety. The world of *Hamlet* is a world where one has lost one's way. The Prince also has no doubt lost his, and we can tell the precise moment at which he finds it again. 'Not a whit. We defy augury. There's a special providence in the fall of a sparrow. If it be now, 'tis not to come: if it be not to come, it will be now: if it be not now, yet it will come: the readiness is all: since no man has aught of what he leaves, what is't to leave betimes?'[1]

If I wanted to make one more addition to the gallery of Hamlet's portraits I should trace his hesitation to the fear of death; not to a physical fear of dying, but a fear of being dead. And I think I should get on quite comfortably. Any serious attention to the state of being dead, unless it is limited by some definite religious or anti-religious doctrine, must, I suppose, paralyse the will by introducing infinite uncertainties and rendering all motives inadequate. Being dead is the unknown *x* in our sum. Unless you ignore it or else give it a value, you can get no answer. But this is not what I am going to do. Shakespeare has not left in the text clear lines of causation which would enable us to connect Hamlet's hesitations with this source. I do not believe he has given us data for any portrait of the kind critics have tried to draw. * * *

For what, after all, is happening to us when we read any of Hamlet's great speeches? We see visions of the flesh dissolving into a dew, of the world like an unweeded garden. We think of memory reeling in its 'distracted globe.' We watch him scampering hither and thither like a maniac to avoid the voices wherewith he is haunted. Someone says 'Walk out of the air,' and we hear the words 'Into my grave' spontaneously respond to it. We think of being bounded in a nut-shell and king of infinite space: but for bad dreams. There's the trouble, for 'I am most dreadfully attended.' We see the picture of a dull and muddy-mettled rascal, a John-a-dreams, somehow unable to move while ultimate dishonour is done him. We listen to his fear lest the whole thing may be an illusion due to melancholy. We get the sense of sweet relief at the words 'shuffled off this mortal coil' but mixed with the bottomless doubt about what may follow then. We think of bones and skulls, of women breeding sinners, and of how some, to whom all this

---

1. I think the last clause is best explained by the assumption that Shakespeare had come across Seneca's *Nihil* *perdis ex tuo tempore, nam quod relinquis alienum est* (Epist. lxix).

experience is a sealed book, can yet dare death and danger 'for an egg-shell.' But do we really enjoy these things, do we go back to them, because they show us Hamlet's character? Are they, from *that* point of view, so very interesting? Does the mere fact that a young man, literally haunted, dispossessed, and lacking friends, should feel thus, tell us anything remarkable? Let me put my question in another way. If instead of the speeches he actually utters about the firmament and man in his scene with Rosencrantz and Guildenstern Hamlet had merely said, 'I don't seem to enjoy things the way I used to,' and talked in that fashion throughout, should we find him interesting? I think the answer is 'Not very.' It may be replied that if he talked commonplace prose he would reveal his character less vividly. I am not so sure. He would certainly have revealed *something* less vividly; but would that something be himself? It seems to me that 'this majestical roof' and 'What a piece of work is a man' give me primarily an impression not of the sort of person he must be to lose the estimation of things but of the things themselves and their great value; and that I should be able to discern, though with very faint interest, the same condition of loss in a personage who was quite unable so to put before me what he was losing. And I do not think it true to reply that he would be a different character if he spoke less poetically. This point is often misunderstood. We sometimes speak as if the characters in whose mouths Shakespeare puts great poetry were poets: in the sense that Shakespeare was depicting men of poetical genius. But surely this is like thinking that Wagner's Wotan is the dramatic portrait of a baritone? In opera song is the medium by which the representation is made and not part of the thing represented. The actors sing; the dramatic personages are feigned to be speaking. The only character who sings dramatically in *Figaro* is Cherubino. Similarly in poetical drama poetry is the medium, not part of the delineated characters. While the actors speak poetry written for them by the poet, the dramatic personages are supposed to be merely talking. If ever there is occasion to *represent* poetry (as in the play scene from *Hamlet*), it is put into a different metre and strongly stylized so as to prevent confusion.

I trust that my conception is now becoming clear. I believe that we read Hamlet's speeches with interest chiefly because they describe so well a certain spiritual region through which most of us have passed and anyone in his circumstances might be expected to pass, rather than because of our concern to understand how and why this particular man entered it. I foresee an objection on the ground that I am thus really admitting his 'character' in the only sense that matters and that all characters whatever could be equally well talked away by the method I have adopted. But I do really find a distinction. When I read about Mrs. Proudie I am not in the least interested in seeing the world from her point of view, for her point of view is not interesting; what does interest me is precisely the sort of person she was. In *Middlemarch* no reader wants to see Casaubon through Dorothea's eyes; the pathos, the comedy, the value of the whole thing is to understand Dorothea and see how such an illusion was inevitable for her. In Shakespeare himself I find Beatrice to be a character who could not be thus dissolved. We are interested not in some vision seen through her eyes, but precisely in the wonder of her being the girl she is. A comparison of the sayings we remember from her part with those we remember from Hamlet's brings out the contrast. On the one hand, 'I wonder that you will still be talking, Signior Benedick,' 'There was a star danced and under that I was born,' 'Kill Claudio'; on the other, 'The undiscovered country from whose bourne no traveller returns,' 'Use every man after his desert, and who should 'scape whipping?', 'The rest is silence.' Particularly noticeable is the passage where Hamlet professes to be describing his own character. 'I am myself indifferent honest: but yet I could accuse me of such things that it were better my mother had not borne me. I am very proud, revengeful, ambitious.' It is, of course, possible to devise some theory which explains these self-accusations in terms of character. But long before we have done so the real significance of the lines has taken possession of our imagination for ever. 'Such fellows as I' does not mean 'such fellows as Goethe's Hamlet, or Coleridge's Hamlet, or any Hamlet': it means *men*— creatures shapen in sin and conceived in iniquity—and the vast, empty vision of them 'crawling between earth and heaven' is what really counts and really carries the burden of the play.

* * *

ERNEST JONES

Tragedy and the Mind of the Infant†

* * *

As a child Hamlet had experienced the warmest affection for his mother, and this, as is always so, had contained elements of a

† From *Hamlet and Oedipus* (New York: W. W. Norton & Company, Inc.), pp. 80–91. Copyright © 1949 by Ernest Jones. Reprinted by permission of the publisher, Mrs. Katherine Jones and the Hogarth Press, Ltd.

disguised erotic quality, still more so in infancy. The presence of two traits in the Queen's character accord with this assumption, namely her markedly sensual nature and her passionate fondness for her son. The former is indicated in too many places in the play to need specific reference, and is generally recognized. The latter is also manifest: Claudius says, for instance (Act IV, Sc. 7), "The Queen his mother lives almost by his looks". Nevertheless Hamlet appears to have with more or less success weaned himself from her and to have fallen in love with Ophelia. The precise nature of his original feeling for Ophelia is a little obscure. We may assume that at least in part it was composed of a normal love for a prospective bride, though the extravagance of the language used (the passionate need for absolute certainty, etc.) suggests a somewhat morbid frame of mind. There are indications that even here the influence of the old attraction for the mother is still exerting itself. Although some writers, following Goethe, see in Ophelia many traits of resemblance to the Queen, perhaps just as striking are the traits contrasting with those of the Queen. Whatever truths there may be in the many German conceptions of Ophelia as a sensual wanton * * * still the very fact that it needed what Goethe happily called the "innocence of insanity" to reveal the presence of any such libidinous thoughts demonstrates in itself the modesty and chasteness of her habitual demeanour. Her naïve piety, her obedient resignation, and her unreflecting simplicity sharply contrast with the Queen's character, and seem to indicate that Hamlet by a characteristic reaction towards the opposite extreme had unknowingly been impelled to choose a woman who should least remind him of his mother. A case might even be made out for the view that part of his courtship originated not so much in direct attraction for Ophelia as in an unconscious desire to play her off against his mother, just as a disappointed and piqued lover so often has resort to the arms of a more willing rival. It would not be easy otherwise to understand the readiness with which he later throws himself into this part. When, for instance, in the play scene he replies to his mother's request to sit by her with the words "No, good mother, here's metal more attractive" and proceeds to lie at Ophelia's feet, we seem to have a direct indication of his attitude; and his coarse familiarity and bandying of ambiguous jests with the woman he has recently so ruthlessly jilted are hardly intelligible unless we bear in mind that they were carried out under the heedful gaze of the Queen. It is as if his unconscious were trying to convey to her the following thought: "You give yourself to other men whom you prefer to me. Let me assure you that I can dispense with your favours and even prefer those of a woman whom I no longer love." His extraordinary outburst of bawdiness on this occasion, so unexpected in a man of obviously fine feeling, points unequivocally to the sexual nature of the underlying turmoil.

Now comes the father's death and the mother's second marriage. The association of the idea of sexuality with his mother, buried since infancy, can no longer be concealed from his consciousness. As Bradley well says: "Her son was forced to see in her action not only an astounding shallowness of feeling, but an eruption of coarse sensuality, 'rank and gross,' speeding post-haste to its horrible delight". Feelings which once, in the infancy of long ago, were pleasurable desires can now, because of his repressions, only fill him with repulsion. The long "repressed" desire to take his father's place in his mother's affection is stimulated to unconscious activity by the sight of someone usurping this place exactly as he himself had once longed to do. More, this someone was a member of the same family, so that the actual usurpation further resembled the imaginary one in being incestuous. Without his being in the least aware of it these ancient desires are ringing in his mind, are once more struggling to find conscious expression, and need such an expenditure of energy again to "repress" them that he is reduced to the deplorable mental state he himself so vividly depicts.

There follows the Ghost's announcement that the father's death was a willed one, was due to murder. Hamlet, having at the moment his mind filled with natural indignation at the news, answers normally enough with the cry (Act I, Sc. 5):

> Haste me to know't, that I with wings as swift
> As meditation or the thoughts of love,
> May sweep to my revenge.

The momentous words follow revealing who was the guilty person, namely a relative who had committed the deed at the bidding of lust.[1] Hamlet's second guilty wish had thus also been realized by his uncle, namely to procure the fulfilment of the first—the possession of the mother—by a personal deed, in fact by murder of the father. The two recent events, the father's death and the mother's second marriage, seemed to the world to have no inner causal relation to each other, but they represented ideas which in Hamlet's unconscious fantasy had always been closely associated. These ideas now in a moment forced their way to conscious recognition in spite of all "repressing forces", and found immediate expression in his almost reflex cry: "O my prophetic

1. It is not maintained that this was by any means Claudius' whole motive, but it was evidently a powerful one and the one that most impressed Hamlet.

soul! My uncle?" The frightful truth his unconscious had already intuitively divined, his consciousness had now to assimilate as best it could. For the rest of the interview Hamlet is stunned by the effect of the internal conflict thus re-awakened, which from now on never ceases, and into the essential nature of which he never penetrates.

One of the first manifestations of the awakening of the old conflict in Hamlet's mind is his reaction against Ophelia. This is doubly conditioned by the two opposing attitudes in his own mind. In the first place, there is a complex reaction in regard to his mother. As was explained above, the being forced to connect the thought of his mother with sensuality leads to an intense sexual revulsion, one that is only temporarily broken down by the coarse outburst discussed above. Combined with this is a fierce jealousy, unconscious because of its forbidden origin, at the sight of her giving herself to another man, a man whom he had no reason whatever either to love or to respect. Consciously this is allowed to express itself, for instance after the prayer scene, only in the form of extreme resentment and bitter reproaches against her. His resentment against women is still further inflamed by the hypocritical prudishness with which Ophelia follows her father and brother in seeing evil in his natural affection, an attitude which poisons his love in exactly the same way that the love of his childhood, like that of all children, must have been poisoned. He can forgive a woman neither her rejection of his sexual advances nor, still less, her alliance with another man. Most intolerable of all to him, as Bradley well remarks, is the sight of sensuality in a quarter from which he had trained himself ever since infancy rigorously to exclude it. The total reaction culminates in the bitter misogyny of his outburst against Ophelia, who is devastated at having to bear a reaction so wholly out of proportion to her own offence and has no idea that in reviling her Hamlet is really expressing his bitter resentment against his mother.[2] "I have heard of your paintings too, well enough; God has given you one face, and you make yourselves another; you jig, you amble, and you lisp, and nickname God's creatures, and make your wantonness your ignorance. Go to, I'll no more on 't; it hath made me mad" (Act III, Sc. 1). On only one occasion does he for a moment escape from the sordid implication with which his love

2. His similar tone and advice to the two women show plainly how closely they are identified in his mind. Cp. "Get thee to a nunnery: why wouldst thou be a breeder of sinners?" (Act III, Sc. 2) with "Refrain to-night; And that shall lend a kind of easiness To the next abstinence" (Act III, Sc. 4).

The identification is further demonstrated in the course of the play by Hamlet's killing the men who stand between him and these women (Claudius and Polonius).

has been impregnated and achieve a healthier attitude towards Ophelia, namely at the open grave when in remorse he breaks out at Laertes for presuming to pretend that his feeling for her could ever equal that of her lover. Even here, however, as Dover Wilson has suggested, the remorse behind his exaggerated behaviour springs not so much from grief at Ophelia's death as from his distress at his bad conscience that had killed his love—he acts the lover he fain would have been.

Hamlet's attitude towards Ophelia is still more complex. Dover Wilson has adduced good evidence for thinking that Hamlet is supposed to have overheard the intrigue in which Polonius "looses" his daughter to test her erstwhile lover, a suggestion which had previously been made by Quincy Adams. This is probably an echo of the old (Saxo) saga in which the girl is employed by the king to test his capacity for sexual love and so decide whether he is an imbecile or a cunning enemy. It certainly helps to explain the violence with which he attacks her feminine charms and treats her worse than a paid prostitute. He feels she is sent to lure him on and then, like his mother, to betray him at the behest of another man. The words "Get thee to a nunnery"[3] thus have a more sinister connotation, for in Elizabethan, and indeed in later, times this was also a term for a brothel; the name "Covent Garden" will elucidate the point to any student of the history of London.

The underlying theme relates ultimately to the splitting of the mother image which the infantile unconscious effects into two opposite pictures: one of a virginal Madonna, an inaccessible saint towards whom all sensual approaches are unthinkable, and the other of a sensual creature accessible to everyone. Indications of this dichotomy between love and lust (Titian's Sacred and Profane Love) are to be found later in most men's sexual experiences. When sexual repression is highly pronounced, as with Hamlet, then both types of women are felt to be hostile: the pure one out of resentment at her repulses, the sensual one out of the temptation she offers to plunge into guiltiness. Misogyny, as in the play, is the inevitable result.

The intensity of Hamlet's repulsion against woman in general, and Ophelia in particular, is a measure of the powerful "repression" to which his sexual feelings are being subjected. The outlet for those feelings in the direction of his mother has always been firmly dammed, and now that the narrower channel in Ophelia's direction has also been closed the increase in the original direction

---

3. This exhortation (with its usual connotation of chastity) may be equated with the one addressed later to his mother, "Go not to my uncle's bed", indicating Hamlet's identification of the two women in his feelings.

consequent on the awakening of early memories tasks all his energy to maintain the "repression". His pent-up feelings find a partial vent in other directions. The petulant irascibility and explosive outbursts called forth by his vexation at the hands of Guildenstern and Rosencrantz, and especially of Polonius, are evidently to be interpreted in this way, as also is in part the burning nature of his reproaches to his mother. Indeed, towards the end of his interview with his mother the thought of her misconduct expresses itself in that almost physical disgust which is so characteristic a manifestation of intensely "repressed" sexual feeling.

> Let the bloat king tempt you again to bed,
> Pinch wanton on your cheek, call you his mouse,
> And let him for a pair of reechy kisses,
> Or paddling in your neck with his damn'd fingers,
> Make you to ravel all this matter out   (Act III, Sc. 4)

Hamlet's attitude towards Polonius is highly instructive. Here the absence of family tie and of other similar influences enables him to indulge to a relatively unrestrained extent his hostility towards what he regards as a prating and sententious dotard.[4] The analogy he effects between Polonius and Jephthah is in this connection especially pointed. It is here that we see his fundamental attitude towards moralizing elders who use their power to thwart the happiness of the young, and not in the over-drawn and melodramatic portrait in which he delineates his father: "A combination and a form indeed, where every god did seem to set his seal to give the world assurance of a man".

It will be seen from the foregoing that Hamlet's attitude towards his uncle-father is far more complex than is generally supposed. He of course detests him, but it is the jealous detestation of one evil-doer towards his successful fellow. Much as he hates him, he can never denounce him with the ardent indignation that boils straight from his blood when he reproaches his mother, for the more vigorously he denounces his uncle the more powerfully does he stimulate to activity his own unconscious and "repressed" complexes. He is therefore in a dilemma between on the one hand allowing his natural detestation of his uncle to have free play, a consummation which would stir still further his own horrible wishes, and on the other hand ignoring the imperative call for the vengeance that his obvious duty demands. His own "evil"

---

4. It is noteworthy how many producers and actors seem to accept Hamlet's distorted estimate of Polonius, his garrulity being presumably an excuse for overlooking the shrewdness and soundness of his worldly wisdom. After all, his diagnosis of Hamlet's madness as being due to unrequited love for Ophelia was not so far from the mark, and he certainly recognized that his distressful condition was of sexual origin.

prevents him from completely denouncing his uncle's, and in continuing to "repress" the former he must strive to ignore, to condone, and if possible even to forget the latter; *his moral fate is bound up with his uncle's for good or ill.* In reality his uncle incorporates the deepest and most buried part of his own personality, so that he cannot kill him without also killing himself. This solution, one closely akin to what Freud has shown to be the motive of suicide in melancholia, is actually the one that Hamlet finally adopts. The course of alternate action and inaction that he embarks on, and the provocations he gives to his suspicious uncle, can lead to no other end than to his own ruin and, incidentally, to that of his uncle. Only when he has made the final sacrifice and brought himself to the door of death is he free to fulfil his duty, to avenge his father, and to slay his other self— his uncle.

There are two moments in the play when he is nearest to murder, and it is noteworthy that in both the impulse has been dissociated from the unbearable idea of incest. The second is of course when he actually kills the King, when the Queen is already dead and lost to him for ever, so that his conscience is free of an ulterior motive for the murder. The first is more interesting. It is clear that Hamlet is a creature of highly charged imagination; Vischer, for instance, quite rightly termed him a "Phantasiemensch". As is known, the danger then is that phantasy may on occasion replace reality. Now Otto Rank, who uses the same term, has plausibly suggested that the emotionally charged play scene, where a nephew kills his uncle(!), and when there is no talk of adultery or incest, is in Hamlet's imagination an equivalent for fulfilling his task.[5] It is easier to kill the King when there is no ulterior motive behind it, no talk of mother or incest. When the play is over he is carried away in exultation as if he had really killed the King himself, whereas all he has actually done is to warn him and so impel him to sign a death warrant. That his pretext for arranging the play—to satisfy himself about Claudius' guilt and the Ghost's honesty—is specious is plain from the fact that *before* it he had been convinced of both and was reproaching himself for his neglect. When he then comes on the King praying, and so to speak finds him surprisingly still alive, he realizes that his task is still in front of him, but can only say "Now *might* I do

5. There is a delicate point here which may appeal only to psychoanalysts. It is known that the occurrence of a dream within a dream (when one dreams that one is dreaming) is always found when analysed to refer to a theme which the person wishes were "only a dream", i.e. not true. I would suggest that a similar meaning attaches to a "play within a play", as in "Hamlet". So Hamlet (as nephew) can kill the King in his imagination since it is "only a play" or "only in play".

it" (not "will"). He then expresses openly the unconscious thoughts of his infancy—the wish to kill the man who is lying with his mother ("in th' incestuous pleasure of his bed")—but he knows only too well that his own guilty motive for doing so would always prevent him. So there is no way out of the dilemma, and he blunders on to destruction.

The call of duty to kill his stepfather cannot be obeyed because it links itself with the unconscious call of his nature to kill his mother's husband, whether this is the first or the second; the absolute "repression" of the former impulse involves the inner prohibition of the latter also. It is no chance that Hamlet says of himself that he is prompted to his revenge "by heaven and hell".

In this discussion of the motives that move or restrain Hamlet we have purposely depreciated the subsidiary ones—such as his exclusion from the throne where Claudius has blocked the normal solution of the Oedipus complex (to succeed the father in due course)—which also play a part, so as to bring out in greater relief the deeper and effective ones that are of preponderating importance. These, as we have seen, spring from sources of which he is quite unaware, and we might summarize the internal conflict of which he is the victim as consisting in a struggle of the "repressed" mental processes to become conscious. The call of duty, which automatically arouses to activity these unconscious processes, conflicts with the necessity of "repressing" them still more strongly; for the more urgent is the need for external action the greater is the effort demanded of the "repressing" forces. It is his moral duty, to which his father exhorts him, to put an end to the incestuous activities of his mother (by killing Claudius), but his unconscious does not want to put an end to them (he being identified with Claudius in the situation), and so he cannot. His lashings of self-reproach and remorse are ultimately because of this very failure, i.e. the refusal of his guilty wishes to undo the sin. By refusing to abandon his own incestuous wishes he perpetuates the sin and so must endure the stings of torturing conscience. And yet killing his mother's husband would be equivalent to committing the original sin himself, which would if anything be even more guilty. So of the two impossible alternatives he adopts the passive solution of letting the incest continue vicariously, but at the same time provoking destruction at the King's hand. Was ever a tragic figure so torn and tortured!

Action is paralysed at its very inception, and there is thus produced the picture of apparently causeless inhibition which is so inexplicable both to Hamlet and to readers of the play. This paralysis arises, however, not from physical or moral cowardice, but from that intellectual cowardice, that reluctance to dare the exploration of his inmost soul, which Hamlet shares with the rest of the human race. "Thus conscience does make cowards of us all."

HARRY LEVIN

An Explication of the Player's Speech†

I

The text before us [II.ii.446–512] is a purple passage, not because it has been admired, but because it stands out from the rest of the play. On the whole it has aroused, in Shakespearean commentators, less admiration than curiosity and less curiosity than bewilderment. Some of them, like Polonius, have been quite frankly bored with it; many of them, unlike Hamlet himself, have considered it highly bombastic. Those who discern the hand of another playwright, whenever Shakespeare's writing presents a problem, have fathered it upon Marlowe, Chapman, Kyd, and even unlikelier authors. Others, hesitating to assume that Shakespeare would cite a fellow playwright at such length, have interpreted the speech as parody or satire—although who is being parodied, or what is being satirized, or how or why, is again a matter of diverging opinion. Still others have explained the incongruity, between these high-pitched lines and the ordinary dialogue, by assuming that Shakespeare had taken occasion to foist upon his patient audience a fragment of his earlier journeywork. * * * More rigorous scholarship tends to support the integrity of Shakespeare's text, just as more perceptive criticism emphasizes the consciousness of his artistry. Appealing to the authority of Sir Edmund Chambers, as well as to the insight of A. C. Bradley, we can proceed from the assumption that the passage at hand is both authentic and advised. But is it well advised? is it really significant? and what, if so, does it signify?

We can scarcely become aware of its significance without some preliminary awareness of its context: not only the intrinsic place that it occupies within the dramatic economy of *Hamlet*, but the stream of extrinsic associations that it carries along with it into

† From *The Question of Hamlet*, by Harry Levin (New York: Oxford University Press, 1959), pp. 141–62. Copyright © 1959 by Oxford University Press, Inc. Reprinted by permission.

the drama. The player who, at Hamlet's request, gives us this demonstration of his professional skill, this 'taste' of his 'quality,' is cast in a functional role; for in the next act he and his fellows are destined to perform the play that will 'catch the conscience of the King.' Meanwhile Shakespeare, who seldom misses an opportunity to talk about his craft, indulges in two of his fullest discussions on the theater. These are often regarded as digressions, and one of them is usually cut on the stage. * * * But Goethe, who took a producer's point of view, saw how that 'passionate speech' served a psychological purpose by planting the suggestion in Hamlet's mind that leads to his experiment upon Claudius. And the late Harley Granville-Barker, perhaps the most pragmatic of all Shakespeareans, observed that the name of Hecuba was not only a necessary link between the First Player's scene and Hamlet's ensuing soliloquy, but also an implicit commentary on the Queen. To underline that observation: if the Player is nothing to Hecuba, or she to him, it follows *a fortiori* that Hamlet should feel and show a much deeper grief, and that Gertrude has failed abysmally to live up to the standard of royal motherhood.

* * * By requesting the account of 'Priam's slaughter' as it was told in 'Aeneas' tale to Dido,' Hamlet refers us to what might be called the official version: the retrospective story that Vergil tells in the second book of his *Aeneid* (506–58). * * * Further and closer scrutiny of Shakespeare's treatment reveals that—although he elaborated a few small Vergilian details, such as the useless sword (*'inutile ferrum'*)—he is actually less indebted to Vergil than to his favorite among the Latin poets, Ovid. * * *

In shifting his attention from Priam to Hecuba, and his source from Vergil to Ovid, Shakespeare turns from the sphere of the epic to the lyric, and from events to emotions. It is Ovid, too, who inspires his final appeal to the gods themselves: '. . . *illius fortuna deos quoque moveret omnes.*' But the lyrical note can prevail no more than the epical, since Shakespeare's form is basically tragic. * * * The tone of [the Player's] speech is that of the *nuntius*, the Senecan messenger who enters to make a morbidly protracted recital of bad news from offstage—or, for that matter, the Sergeant in *Macbeth* (i.ii.8–42), whose sanguinary report makes the merciless Macdonwald a blood brother to the rugged Pyrrhus. Among the disheveled heroines of Seneca's tragedies, Hecuba looms particularly large as the archetype of maternal woe and queenly suffering. How she was metamorphosed into a dog, after the destruction of Troy, is recollected when, in Seneca's *Agamemnon*, she 'barketh as a bedlam bitch about her strangled chylde.' * * *

Since the Elizabethans conceived of tragedy as a spectacular descent from the heights to the depths, they could conceive of no more tragic worthies than the King and Queen of Troy. Hence the object-lesson of the first English tragedy, *Gorboduc*, is driven home by identifying the heroine with 'Hecuba, the wofullest wretch / That euer lyued to make a myrrour of.' And in the most popular of all Elizabethan plays, *The Spanish Tragedy*, the hero, instructing a painter to 'shew a passion,' volunteers to pose for his portrait 'like old *Priam of Troy*, crying: "the house is a fire . . ."' But tragedy was more than a sad story of the death of kings and the weeping of tristful queens; it chronicled the fall of dynasties, the destruction of cities, the decline of civilizations. * * *

The matter of Troy—which Caxton had popularized, which English ballads celebrated, which poets and artists could draw upon as freely as the matter of England itself—served Shakespeare most effectively by helping to frame his characters and outline his situations. It figured upon a tapestry, as it were, backing the literal episodes of English history with a deeper dimension. The conflict between the houses of York and Lancaster was inevitably viewed in the light of the struggle between the Greeks and the Trojans. The father who accidentally slays his son in *3 Henry VI* (II.v.120), like Northumberland when he learns of Hotspur's death in *2 Henry IV* (I.i.70–74), is bound to see himself in Priam's role. Similarly, the Roman mother in *Coriolanus* (I.iii.43–6) and the cursing wife in *Cymbeline* (IV.ii.311–12) associate their grief with Hecuba's. It is not surprising, then, that the impassioned father wants to be painted as Priam in *The Spanish Tragedy*, or that the outraged wife in *The Rape of Lucrece* seeks consolation in a painting of the siege of Troy, more especially in its depiction of Hecuba (1450–51):

> In her the painter had anatomiz'd
> Time's ruin, beauty's wrack, and grim care's reign . . .

When Lucrece surveys the picture, discovering in it a precedent for her sorrows, its dumbness stimulates her to become vocal and its flatness puts her feelings into iconographic relief (1492): 'Here feelingly she weeps Troy's painted woes.' In similar fashion, all occasions inform against Hamlet, who rediscovers his own plight in the verbal painting, the theatrical mirror of the Player's speech. The narrator, pious Aeneas, recalls him to his filial duty. The King, his father, like Priam, has been slaughtered. The Queen his mother, ironically unlike Hecuba, refuses to play the part of the mourning wife. As for the interloping newcomer—whether you call him Pyrrhus, Neoptolemus, or Fortinbras—he too is prompted by the unquiet ghost of his father, Achilles. His destiny, too, is to bring down the revenge of a dead hero upon the unheroic heads of the living.

II

But these apparitions hover in the background until the words are pronounced that summon them. * * * The cruelty of Pyrrhus is symbolized by his heraldic trappings. Knightly prowess ordinarily finds its outward symbol in armorial panoply, which is frequently contrasted with the reality of blood, sweat, and tears—notably in the characterization of Hotspur. Here, where that situation is reversed, bloodshed is treated as if it were decoration. The sable arms of Pyrrhus resemble his funereal purpose, and also the night —which is not a generic night, but the particular, portentous, claustral night that he and his companions have just spent in the wooden horse. The repeated adjective 'black' (1. 424, 426) is an elementary manifestation of evil, like the 'Thoughts black' of the poisoner in the play-within-the-play; yet it hints at that 'power of blackness' which Melville discerned more fully in Shakespeare's works than anywhere else. But the scene does not appear in its true color until its dark surfaces are 'o'ersized' (433), covered with sizing, dripping with redness. Red, unrelieved by quartering, is 'total gules' in the unfeeling jargon of heraldry, which Shakespeare deliberately invokes to describe the clotted gore of others shed by Pyrrhus—of parents and children whose family relationships are feelingly specified by way of contrast (429), a contrast which ultimately juxtaposes esthetic and ethical values. He is tricked out, dressed up in the unnatural colors of Marlowe's Tamburlaine—in black and red and in a carbuncular brightness which flickers against the darkness, as opposed to the hues of nature, the blues and browns and greens that Shakespeare has more constantly in mind. Thence the metaphor shifts from light to heat, from visual to tactile images, and to a zeugma which holds in suspension both physical fire and psychological wrath (432). * * *

At this point, the appropriate point where Pyrrhus encounters Priam, the Player takes up the story and—in a manner of speaking —the monologue becomes a dialogue. It should not be forgotten that 'anon' (439) is one of those adverbs whose force has been weakened by time: in this case it means 'very soon' rather than later on.' It reinforces the series of 'nows,' which in their turn reinforce the employment of the present tense, and convey the impression of breathless immediacy: we might almost be listening to the play-by-play account of a sporting event. The ineffectuality of the old grandsire's antique sword (440), whose fall prefigures his (445), is motivated by the spirit of general mutiny. The angry swing of his assailant—which, though it goes wild, deprives the father of his remaining strength, unnerves him—rends the air with ten onomatopoetic monosyllables: 'But with the whiff and wind of his fell sword . . .' (444). * * * And though the poet hesitates to indulge in a pathetic fallacy, to attribute sensation or sensibility to the city itself, he interprets the crash of its top-less towers as a comment on the downfall of its king. Troy, how-ever, has its momentary and metaphorical revenge upon Pyrrhus when the noise, by capturing his ear, arrests his motion. At that fatal moment everything stops; the narrative is transposed to the past tense; and the interjection 'lo!' (448) points a moral and pictorial contrast between the bloody tyrant and his 'milky' victim (449). * * *

It is only during this uncharacteristic standstill that Pyrrhus, the unthinking avenger, shows any likeness to his polar opposite, Hamlet. Standing there for the nonce in a cataleptic state of neutrality, as if he had no control over mind or body, equally de-tached from his intention and his object, he 'did nothing'—and the pause is rounded out by an unfilled line (453). Then as he swings into action by way of an epic simile, sight is commingled with sound—or rather, with the absence of sound, since we are asked to visualize a silence (455). And as our gaze is deflected from the clouds to the earth, a second simile takes its departure from the first, and perceives an omen of death in the silent atmos-phere (457). Anon—that is, suddenly—like the awaited thunder-clap, vengeance is resumed; the retarded decline of the sword (463), with its Homeric reverberation (460), now parallels the dying fall of Priam and of his sword. The word 'fall,' coming twice in pairs, accentuates the rhythm and underlines the theme. The classical allusion, a preliminary glimpse of 'Vulcan's stithy,' though somewhat archaically expressed, would be commonplace if it were not for the violence of Shakespeare's application. He uses a favorite stylistic device of his predecessors, the University Wits, who seldom made a comparison without making it in-vidious: their characters are more beautiful than Venus, as pow-erful as Jove, no weaker than Hercules. After all, there could be no more remorseless task than to beat out indestructible armor for the god of war. To display as little or less remorse, while strik-ing down a disarmed graybeard, was to be as devoid of sympathy —as ready to inflict suffering and unready to feel it—as any human being could expressibly be.

* * * Leaving the senseless Priam to the insensate Pyrrhus,

after another hiatus of half a line (463), the speech addresses
violent objurgations to the bitch-goddess Fortune, about whom
Hamlet has lately cracked ribald jokes with Rosencrantz and Guildenstern; whose buffets and rewards he prizes Horatio for suffering with equanimity; against whom he will, in the most famous
of all soliloquies, be tempted to take arms. An appeal is addressed
to the gods, who are envisaged as meeting in epic conclave, to
destroy the source of her capricious authority. It is urged that
her proverbial wheel, whose revolution determines the ups and
downs of individual lives, be itself dismantled; and that its com-
ponents suffer the destiny to which they have so often carried
mortals—to fall, as the angels did in the world's original tragedy,
from paradise to hell. To catch the gathering momentum of that
descent, Shakespeare again resorts to words of one syllable (not
excepting 'heav'n'), and relies—as he does throughout—upon
assonances and alliterations (467, 468): 'And bowl the round
nave down the hill of heaven/ As far as to the fiends.' The same
image, that of 'a massy wheel,' disintegrating as it rolls downhill,
is later likened by Rosencrantz to 'the cesse of majesty,' the death
of the king involving 'the lives of many' attached to its spokes:

> . . . when it falls,
> Each small annexment, petty consequence,
> Attends the boist'rous ruin.

The fact that the twenty-three foregoing lines (445–468) are
frequently omitted from acting versions, notably from the First
Quarto, supports the view that they constitute a rhapsodic excur-
sion from the narrative. Shakespeare cleverly obviated boredom on
the part of his audience by allowing Polonius to complain and
Hamlet to gibe at him. By laughing with Hamlet at Polonius,
whose own tediousness is the butt of so many gibes, the audience
is pledged to renew its attention. Hamlet, of course, has personal
motives for echoing the Player's mention of Hecuba. Thereupon
Polonius, who fancies himself as a critic, and who has said of
Hamlet's letter to Ophelia that ' "beautified" is a vile phrase,'
seeks to propitiate Hamlet by voicing judicious approval of a
peculiarly inept expression: ' "Mobled queen" is good.' Has im-
pressionistic criticism ever said more?

The barefoot queen remains mobled, or muffled, for better or
for worse, in spite of editors who prefer 'mob-led' or 'ennobled.'
Her special poignance depends upon her abdication of queenly
dignity, upon the antitheses between 'diadem' (478) and 'clout'
(477) and between 'robe' (478) and 'blanket' (480). * * * The
concept of royalty has been debased: 'Hyperion to a satyr,' goddess

to fishwife. The sword, on its fourth and last appearance, is not unlike a kitchen-knife; while the final outburst of Hecuba is like Homer's portrayal of Helen, in one respect if in no other, since it registers its emotional impact on the spectators. Fortune, it would appear, is still so securely entrenched that the impulse to denounce her is a poisonous subversion of things as they are (482). To appeal once more to the gods is to admit—more skeptically than Ovid—that they may exhibit an Olympian disregard for the whole situation: such is the question that Shakespeare explored in *King Lear*, and which such modern writers as Thomas Hardy have reconsidered. Yet if heaven takes any interest whatsoever in man's affairs, it might be expected to respond to so harassed an incarnation of feminine frailty, and its presumptive response inspires a last downward sweep of sinking metaphor. Its tears, burning like the lurid eyes of Pyrrhus, turning into milk like the revered hair of Priam, and associated by that maternal essence with Hecuba's 'o'erteemed loins' (479), might produce a downpour more blinding than her 'bisson rheum' (477) and thereby extinguish the holocaust of Troy. What commenced in firelight concludes in rainfall. Recoiling before this bathetic *Götterdämmerung*, Dryden remarks: 'Such a sight were indeed enough to have rais'd passion in the Gods, but to excuse the effects of it [the poet] tells you perhaps they did not see it.'

III

To break off the speech is to awaken Hamlet from what he calls 'a dream of passion'—a glaring nightmare of smoke and screams and ruins—to the light of day. But somber northern daylight renews 'the motive and the cue for passion' in his own life, and the Trojan retrospect becomes a Danish omen, joining the echoes of Caesar's assassination and other portents of Hamlet's tragedy. None of the others, however, could have seemed as epoch-making or epoch-shattering as the evocation of Priam, no less a byword for catastrophe to the Elizabethans than the name of Hiroshima seems to us. 'O what a fall was there, my countrymen.' The catastrophic mood that overtook sensitive Englishman during the latter years of Elizabeth's reign, particularly after the downfall of Essex, had set the key for the play. From the long-echoing lament of Hecuba, as enunciated by Ovid, Shakespeare had learned the rhetorical lesson of copiousness. It is also probable that his books of rhetoric had taught him an old argument of Quintilian's: that the orator who pens his own speeches would move his hearers more profoundly than the mere elocutionist who recites what someone else has felt and thought and written. At all events, the surface of the drama is undisturbed by the Player's elocution. Again he is merely a player; Polonius is quite unaffected; and Hamlet completes his arrangements for the morrow's performance of the play that will affect Claudius as— it soon appears—this foretaste has affected him. Hitherto constrained from weeping or speaking his mind, he now reveals that the player has wept and spoken for him. The deeply revealing soliloquy that completes the Second Act and sets the scene for the Third, 'O what a rogue and peasant slave am I,' pulls aside the curtain of heavily figured declamation that has just been spread before us for that very purpose.

To be more precise, the soliloquy is the mirror-opposite of the speech. Both passages are very nearly of the same length, and seem to be subdivided into three movements which run somewhat parallel. But where the speech proceeds from the slayer to the slain, and from the royal victim to the queenly mourner, the soliloquy moves from that suggestive figure to another king and finally toward another villain. And where the speech leads from action to passion, the soliloquy reverses this direction. Where the Player's diction is heavily external, underlining the fundamental discrepancy between words and deeds, Hamlet's words are by convention his thoughts, directing inward their jabs of self-accusation. Midway, where the Player curses Fortune as a strumpet, Hamlet falls 'a-cursing like a very drab.' Well may he hesitate, 'like a neutral to his will and matter,' at the very point where even the rugged Pyrrhus paused and did nothing. Though we need not go so far as Racine, who refined that model of bloody retribution into the gallant lover of Andromaque (*'violent mais sincère'*), we may cite the precedent as a justification—if further justification still be needed—for Hamlet's often criticized delay. While he must hold his tongue, so long as he 'cannot speak' his genuine sentiments, the Player is vocal on his behalf. Since he is all too literally 'the observed of all observers,' he must enact a comedy and so must they: the courtly comedy of fashionable observance. He offers Rosencrantz and Guildenstern the same treatment that he accords the Players, to whom he also must 'show fairly outwards.' Polonius, who has acted in his youth, ends—all too ironically—as Hamlet's 'audience.' And while the courtiers watch Hamlet, he watches Claudius, the most subtle impersonator of them all, who conceals his villainy behind a smile and only reveals it while watching a dramatic performance.

Afterwards, when Hamlet confronts his mother with her 'act,' he undertakes to show her 'a glass/ Where you may see the inmost part of you.' The Elizabethan conception of art as the glass of nature was ethical rather than realistic; for it assumed that, by contemplating situations which reflected their own, men and women could mend their ways and act with greater resolution thereafter. To the observer who is painfully learning the distinction between *seems* and *is*, the hideous pangs of the Trojan Queen are the mirrored distortions of Gertrude's regal insincerities. The 'damn'd defeat' of Priam, reminding Hamlet of his father, prompts him to renounce his hitherto passive role, to soliloquize on the Player's example, and finally to evolve his plan of action. Thus his soliloquy departs from, and returns to, the theatrical sphere. 'The play's the thing'—the play-within-the-play, where the Player's 'passionate speech' will be crowned by the Play Queen's 'passionate action,' and the crime will be metaphorically ('tropically') re-enacted, beginning and ending with Hamlet's echoed quotations from two notorious tragedies of revenge. Meanwhile the situation at hand is transcended by the searching question in Hamlet's mind —a question which ponders not only the technique of acting, but the actual nature of the esthetic process. * * * What is the relationship of the player to the play, of the dancer to the dance, of the work of art to its interpretation, or of the interpreter to the audience? How, Shakespeare asks himself in effect, can emotion be communicated by my dramaturgy?

Observe—and here I beg leave to reduce our text for the moment to a paradigm (see Figure 1, page 237)—that he does not present Hecuba's emotions directly. Her passion, unlike Thisbe's, is neither presented nor described. Instead he describes her appearance and appeals to the spectator: 'Who, O who,' he opines —or even more lugubriously, as the Quartos would have it, 'Who, ah woe!'—whoever viewed that spectacle would repudiate destiny itself. Thence the poet appeals the case to a higher court:

> But if the gods themselves did *see* her, then,
> When she [Hecuba] *saw* Pyrrhus make malicious sport,
> In mincing with his sword her husband's [Priam's] limbs—

even they (the GODS) might feel an emotional response, though such a prospect is conditionally stated. Let us meet the condition by recognizing their existence on a highly figurative plane, and by characterizing their attitude as *compassion*: a sympathetic participation in the feelings of Hecuba. * * * HECUBA is likewise an onlooker, tense though the bond of sympathy must be that unites her to the agonies of Priam; it is he who feels, who suffers physically when Pyrrhus acts. PYRRHUS is your man of *action*, in the most epical and extroverted signification of the term: the key to this passage is the emphasis that Shakespeare places upon

his insensibility. Furthermore, no effort is made to present the
sufferings of PRIAM: his falling city sympathizes with him, his
animistic sword rebels against him, but he himself remains inanimate. Tradition depicts him slain upon the altar of Apollo,
and—although Shakespeare makes no point of this circumstance
—it sheds the light of religious ritual upon his sacrifice, and
helps to explain why so many generations could identify it with
their experience. In terms of sheer brutality, or ritualistic fulfilment, the murder might be regarded as a *passion*, and differ-
entiated by an exclamation-point from the question-mark that
might appropriately designate the psychological *passion* of Hecuba.
But even the burden of her grief, as we have noticed, is relayed to
higher authorities: if the gods exist and look down, perhaps their
compassionate overview will gather up the vicarious passions of
the dead Priam, the unfeeling Pyrrhus, and the muffled queen.
And we are left confronting a dizzying hierarchy of externalized
emotion, which continues to refer our query upwards until it is out
of sight.

Let us therefore look in the other direction, downwards—from
the eyes of the gods, past Hecuba and the murderer and the murdered, to the voice of the narrator. When all is said and done,
we must not forget that it is AENEAS who speaks: a surviving
eye-witness who relives the tale as he tells it to Dido. Since she is
not represented, its impact on her goes unregistered. But since the
epic has been adapted to the drama, *narration* has become *action*
in quotation-marks, simulated actuality; while Aeneas is enacted
by the PLAYER. Shakespeare exploits the ambiguity of the verb
'to act,' which alternates between 'doing' and 'seeming,' between
the brutal deeds of Pyrrhus and the verbal hypocrisies that Hamlet
dwells on: 'For they are actions that a man might play . . .' By
means of his acting, the Player simulates *passion*, again in quotation-marks; he functions as a surrogate for the various mythical
figures whose respective sorrows he personifies, and bridges the
gap between their world and Hamlet's. * * *

Since the theater perforce exaggerates, amplifying its pathos and
stylizing its diction, it takes a specially marked degree of amplifica-
tion and stylization to dramatize the theatrical, as Schlegel realized.
Conversely, when matters pertaining to the stage are exhibited
upon the stage, to acknowledge their artificiality is to enhance the
realism of everything else within view. The contrasting textures
of the Player's fustian and Hamlet's lines, like the structural contrast between the prevailing blank verse and the rhyming couplets
of the play-within-the-play, bring out the realities of the situation
by exposing its theatricalities. By exaggeration of drama, by 'smell-

ing a little too strongly of the buskin' in Dryden's phrase, Shakespeare achieves his imitation of life. Yet the play itself—not 'The Murder of Gonzago' but *The Tragedy of Hamlet, Prince of Denmark*—is 'a fiction,' an illusion which we accept on poetic faith. Hamlet's passion is sincere and sentient as compared to the Player's, which—though externalized and factitious—has aroused Hamlet from passivity to action. And of course he is not, in the very last analysis, 'passion's slave'; he is, he becomes, an agent of revenge; he suits 'the word to the action.' Nor is he a recorder to be played upon, though he succeeds in playing upon Claudius. The implied comparison with Aeneas would be completed by Dido's counterpart in the neglected person of Ophelia, but dalliance in either case is resolutely cut off. When Hamlet hits upon his ingenious plot, it projects him in two directions at once: back to the plane of intradramatic theatricals, and forward to the plane of his audience. A spectator of the players, he has his own spectators, who turn out to be ourselves, to whom he is actually an ACTOR. Here we stand in relation to him—that is, to his interpreter, be he Garrick or Gielgud—where he stands in relation to the Player. The original emotion, having been handed down from one level to another of metaphor and myth and impersonation and projection, reaches the basic level of *interpretation*, whence the expression can make its impression upon our minds. There the reality lodges, in the *reaction* of the AUDIENCE: the empathy that links our outlook with a chain of being which sooner or later extends all the way from the actors to the gods.

* * *

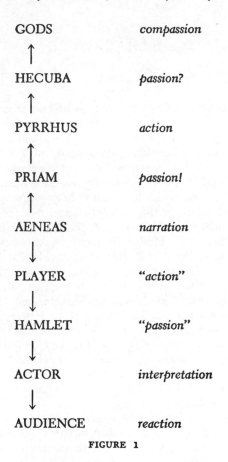

FIGURE 1

G. B. HARRISON

Hamlet†

So much has been written about *Hamlet* that it is hardly possible for an educated person nowadays to come to a reading or a performance of the play without prejudice, without a feeling that he ought somehow to be baffled, dissatisfied, intrigued by a sense of mystery. The critic is therefore at some disadvantage if he begins his examination by observing certain facts about the play itself and the type of drama to which it belongs. Nevertheless, an objective consideration of the facts will dispel most of the fancies and leave *Hamlet* unencumbered of the excessive tributes and speculations which have hidden its greater excellencies.

The first fact, so easily and often forgotten, is that *Hamlet* is a play, and not a treatise on philosophy, psychiatry, Elizabethan history, or social ethics. It was a popular play, and therefore gave the public what it wanted. Moreover, Shakespeare's play was not the first to be written on the Hamlet story. There is some evidence that an earlier *Hamlet* play was in existence in 1589, and actual records that it was being played in 1594 and 1596. In the form that we now know it, Shakespeare's *Hamlet* was mostly written between 1598 and 1602. From the first it was a great success and at least twice Shakespeare partially re-wrote it or added some considerable passages.

There are, indeed, four versions even of Shakespeare's *Hamlet*. The first came out in 1603; a botched dishonest pirated affair, put together either from memory or from the shorthand version of a bungler with an elementary knowledge of his craft. This version, known as the First Quarto, is about half the length of the play as we know it; but it contains at least 240 lines which do not appear in any of the other versions, and it has considerable interest. It may, indeed, preserve a form of the play in a transition stage before Shakespeare had finally rewritten the old play of 1594; it certainly records in its stage directions some very interesting notes of what actually happened on the stage.

The second version—the Second Quarto—came out in 1604; it gives the completest version of the play. Probably it was printed

† From *Shakespeare's Tragedies*, by G. B. Harrison (New York: Oxford University Press, 1951), pp. 88–109. Copyright © 1951 by George Bagshawe Harrison. Reprinted by permission of the publisher and David Higham Associates, Ltd.

direct from Shakespeare's own manuscript; but if so by an un-skilled printer who found great difficulty in reading Shakespeare's handwriting, for it is full of mistakes. Nearly twenty years later, when *Hamlet* was printed with the others in the First Folio, the text was again different; apart from minor changes of reading, two hundred lines were omitted, eighty-five were added.

Then there is the modern version, which most readers know, a compound of all that is in the Second Quarto and in the First Folio; and, where there is a difference of reading, that which seems best to the Editor. We must step warily; if Shakespeare himself altered *Hamlet* the critics, too, may hold a variety of opinions.

Hamlet was not first invented by Elizabethan dramatists. Be-hind the play, versions of the tale are known which go back at least to the thirteenth century; but in all versions the theme is the same—revenge. Elizabethan playgoers had a peculiar delight in this theme, and there are many revenge plays. Most of them fol-low a pattern, just as in these days the crime and detective thriller runs to type.

In the thriller there is first the crime (and usually the corpse, in various stages of preservation). The master mind is stimulated and begins to rotate. Then follow the false clues, all set out according to the elaborate rules of the game, the triumphant but unexpected solution, the analysis of the evidence, and—as a per-functory tribute to morality in the last half page—the punishment of the guilty.

Revenge plays also have their pattern. It occurs first in *The Spanish Tragedy*, which was the father of all Revenge Plays, and in an even more extravagant specimen, exactly contemporary with *Hamlet*, Marston's *Antonio's Revenge*.

The story of the Revenge Play begins with the crime, usually murder, but with varying motives. The duty of vengeance is laid on the next of kin, who is faced with the problem of identifying the murderer, a matter of some difficulty. He encounters many impediments to vengeance. Finally, in the last Act, comes the triumphant conclusion when the original murderer is appropriately dispatched, and, since playgoers liked their tragedies to be richly coloured, the venger and all others nearly concerned perish to-gether in one red ruin.

There was, moreover, an etiquette, a morality, in revenge. Vengeance was a pious duty laid on the next of kin; it was wild justice, but to be satisfactory and successful something more than strict justice was needed. The Old Law claimed an eye for an eye and a tooth for a tooth; vengeance demanded both eyes, a jaw

240 · *G. B. Harrison*

full of teeth, and above all that the victim, after exquisite torments of body and mind, should go straight to Hell there to remain in everlasting torment. A perfect revenge required, therefore, great artistry.

The pattern can be illustrated from John Marston's *Antonio's Revenge*, the sequel to *Antonio and Mellida*; both parts were written in 1599. There are, indeed, certain similarities with Shakespeare's *Hamlet* which seem to be more than coincidence.[1]

The story runs thus: Years ago Piero, Duke of Venice, and Andrugio, Duke of Milan, had both loved the Lady Maria. Andrugio won her and ever since Piero has been nursing an implacable lust for revenge. When the first play opens, Piero has recently defeated Andrugio in a sea fight; but Andrugio and his son Antonio have survived. Antonio is in love with Mellida, Piero's daughter; and the first part ends as a comedy with Piero apparently reconciled to his old enemy and Antonio betrothed to Mellida.

Antonio's Revenge is a very different play. It opens well, with a promising stage direction: *Enter Piero, unbraced, with his arms bare, smeared in blood, a poniard in one hand bloody, and a torch in the other; Strotzo—his minion—following him with a cord.* Piero has had a very enjoyable evening. He has poisoned Andrugio, stabbed a too freely-spoken courtier called Feliche and hung the body in Mellida's bedchamber, and, to complete the triumph, Maria, Andrugio's Duchess, is due to arrive that very morning.

The corpse of Andrugio is solemnly interred and at once Piero makes love to the lady; but when Antonio comes to pay reverence to the tomb of his father, Andrugio's Ghost rises, cries out for vengeance, reveals the murder, and warns the son that his mother is yielding to Piero. Antonio is eager for revenge. Piero passes by with his little son, Julio. The boy, who is fond of Antonio, lingers behind. Here is a chance for vengeance, the exchange of a son for a father. Antonio seizes the boy and cuts his little throat, whereat, as the stage direction expresses it, *from under the stage a groan.* Antonio then sprinkles the hot blood over the tomb and utters an appropriate soliloquy which ends:

> Lo thus I heave my blood-dyed hands to heaven,
> Even like insatiate hell still crying, More!
> My heart hath thirsting dropsies after gore.
> Sound peace and rest to church, night-ghosts, graves:
> Blood cries for blood, and murder murder craves.

That night Maria is abruptly brought to her senses. As she draws aside the bed curtains she sees before her the Ghost of her

---

1. And if so, the learned must admit either that Shakespeare owed something to Marston, or that *Hamlet* was written for the most part before 1599.

husband sitting on the bed and waiting to utter a stern admonishment. Mellida meanwhile has been accused of adultery. She puts up a brave fight for her own honour until she is falsely told that her Antonio is dead, when she dies of a broken heart.

Final vengeance is now ready for Piero. The last Act opens in revelry. Piero is about to marry Maria and the wedding mask is in progress. Certain of the maskers persuade Piero to dismiss his attendants, for they would honour him alone. Piero is thus at their mercy when Antonio and his companions reveal themselves. They bind Piero, pluck out his tongue and triumph over him. Then they present a dish which contains the limbs of little Julio. They level their rapiers, run at him, but stop short. At length one by one the vengers, each with appropriate comment, stab home, and the Ghost of Andrugio which has been watching events from above withdraws satisfied.

That was the meaning of revenge to an Elizabethan playgoer. That also is what revenge meant to the Ghost of the late King Hamlet when it so sternly demanded that Hamlet should fulfil his pious duty. Our ideas on this matter, at least among those whose native language is English, have changed.

The theme of the Hamlet story in all its versions is how a King was killed by his brother and how the King's son ultimately took vengeance on the murderer. It is therefore bound by the normal conventions of the theme.

The plot of Shakespeare's *Hamlet* is neat, admirably worked out, symmetrical, and using the word in the Jonsonian—or complimentary—sense, 'artificial'. It is also highly improbable. A brother kills a king and marries the widow; and hence the King's son has double cause to hate the uncle and a filial obligation to avenge the dead. But, if the final vengeance is to be satisfactory, the son should also perish; and there must be an adequate cause for his end other than mere accident. So the son of the murdered King also kills a father; and on that father's son too is laid the duty of vengeance; and by a supremely artistic device the double vengeances come to a point at the same moment. That, however, will mean that at the end of the play the murderer-Uncle will be dead and the son-venger will be dead; but the other venger and the Queen who was the cause of all the trouble will survive. Such an ending is contrary to good form. Some means must therefore be devised to despatch these two at the same time. The poisoned rapier, exchanged in the heat of combat, whereby both vengers are killed with the same weapon is most satisfactory; and for the Queen, the accidental cup of poison intended for the nephew but destroying the erring wife and mother is a very effective touch, full of grim irony.

This conclusion, however, will leave the practical problem that the royal family of Denmark has been entirely wiped out. Someone must take charge or the audience will leave the theatre unsatisfied, and wondering what happened next. Let someone come in with an army and then there will be a fine military funeral for Hamlet and a general feeling that the state of Denmark is at last in strong hands.

But that solution will introduce other problems, for this army and its commander must be introduced naturally; at such a late point in the action the play must neither be delayed nor diverted for explanations. If this commander is a rival Prince who has a claim on the throne then there is a rounded and satisfactory ending. There is, however, another difficulty; somehow this Prince must have been introduced early and kept constantly in mind so that his entry at the end is quite natural and, indeed, inevitable.

There are still a few loose ends. How does the son find out about the murder? The discovery is usually one of the major incidents in a Revenge Play. One method is the ghost of the murdered man; no Revenge Play is complete without at least one ghost.

And still something is lacking. There is no love interest. Prince Hamlet must be provided with a lady; and if she can be the sister of the man who ultimately kills him it will add greatly to the piquancy of the situation. It would, of course, be best to have her dead before the last Act, for as things are now planned we have already four corpses, which is as many as we can conveniently handle if there are to be enough actors left over for the army. Let the poor girl go mad; we always have a mad scene in a Revenge Play; and then let her kill herself in the fourth Act.

These, then, are the stock incidents of an exciting melodrama; incidents which are used over and over again in any Revenge Play; and these Shakespeare transmuted into his *Hamlet*. It is worth watching him at work, for the mechanics of the making of *Hamlet* are magnificent.

* * *

The prevailing feeling in Hamlet's mind is disgust, a young man's unreasonable disgust when he discovers that his elders are as strongly sexed as himself. Hamlet, in Shakespeare's play, is thus an impetuous, highly strung young man, bewildered and frustrated, for he can do nothing and say nothing; indeed, as yet he knows nothing more than anyone else in the Court of Denmark.

To Hamlet in this mood come Horatio and Marcellus with

their strange story of the midnight apparition. Here at least is something to do, a chance to get away from Claudius and his interminable drinking parties. The excitement begins to rise; will the Ghost be more communicative to Hamlet than to Horatio?

Now, partly to keep us impatient, partly to show us something of the lady who is Hamlet's fancy, and partly to provide a complete contrast of mood, Shakespeare thrusts in a scene of the Polonius family. Laertes is about to embark for Paris, but before he goes he must deliver a little homily to his sister Ophelia; brother and sister are genuinely fond of each other and he is afraid that Hamlet may lead her astray. But Laertes in his turn is justly caught, and must listen to yet another lecture from his old father, Polonius.

This old diplomat and statesman, who has no faith in human nature, is one of the most masterly pieces of characterization in all Shakespeare. Naturally, Polonius cannot believe that Prince Hamlet can seriously be in love with such a simple unsophisticated girl. It is a marvellous picture of middle-aged respectability, full of high-sounding platitudes, worldly wisdom, and a complete lack of faith in human beings, especially the young. * * *

After this domestic scene of pure comedy we are taken back to the battlements. Again the Ghost appears, but this time it leads Hamlet away, tells him the whole story of the murder in the orchard, and demands a full-blooded revenge. When the Ghost has faded away Hamlet is for some time left alone in a state of shocked horror before his companions catch up with him. He swears them to secrecy and the first part of the play ends.

* * *

The second part of the play shows how Hamlet proved his uncle guilty. Some time has elapsed—about four months. The passing of time is indicated by another scene of comedy. Shakespeare introduces Polonius sending his man Reynaldo to Paris with the next instalment of Laertes' allowance; and of course with instructions to spy on the boy's behaviour. We learn that Hamlet has taken Ophelia's rejection very hardly and is showing all signs of being mad at rejected love—recognized as a common form of neurosis. This, coupled with the letters which Ophelia has handed over, lead Polonius to think that he fully understands the cause of Hamlet's apparent madness.

As for Hamlet, he is still involved in the same haunting situation as at the beginning of the play, but worse, for although he is burdened with this horrible suspicion, still he can do nothing. The King also is alarmed, for though as yet he has no fear that

244 · G. B. Harrison

his guilty secret has been betrayed, he is naturally uneasy. So Rosencrantz and Guildenstern are summoned to play the spy; everyone is spying in this court. Then, by chance—the only incident that does occur by chance in the play, and yet how naturally —the players on tour present themselves at the palace to offer a play.

Here is Hamlet's opportunity of proving once and for all whether this horrible story is true or whether it is a figment of a diseased imagination. The idea comes to him after he has asked for a trial speech from the first player. He realizes that if the mere fiction of Hecuba and the sack of Troy can so move him, the King must inevitably be forced to betray emotion by a close imitation of the murder itself. The soliloquy that Hamlet utters after the players have left him is worth careful note. As usual, indeed as the convention of the soliloquy demanded, Hamlet quite literally reveals his own mind. He is powerfully stirred; and he falls, as do all men of impetuous nature when frustrated, into self-condemnation. And then the idea comes to him:

> I have heard, that guilty creatures sitting at a play
> Have by the very cunning of the scene,
> Been struck so to the soul, that presently
> They have proclaim'd their malefactions.
> For murther, though it have no tongue, will speak
> With most miraculous organ. I'll have these Players,
> Play something like the murder ,of my father,
> Before mine uncle. I'll observe his looks,
> I'll tent him to the quick; if he but blench
> I know my course. The spirit that I have seen
> May be the Devil, and the Devil hath power
> T'assume a pleasing shape, yea and perhaps
> Out of my weakness, and my melancholy,
> As he is very potent with such spirits,
> Abuses me to damn me. I'll have grounds
> More relative than this: the play's the thing,
> Wherein I'll catch the conscience of the King.

This emphasis on the Devil and melancholy as the cause of delusions is a literal statement of psychological theory as believed by Shakespeare's contemporaries. The word melancholy covered many forms of mental disease; extreme cases suffered not only horrible nightmares but even hallucination. Hamlet's reluctance to believe in the Ghost's word was thus normal prudence. On these matters the *Demonology* of King James the Sixth and Burton's *Anatomy of Melancholy* are worth consulting.

Hamlet, therefore, anticipating by some centuries a modern

device called the lie-detector, determines to apply the decisive test to his uncle. Meanwhile the King is becoming more uneasy, for he cannot discover what may lie behind Hamlet's behaviour. He is not impressed by Polonius's suggestion that Hamlet is love mad, but at least he agrees to a test. Both sides are now watching each other intently. Ophelia is therefore set as a decoy while the King and her father spy on the meeting from behind the arras. She is also provided with a Book of Devotions as a suitable ornament or camouflage and instructed to accost Hamlet.

Hamlet comes in. As the First Quarto tells us, he is reading a book; and for a long while he is entirely absorbed by his own meditations, as he gives utterance to the much quoted soliloquy, 'To be or not to be'. This speech, be it noted, is not Hamlet brooding on his own possible suicide but meditating on the words before him, which are set out in the normal form of an academic argument, beginning with the usual formula for such exercises— *Quaestio est an* (the question is whether)—followed by the alternative question which is the topic for debate. The matter under discussion is, 'Whether it is nobler to take arms against a sea of troubles or by opposing (that is, by suicide) to end them'. It is quite a common topic for philosophic discussion. This speech has several purposes, but principally to give us the one picture in the play of Hamlet, the scholar, the intellectual, pondering a problem of moral philosophy.

Then for the first time he notices Ophelia. The passage between Hamlet and Ophelia has greatly disturbed critics because Hamlet's language is so very unpleasant. It is a pity that critics of Shakespeare so seldom bring their own experiences of life to the examination of great works of art; for no one who has ever suffered or even watched a violent love affair at close quarters will fail to understand Hamlet's feeling. At this point and indeed whenever Hamlet is on the stage, we must look at the events with his eyes as he sees them.

This, then, is the situation. Hamlet is Prince and heir of Denmark, the most eligible and covetable of bachelors, the observed of all observers. He offers honourable love to a girl who is considerably beneath him in rank, so far below him, indeed, that Polonius suspects that he is planning to seduce her. At first Ophelia encourages Hamlet, and then, for no reason given, the door is slammed, his gifts are refused, and his letters unanswered. When a young man is faced with such a rebuff without warning he is naturally hurt and surprised. There are two likely explanations which would occur to any man; either that he has in some way unwittingly offended his beloved, or that she has acquired another lover. And the second, surely, is the natural and likely explanation as Hamlet interprets events; for we must not forget that although we have seen what passed between Polonius and Ophelia, Hamlet knows nothing of her motives for refusing him. His suspicions are confirmed at this moment when Ophelia so clumsily returns his gifts. The only other woman for whom he cares anything has also turned from him, and has shown herself to be no better than the rest. She too—as he interprets the evidence of her uneasy behaviour—is carrying on an intrigue behind the arras. He is wrong, as we know, but how natural for him to suspect the worst. Hence his bitterness and brutal language; hence Ophelia's breakdown, for she—like other simple-minded daughters who lack the strength of mind to rely on themselves—is the victim of a foolish but well-meaning old father.

* * *

The play is open declaration of war between Hamlet and Claudius, for no one in that audience can miss the gross impertinence of the references to second marriages. There is no withdrawing now, and the excitement rises as Hamlet underlines each point until the grimacing poisoner reproduces the original murder:

He poisons him i' the garden for's estate: his name's Gonzago: the story is extant and writ in choice Italian. You shall see anon how the murtherer gets the love of Gonzago's wife.

Claudius can endure no more; he rushes away. Now Hamlet knows for certain. He has proved his case. It was not the hallucination of a diseased mind but a true Ghost after all; and Claudius stands revealed a murderer. From this moment the whole direction of the play changes, for, at the same time that Hamlet learns for certain that Claudius is indeed guilty, he reveals to Claudius that he knows all. Hitherto, the initiative has been with Hamlet; now it passes to the King, with every advantage on his side. Claudius is quick witted and ruthless; he can act in sure knowledge; his dangerous nephew shall be despatched to England and there immediately liquidated.

* * *

Hamlet now disappears for a long while and the second revenge story—the revenge of Laertes for Polonius—is set in motion. This is the third and last part of the play, which tells how Hamlet and Laertes simultaneously took their vengeance. Some little time— not precisely indicated—has again passed. Ophelia, never very strong minded, has gone quite mad; Laertes has returned from

Paris and is plotting a revolution. But Claudius, however mean his physical gifts, has immense presence of mind and quick wit. When Laertes breaks into the palace, Claudius subdues him by sheer force of personality, and quite quickly wins him round to his own side. He shows the same quick decision when the news comes that Hamlet is not dead in England but alive in Denmark. Claudius immediately works on Laertes to avenge his father and so assume or at least share the responsibility for the murder of Hamlet. Laertes is willing enough.

> 'What would you undertake,' asks Claudius,
> 'To show yourself your father's son indeed,
> More than in words?'

> 'To cut his throat i' th' Church,' cries Laertes—

an act which would be doubly mortal sin.

No place, replies the King, can make a murder holy; *'revenge should have no bounds.'* And that was the normal morality of revenge. Moreover, Laertes's purpose is strengthened by the news of fresh calamity: Ophelia has drowned herself.

So Hamlet comes back to Denmark and destruction draws near. The angle or point of view of the play has somewhat changed. Before Hamlet went to England the action was seen through his eyes; thereafter it was shown rather from the angle of Claudius. Now Hamlet again takes his place in the centre. And once more at a moment when the excitement is mounting, Shakespeare holds us back. The play is growing more gloomy, and to brighten the darkness he adds some comic 'relief', as it is not always very aptly called. Two new characters enter, two grave-diggers, who are about to prepare a grave for Ophelia.

This scene has several purposes. It gives emotional relief so that the feelings may later be stirred even more deeply; and it provides cynical contrast to Hamlet's lofty philosophies. Hamlet had brooded over man and mortality. The last word with man and woman lies with these two horny-handed sons of Adam. The first grave-digger also is interested in man, not as the beauty of the world or the god-like paragon of animals but as a dead carcass, daily trade, matter for professional observations which he very willingly discusses with Hamlet.

'How long will a man lie i' th' earth ere he rot?' asks Hamlet.
'I' faith, if he be not rotten before he die (as we have many pocky corses nowadays, that will scarce hold the laying in), he will last you some eight year, or nine year. A tanner will last you nine year.'
'Why he, more than another?'

'Why sir, his hide is so tann'd with his trade, that he will keep out water a great while. And your water, is a sore decayer of your whoreson dead body.'

It is another point of view, crude but very sane.

Then comes the funeral of Ophelia; and once more a little scholarship will correct some misapprehensions. The stage directions in the texts give her a magnificent funeral—in the best Hollywood tradition. *Enter Priests, etc., in procession; the corpse of Ophelia, Laertes and Mourners following; King, Queen, their trains, etc.* The First Quarto sets us right here. *Enter King and Queen, Laertes and other Lords, with a Priest after the coffin*—an insultingly simple affair for a lady of her rank, almost sordid, with the reluctant priest, unwilling even to offer a prayer over the grave. From the pathos of this moment, the sudden passions of Laertes and Hamlet flare up and the scene ends with the sinister words of the King:

> This grave shall have a living monument:
> An hour of quiet shortly shall we see;
> Till then, in patience our proceeding be.

The excitement is again growing; and we are held back to make us more impatient and so in a better mood for the end. Yet another new character comes in—Osric, the fashionable courtier, an object of particular detestation to the regular playgoer, a pretty little man with nothing to recommend him but his wealth, his clothes and his fashionable manners; yet a fascinating object in itself. He comes to carry the King's request that Hamlet shall fence with Laertes. We know, but Hamlet does not, that this will be the end. * * *

At last all the characters are assembled; Claudius, Gertrude, Hamlet, Horatio, Laertes, Osric and as many more as the company can collect. The King prepares his poisoned cup. Laertes is ready with his envenomed and sharpened rapier. Everything is going smoothly according to plan for Claudius when, by a sudden quirk of Fate, the wheel turns. The Queen takes up the poisoned cup to drink to Hamlet. Claudius has but a second to make a decision; to save his Queen by snatching the cup from her and so to betray himself, or to let Fate take its course. He hesitates, and is doubly damned, for he has killed the woman for whom he has contrived two murders, and with his own weapon, and he can only wait for the end. Even before that end he is already suffering the torments of the damned. From this moment he loses all power of will.

Laertes, indeed, at last wounds Hamlet but in the change of

weapons is himself wounded. Gertrude, as the poison works and chokes her utterance, has one flash of horrible revelation. In the few seconds before the dark, she realizes that this man, whom she had so complacently preferred to her own royal husband, has murdered her in the act of murdering her only son. It is a fine dramatic moment, invariably lost on the stage because of the greediness of every actor who plays Hamlet lest the attention should be diverted from himself even for an instant.

So Hamlet at last leaps to his revenge, and Claudius joins his victims. It is not quite so deliberate and artistic a vengeance as is usual in Revenge Plays, but quite adequate nevertheless, for there can be little doubt that Claudius has been surely caught in a moment that has no relish of salvation in it. Hamlet himself survives the rest but a few moments, and before he dies, there is heard the roll of drums which heralds the end of the old story and the beginning of the new.

And so we come to the winding up of the drama. Fortinbras appears; we have no need to be told why he is here or how he stands in the present state of affairs. He has some rights of memory in this Kingdom and he takes command.

Shakespeare never ends his plays at the moment of death. Feelings are at their height; they must be brought down to a more normal level or the audience will leave the theatre with the emotions seared and raw. In Shakespeare's tragedies it is usual for the chief survivor to sum up the story and to give a farewell to the hero with a final comment on his character. What is Fortinbras's epitaph? Hamlet the failure? the dreamer? the philosopher, too sensitive to carry out a ruthless deed? too high-minded for a sordid age? Far from it.

> Let four captains
> Bear Hamlet like a soldier to the stage,
> For he was likely, had he been put on
> To have prov'd most royally: and for his passage,
> The soldiers' music, and the rites of war
> Speak loudly for him.
> Take up the body; such a sight as this
> Becomes the field, but here shows much amiss.
> Go, bid the soldiers shoot.

The last thought on Hamlet, thrice stressed, is that he was a soldier; and the soldierly virtues are courage, intelligence, resolution, quick determination, ruthlessness. Hamlet was endowed with them all.

Hamlet is usually considered a play of problems; and the problem which has chiefly exercised the critics is why did he delay? To

which the answer is that in the play which Shakespeare wrote there
was no delay.

* * *

H. D. F. KITTO

Providence in *Hamlet*†

What we are to be concerned with is the madness and then
the death of Ophelia, the return of Laertes, the willingness of 'the
false Danish dogs' to rebel against Claudius, the failure of his
present plot against Hamlet, and the hatching of the new double
plot by Claudius and Laertes together. If we try to take, as the
essence of the play, the duel between Hamlet and Claudius, or
the indecision of Hamlet, or any other theme which is only a
part, not the whole, of the play, then much of this act is only
peripheral; but everything coheres closely and organically when
we see that the central theme is the disastrous growth of evil.

How, for instance, does Shakespeare introduce the madness of
Ophelia? In a very arresting way indeed:

> *I will not speak with her.*

These few words reveal much. We last saw Gertrude utterly con-
trite at the sins which Hamlet had revealed to her. She has received a straight hint that she is living with her husband's murderer; she has seen Polonius killed, and his daughter crazed—all
this the direct or indirect consequence of the villainy in which she
has been a partner. No wonder that she would avoid being confronted with this latest disaster: 'I will not speak with her.'

But Horatio tells her that she must, lest worse happen:

> *'Twere good she were spoken with, for she may strew*
> *Dangerous conjectures in ill-breeding minds.*

She gives way, hoping to make the best of it:

> *Let her come in.—*
> *To my sick soul, as sin's true nature is,*
> *Each toy seems prelude to some great amiss.*
> *So full of artless jealousy is guilt,*
> *It spills itself in fearing to be spilt.*

† From *Form and Meaning* in Drama
by H. D. F. Kitto (London: Methuen
& Co., Ltd., 1956), pp. 321–28. Copyright © 1956 by Methuen & Co., Ltd.
Kitto's footnotes are here omitted.

She is frightened by her knowledge of her own guilt, but against this she sets the thought that too great consciousness of guilt, and too great circumspection in hiding it, may of themselves reveal that guilt to the world. It is one of the themes that run through the play, that sin breaks through every attempt to keep it secret: 'Foul deeds will rise.' The oath of the cellarage-scene was sworn in vain.

After this it is the King's turn to show what offspring his own sins are breeding for him, and what he says does but repeat, more urgently, what he has said before.

> *When sorrows come, they come not single spies,*
> *But in battalias.*

Polonius is dead, Hamlet gone, the people mudded—

> *and we have done but greenly*
> *In hugger-mugger to inter him—*

and Laertes has come secretly from France, to hear 'pestilent speeches of his father's death'.

> *O my dear Gertrude, this,*
> *Like to a murdering-piece, in many places*
> *Gives me superfluous death.*

Immediately upon this comes Laertes, at the head of an incipient rebellion. The Court may be subservient and complaisant, but among the people Claudius commands little respect:

> *Thick and unwholesome in their thoughts and whispers*
> *For good Polonius' death,*

and bearing 'great love' for the exiled Prince. Claudius has given a handle to any enemy he may have, and the people are willing to take from him the crown which he has done so much to win. But he is equal to the occasion; Hamlet has gone to his death, and Laertes can be talked over.

With Laertes he has little trouble:

LAERTES: *And so have I a noble father lost;*
> *A sister driven into desperate terms,*
> *Whose worth, if praises may go back again,*
> *Stood challenger on mount of all the age.*
KING: *Break not your sleeps for that: you must not think*
> *That we are made of stuff so flat and dull,*
> *That we can let our beard be shook with danger,*
> *And think it pastime. You shortly shall hear more:*
> *I loved your father, and we love ourself;*
> *And that, I hope, will teach you to imagine—*
> *Enter a Messenger.*

Sophocles too used Messengers in this way. Claudius is confronted with news which we have briefly learned already. His plot has failed; Hamlet is back in Denmark. To Claudius it is incredible:

> How should it be? how otherwise?

The full story of his escape we are still to learn, but we may suspect that there was indeed a cherub that saw the King's purposes. But for the plot that has failed he substitutes another, since he 'loves himself'. Laertes consents—like two other men, now dead—to serve Claudius:

KING: *Will you be ruled by me?*
LAERTES: *I will, my lord,*
So you will not o'errule me to a peace.
KING: *To thine own peace.*

But hardly so, since it involves Laertes first in treachery, then in death.

Again a Messenger interrupts the King:

KING: *. . . wherein but sipping,*
If he by chance escape your venomed stuck,
Our purpose may hold there.—
Enter the Queen.
How now, sweet Queen?
QUEEN: *One woe doth tread upon another's heel,*
So fast they follow.—Your sister's drowned, Laertes.

Death has struck again. It is the fitting climax to this part of the play. Since it began, with the Queen's vain declaration: 'I will not speak with her', our thoughts have not been encouraged to stray very far from the idea of evil breeding evil, and leading to ruin. Each toy *is* prelude to some great amiss. The present one reaches its consummation in the scene that follows; and the horrible spectacle of Hamlet and Laertes struggling with each other beside the grave points the way to the end. * * *

At the end of the Churchyard-scene we are told what happened on the North Sea. We last saw Hamlet being sent away, under guard, for 'instant death'. It looked as if Claudius might triumph. But Hamlet is home again. All we know of the manner of his escape is what we have learned from his letter to Horatio; everything turned on the veriest accident—seconded by Hamlet's own impetuous valour. Shakespeare now chooses to amplify the story; and the colour he gives it is surely a definite and significant one. and entirely harmonious with the colours of the whole play.

> *Sir, in my heart there was a kind of fighting*
> *That would not let me sleep.*

This time, as when he killed Polonius, and as always henceforth, Hamlet yields to the prompting of the occasion:

> HAMLET: *Rashly—*
> *And praised be rashness for it: let us know*
> *Our indiscretion sometimes serves us well*
> *When our deep plots do pall; and that should teach us*
> *There's a divinity that shapes our ends*
> *Rough-hew them how we will,—*
> HORATIO: *That is most certain.*
> HAMLET: *Up from my cabin . . .*

This is a very different Hamlet from the one who sought confirmation—or disproof—of what the Ghost had told him, and who sought more than mere death for Claudius. It is the Hamlet who did the 'rash and bloody deed' on Polonius, where also 'rashness' serves the ends of Providence.

As for what Hamlet did to Rosencrantz and Guildenstern, we must be on our guard against seeing the obvious and missing what is significant. There is no irrelevant reproof in Horatio's brief comment:

> *So Rosencrantz and Guildenstern go to 't.*

Hamlet continues:

> *Why, man, they did make love to this employment:*
> *They are not on my conscience; their defeat*
> *Doth by their own insinuation grow.*
> *'Tis dangerous when the baser nature comes*
> *Between the pass and fell incensèd points*
> *Of mighty opposites.*

This is not Hamlet trying to exculpate himself. Shakespeare is not interested in that kind of thing here. He is saying: 'This is what happens in life, when foolish men allow themselves to be used by such as Claudius, and to get themselves involved in desperate affairs like these.' To prove that this is what he meant, we may once more reflect what Horatio might have said, and then listen to what he does say:

> *Why, what a King is this!*

How could Shakespeare more decisively draw our attention away from a nice and private appraisal of Hamlet's character, as expressed in this affair, and direct it to the philosophic or 'religious' framework in which it is set? Horatio says just what Laertes says later: 'The King! the King's to blame.'

It was a lucky chance, though not an unlikely one, that Hamlet had his father's signet in his purse; but this is how Hamlet puts it:

> Why, even in this was Heaven ordinant.

It was also a lucky chance that the pirate ship caught up with them at this time; and our natural response is: Here too Heaven was ordinant. But it was no lucky chance that Hamlet (with his well-known indecision) was the first and only man to board the pirate.

* * *

Once more Hamlet and Claudius confront each other, and Claudius, we know, has another deadly plot ready. Horatio warns Hamlet that the time is short; but Hamlet replies 'The interim is mine'.

But there is no interim at all; the tide has run out, and Hamlet seems to feel it: 'If his fitness speaks, mine is ready.' That Claudius is fit for death is plain enough; but what of Hamlet? 'I will forstall their repair hither,' says Horatio, 'and say you are not fit.' Every word in this dialogue makes us feel that the tragic action is at last poised, ready for the catastrophe. Hamlet has his 'gaingiving', but he defies augury: 'Mine is ready.' Even more forcibly we are made to feel that Providence is working in the events; an eternal Law is being exemplified: 'There is a special providence in the fall of a sparrow.' But if Providence is working, what is the catastrophe intended to reveal?

The significant design of the catastrophe is unmistakable. The action of the play began with poison, and it ends with a double poison, that of Claudius and that of Laertes. Gertrude, left to Heaven as the Ghost had commanded, drinks Claudius's poison literally as she had once done metaphorically. Claudius is killed by both, for Hamlet first runs him through with Laertes' poisoned sword, and then makes him drink his own poisoned cup. Laertes himself confesses: 'I am most justly slain by my own treachery'; and in his dying reconciliation with Hamlet he accepts, in effect, what Hamlet had said to him earlier in his own defence:

> Hamlet does it not, Hamlet denies it.
> Who does it then? His madness. If 't be so,
> Hamlet is of the faction that is wronged.

For Hamlet's 'madness' was but the reflection of the evil with which he found himself surrounded, of which Claudius was the most prolific source. So Laertes declares: 'The King! The King's to blame.' Hamlet's death shall not come on Laertes, nor the death of Polonius on Hamlet, but both on Claudius. Horatio, on the other hand, is forcibly prevented from sharing in this common death. He has stood outside the action; he has not been tainted. * * * Hamlet is destroyed not because evil works mechanically, but because his nature was such that he could not confront it until too late.

> *Fie, 'tis an unweeded garden,*
> *That grows to seed; things rank and gross in nature*
> *Possess it merely.*

Weeds can choke flowers. These weeds have choked Ophelia, and at last they choke Hamlet, because he could not do the coarse work of eradicating them. First, his comprehensive awareness of evil, reversing every habit of his mind, left him prostrate in anguish and apathy; then, the desire for vengeance being aroused, he missed everything by trying to encompass too much; finally, pursuing Honour when it was nearly too late, he found it, but only in his own death. So finely poised, so brittle a nature as Hamlet's, is especially vulnerable to the destructive power of evil.

In the first act, the sinister Claudius drank to Hamlet's health, and guns proclaimed to Heaven and Earth the 'heavy-headed revel'. Now in the last scene the guns roar again: Claudius is drinking to Hamlet's death. The action has completed its circle. The guns remind us of what Hamlet said when first they spoke: some vicious mole of nature, like their birth, wherein they are not guilty; the overgrowth of some complexion that breaks down the pales and forts of reason; some habit that o'erleavens, or works too strongly for, plausive manners—all these bring corruption to a man whose virtues else may be 'pure as grace, as infinite as man may undergo'. All this we see fulfilled in Hamlet. Gertrude's sin, his 'birth', has worked in his mind to spoil it; his philosophic 'complexion', too absolute, was overthrown and turned to 'madness'; his habit of 'godlike reason' betrayed him at the great crisis.

But does Hamlet 'in the general censure take corruption'? This is a question which Shakespeare answers by letting off guns for a third time.

> *Let four captains*
> *Bear Hamlet, like a soldier, to the stage;*
> *For he was likely, had he been put on,*
> *T' have proved most royally: and for his passage*
> *The soldiers' music and the rites of war*
> *Speak loudly for him.*

This time the guns proclaim neither swinish coarseness nor black treachery, but Honour.

REBECCA WEST

The Nature of Will†

Yet Hamlet recognizes the value of tradition. That is made clear by the courage he shows in choosing to meet the ghost and in casting off the hands of his companions when it bids him follow it and they seek to hold him back. But he feels no real reverence for tradition. That is a very strange scene, when he swears his companions to secrecy on his sword, and the ghost raps upward on the earth they stand on, and Hamlet says, "You hear this fellow in the cellarage" (I.5.150). The root of this disrespect becomes explicable when we inquire into Hamlet's attitude to humanity. For tradition is the distillation of human experience, and it must be condemned if humanity is condemned; and Hamlet was disgusted by his own kind.

There are other crimes afoot in Elsinore, in the world, as well as murder. The ghost wishes Hamlet to avenge his murder and also to put an end to the unholy offense of the marriage between his widow and his murderer. But when Hamlet talks of these matters with his mother he loses all interest in that part of the command which relates to his father's murder, and in the course of over eighty lines addressed to her he devotes only three to a perfunctory mention of the fact that her present husband murdered her previous husband, and when she shows that she did not know that any such crime had been committed he does not take the opportunity of enlightening her. He simply tells her that she is behaving reprehensibly in living with her present husband, not because he had murdered her dead husband and his own brother, but because he was not so good looking as her dead husband. It is not surprising, though it is always comic, that the ghost should then reappear in order to ask Hamlet to stick to the point. "Do not forget: this visitation Is but to whet thy almost blunted purpose" (III.4.112). But a revelation is made in the course of the scene. The Queen admits the charge of sensuality (III.4.89):

† From *The Court and the Castle*, by Rebecca West (New Haven: Yale University Press, 1958), pp. 17–32. Copyright © 1958 by Yale University Press. Reprinted by permission of Yale University Press, The Macmillan Co. of Canada, Ltd. and Macmillan Co., Ltd., London.

Oh, Hamlet, speak no more,
Thou turn'st mine eyes into my very soul,
And there I see such black and grained spots
As will not leave their tint.

Claudius is guilty, the Queen is guilty, and so as this scene makes quite plain, is Hamlet. All that he says is smeared with a slime which is the mark of sexual corruption. His curious emphasis on the physical difference between the dead King and the living Claudius hints at a homosexual element in his nature, but that is irrelevant. Hamlet could be neither a heterosexual nor a homosexual lover. Such an egotist would be restricted to lust, for he could not afford the outgoings of love.

This has been indicated earlier in the play by his scenes with Ophelia. There is no more bizarre aspect of the misreading of Hamlet's character than the assumption that his relations with Ophelia were innocent and that Ophelia was a correct and timid virgin of exquisite sensibilities. Probably the conception would not have lasted so long in England had it not been for the popularity of the pre-Raphaelite picture by Sir John Millais which represents her as she floated down the glassy stream, the weeping brook; for his model was his friend Rossetti's bride, the correct, timid, sensitive, virginal, and tubercular Miss Siddal, and she was, poor thing, especially wan during the painting of the picture, for she was immersed in a tin bath full of water kept warm by a lamp placed underneath, like an old-fashioned hot-water dish. We have certainly put Ophelia into the wrong category and into the wrong century. She was not a chaste young woman. That is shown by her tolerance of Hamlet's obscene conversations, which cannot be explained as consistent with the custom of the time. If that were the reason for it, all the men and women in Shakespeare's plays, Romeo and Juliet, Beatrice and Benedict, Miranda and Ferdinand, Antony and Cleopatra, would have talked obscenely together, which is not the case. "The marriage of true minds" would hardly, even in the most candid age, have expressed itself by this ugly chatter, which Wilson Knight has so justly described as governed by "infra-sexual neurosis." The truth is that Ophelia was a disreputable young woman: not scandalously so, but still disreputable. She was foredoomed to it by her father, whom it is a mistake to regard as a simple platitudinarian. Shakespeare, like all major writers, was never afraid of a good platitude, and he would certainly never have given time to deriding a character because his only attribute was a habit of stating the obvious. Polonius is interesting because he was a cunning old intriguer who, like

an iceberg, only showed one-eighth of himself above the surface.
The innocuous sort of worldly wisdom that rolled off his tongue
in butter balls was a very small part of what he knew. It has been
insufficiently noted that Shakespeare would never have held up
the action in order that Polonius should give his son advice as
to how to conduct himself abroad, unless the scene helped him
to develop his theme. But "This above all—to thine own self
be true; And it must follow, as the night the day, Thou canst not
then be false to any man" (I.3.78), has considerable contrapuntal
value when it is spoken by an old gentleman who is presently
going to instruct a servant to spy on his son, and to profess great
anxiety about his daughter's morals, when plainly he needed to
send her away into the country if he really wanted her to retain
any.

There is no mistaking the disingenuousness of his dealings with
his daughter. When Ophelia comes to him with her tale of how
Hamlet had come to her as she was sewing in her chamber, "with
his doublet all unbraced," and had looked madly on her, Polonius
eagerly interprets this as "the very ecstasy of love," and asks her
"What, have you given him any hard words of late?" Ophelia
answers (II.1.108):

> No, my good Lord; but as you did command
> I did repel his letters, and denied
> His access to me.

At that Polonius purrs in satisfaction:

> That hath made him mad.
> I am sorry that with better heed and judgment
> I had not quoted him: I fear'd he did but trifle,
> And meant to wrack thee; but beshrew my jealousy!
> It seems it is as proper to our age
> To cast beyond ourselves in our opinions
> As it is common for the younger sort
> To lack discretion. Come, go we to the king.
> This must be known; which, being kept close, might move
> More grief to hide than hate to utter love.
> Come.

This is the Court Circular version of Pandarus. The girl is not to
be kept out of harm's way. She is a card that can be played to take
several sorts of tricks. She might be Hamlet's mistress; but she
might be more honored for resistance. And if Hamlet was himself
an enemy of the King, and an entanglement with him had ceased
to be a means of winning favor, then she can give a spy's report
on him to Claudius. Surely Ophelia is one of the few authentic

portraits of that army of not virgin martyrs, the poor little girls who were sacrificed to family ambition in the days when a court was a cat's cradle of conspiracies. Man's persuasion that his honor depends on the chastity of his women folk has always been liable to waste away and perish within sight of a throne. Particularly where monarchy had grown from a yeasty mass of feudalism, few families found themselves able to resist the temptation to hawk any young beauty in their brood, if it seemed likely that she might catch the eye of the king or any man close to the king. Unfortunately the king's true favorite was usually not a woman but an ideology. If royal approval was withdrawn from the religious or political faith held by the family which had hawked the girl, she was as apt to suffer fatality as any of her kinsmen. The axe has never known chivalry. Shakespeare, writing this play only three reigns from Henry the Eighth, had heard of such outrages on half-grown girls from the lips of those who had seen the final blood-letting. He wrote elsewhere of Anne Boleyn; and he must have heard much of the worse case, which did not excite so much compassion because the edge of the tragedy had been taken off by repetition, the case of Katherine Howard. She, who had been beheaded half a century before, was one of the Catholic Howards, a poor relative of the Duke of Norfolk, and had grown up in the attics and passages and antichambers of a disordered country seat, where maturing beauty brought her several lovers, one of whom she loved. But she did not marry him, because she was presently procured for the King, whom she pleased so well that he made her Queen. Pleasure, however, was not the most important issue involved. The marriage was a token of Henry's temporary softening toward Rome. But he hardened his heart again and turned again toward the innovators of Protestantism, and so the Howards fell out of favor, and Katherine's head was cut off when she was twenty years old.

Shakespeare had pondered on such massacres of the innocent, and he had thought it one of the worse offenses of the court (and he hated courts) that by the time the innocents were massacred, they were no longer innocent. The scene between Anne Boleyn and the bawdy old lady in the part-Shakespearean *Henry the Eighth* has an obvious pathos, because he knows and we know that the girl is doomed to die by the headsman's axe. But it is even more pathetic that she is deprived not only of her life, but of a noble death; for however bravely she bore herself when she laid her head on the block, she had nevertheless found her way there by a greedy intrigue which sought to snatch profit from the fall of an authentic queen. Like Anne Boleyn, Ophelia has lost her integrity. She fiddles with the truth when she speaks of Hamlet to her father, and she fiddles with the truth when she talks to Hamlet as her father and Claudius eavesdrop; and she contemplates without surprise or distaste Hamlet's obscenity, the scab on his spiritual sore.

Surely the picture of Ophelia shows that Shakespeare, who wrote more often of cruelty than any other great writer, was not a cruel man, and was great in pity, that rare emotion. He shows the poor little creature, whom the court had robbed of her honesty, receiving no compensation for the loss, but being driven to madness and done to death. For the myth which has been built round Hamlet is never more perverse than when it pretends that Ophelia went mad for love and killed herself. No line in the play suggests that she felt either passion or affection for Hamlet. She never mentions him in the mad scene, and Horatio says of her, "She speaks much of her father." Indeed she was in a situation which requires no sexual gloss. Her father had been murdered by a member of the royal house, and she found herself without protection, since her brother Laertes was in France, in the midst of a crisis such as might well send her out of her wits with fear. For the Danes hostile to the royal house made of her wrong a new pretext for their hostility, and the royal house, noting this, turned against her, helpless though she was. Claudius speaks of a general resentment (IV.5.79):

> . . . The people muddied,
> Thick and unwholesome in their thoughts and whispers,
> For good Polonius' death; and we have done but greenly
> In hugger-mugger to inter him . . .

When Ophelia wanders to the Castle and asks that the Queen should receive her, she is refused. The Queen says, "I will not speak with her." But Horatio tells her she is not wise (IV.5.4):

> She speaks much of her father; says she hears
> There's tricks i' th' world; and hems, and beats her heart;
> Spurns enviously at straws; speaks things in doubt,
> That carry but half sense; her speech is nothing.
> Yet the unshaped use of it doth move
> The hearers to collection; they aim at it,
> And botch the words up fit to their own thoughts;
> Which, as her winks and nods and gestures yield them,
> Indeed would make one think there might be thought,
> Though nothing sure, yet much unhappily.
> 'Twere good she were spoken with; for she may strew
> Dangerous conjectures in ill-breeding minds.

Courts thus threatened had their own ways of dealing with the threats, as all courtiers knew; and Shakespeare must have heard of women thus dealt with who had been frightened into madness. Lady Rochford, who had helped Katherine Howard to meet her cousin Culpepper after her marriage, was raving mad when she went to her execution.

But neither from fear nor from love did Ophelia kill herself. She did not kill herself at all. The Queen describes her drowning as an accident. "An envious sliver broke," she says, and there is no indication that she was lying. Many things are packed into the passage which begins "There is a willow grows aslant a brook," but insincerity is not among them. These lines achieve a double dramatic value not often exploited in the theater. They are beautiful and expressive verse: their sound suggests heaviness submerging lightness, the soaked clothes dragging down the fragile body they encase, the inanimate flesh grown leaden round the spirit. But the lines are also in character. The Queen is one of the most poorly endowed human beings which Shakespeare ever drew. Very often he created fools, but there is a richness in their folly, whereas Gertrude is simply a stately defective. The whole play depends on her not noticing, and not understanding; and in this passage there are samples of her stupidity. The botanical digression about the long purples is ill-timed, and the epithet "mermaid-like" is not applicable to someone saved from drowning by an amplitude of skirts or to the skirts themselves. But the fusion of perception and obtuseness in these lines, and the contrast between their distinction and the empty rotundity of all the Queen's other speeches, convince us that just once this dull woman was so moved that her tongue became alive. It is not credible that at that moment she would have taken thought to deceive Laertes about the object of her emotion; nor indeed does Shakespeare suggest that she practiced any such deception.

For that Ophelia drowned herself is stated definitely only by two people: the clowns in the graveyard, typical examples of the idiot groundlings gorged on false rumor who appear so often in Shakespeare's plays. Whether we like it or not, we must admit that there is very little in the works of Shakespeare which could be used as propaganda for adult suffrage. For the rest, the priest declares that "her death was doubtful" (V.1.203), and that the doubt was enough to make it necessary that she should be buried with "maimed rites" (V.1.195). But surely we are not intended to believe him, for he is drawn as a bigot, who finds it possible to answer her brother coldly when he asks, "What ceremony else?" (V.1.199), and it is to be presumed that such lack of charity would invent a doubt. Shakespeare will not allow anyone in the graveyard scene, even to the priest, to be without sin. Each of them has helped to dig the girl's grave. Hamlet was the most guilty, for he had been her spurious lover and a tyrant prince, giving her no protection as a mistress or as one of his people; but it was the whole court that had destroyed her. She was a victim of society, which abandons principle for statecraft, for politics, for intrigue, because of its too urgent sense that it must survive at all costs, and in its panic loses cognizance of all the essentials by which it lives. Even her brother Laertes was not fully aware of his sister's tragedy, for he was tainted with the vice which Shakespeare feared most as a distraction: he was subject to lust.

This is indicated clearly enough in the early scene when Laertes warns Ophelia against the nature of Hamlet's courtships and she mocks him (I.3.46):

> But, good my brother,
> Do not as some ungracious pastors do,
> Show me the steep and thorny way to heaven,
> Whilst like a puft and reckless libertine,
> Himself the primrose path of dalliance treads,
> And recks not his own rede.

To this Laertes replies:

> Oh, fear me not.
> I stay too long. But here my father comes.

If Ophelia offers a *tu quoque* defense which we do not usually offer unless we are guilty, Laertes does not trouble to put up a defense at all. These two are no better than they should be; and Polonius, when he instructs his servant Reynaldo to spy on his son in Paris, speaks of drabbing and visiting "a house of sale, Videlicet, a brothel" (II.1.60), as if these were fairly certain to be among his son's activities. When Laertes leaps into his sister's grave, he cries (V.1.227):

> Now pile your dust upon the quick and the dead
> Till of this flat a mountain you have made
> To' o'ertop old Pelion or the skyish head
> Of blue Olympus.

For Shakespeare there was a connection between this outburst and the primrose path, the drabs, and the house of sale, Videlicet, a brothel. In his analysis of love that is not love, the hundred and twenty-ninth sonnet, he uses the word "extreme."

> The expense of spirit in a waste of shame
> Is lust in action; and till action, lust
> Is perjured, murd'rous, bloody, full of blame,
> Savage, extreme, rude, cruel, not to trust.

Laertes' expressions of grief are extreme. His mind rushes away from the dead girl on too long a journey, all the way to blue Olympus, and forgets its true grief in the excitement of travel. The essence of Ophelia has again been ignored, and the waste of a human being not appropriately resented.

It is Shakespeare's contention that the whole of the court is corrupt: society is corrupt. There is a flaw running horizontally through humanity wherever it is gathered together in space. It would seem natural therefore that Hamlet should obey the ghost and punish Claudius, who controls the court, who is an emblem of society. But the flaw runs vertically also; it runs through time, into the past. For Hamlet's father, the ghost, is in purgatory, doing penance for his sins, which were of the same gross kind as those he desires his son to punish. Shakespeare tells us this, stating the fact, and again using bombast to suggest immoderation (I.5.9):

> I am thy father's spirit,
> Doom'd for a certain term to walk the night,
> And for the day confined to fast in fires,
> Till the foul crimes done in my days of nature
> Are burnt and purged away. But that I am forbid
> To tell the secrets of my prison-house,
> I could a tale unfold, whose lighest word
> Would harrow up they soul; freeze thy young blood;
> Make thy two eyes, like stars, start from their spheres,
> Thy knotted and combined locks to part,
> And each particular hair to stand an end,
> Like quills upon the fretful porpentine.

The ghost was indeed a sinner; the voice of tradition speaks from a tainted source. The evil in the world is not the product of the specially corrupt present generation, it has its roots in the generations that went before and also were corrupt; it has its roots in the race. There is no use pretending that we can frustrate our sinful dispositions by calling on tradition, because that also is the work of sinful man. This is the situation of our kind as it is shown to us in *Hamlet*, which is as pessimistic as any great work of literature ever written. The theme of the play could never appear to any reader who kept his eye on the text as the irresolution of Hamlet, his lack of the nerve which forms a hero (as Goethe put it), his failure to achieve a virtue which would consist simply of capacity for action. For what excites Shakespeare in this play is the impossibility of conceiving an action which could justly be termed virtuous, in view of the bias of original sin.

What does Shakespeare see written on the other side of the

ledger? Nothing but beauty. This is the play which more than
any of the others reminds us of the extraordinary advantages which
he enjoyed. For it was his luck to see the human race at one of
the moments, in one of the places, when it blossomed into a state
of exceptional glory; and he moved among men and women who
were beautiful, intelligent, learned, and fearless beyond the habit
of our kind, and whose way of life, with its palaces and its pageants,
was a proper setting for the jewels that they were. Here we ourselves enjoy an extraordinary advantage. Literature cannot always
do its business of rendering an account of life. An age of genius
not of the literary sort must go inadequately described unless there
should happen to exist at the same time a literary genius of the
same degree, who works in circumstances enabling him to accumu-
late the necessary information about his non-literary contemporaries. It happened that the Renaissance man was observed by
Shakespeare. "What a piece of work is man! How noble in reason!
How infinite in faculty! In form and moving how express and
admirable! In action how like an angel! in apprehension how like
a god! The beauty of the world! The paragon of animals!"
(II.2.292). Here is a conicidence. Shakespeare was himself "the
paragon of animals," therefore he could describe to us the man
who was "the beauty of the world." He could write this description
and make the whole character of Hamlet as shown from scene to
scene bear out what he said about man.

All through the play Hamlet speaks with a quick, springing
harmony recognizable as the voice of physical and mental splen-
dor; his mind travels like lightning yet strikes below the surface,
and is impulsive not in surrender to folly but in search of wisdom.
How superior, to use Turgenev's words, he is in mind and temperament, how daring, how proud. In fact, Shakespeare has given
us a picture of the Renaissance man, without the lacuna which
makes the other attempts to portray him, which were made by
the Elizabethan and Jacobean dramatists, notably Ford and Web-
ster. They tried to depict the new man created by the new wealth
of Europe, the new community and continuity of culture, the
new opening of windows on far parts of the globe and on the
minutiae of matter. But they fall into the trap of showing the
Renaissance man at his experiments without explaining why he
felt free to experiment, without bringing forward the good reasons
he had for thinking that he might tamper with the existing moral
world. Even Marlowe took the Faust legend for his great work,
and accounted for his Renaissance man by devil-dealing; but
Shakespeare in Hamlet makes the Renaissance man his own
Mephistopheles, and depicts a being so gifted that he needs no

supernatural being to raise him above the common lot. But Shakespeare, the supreme artist observing this supreme man, immediately adds, "And yet to me what is the quintessence of dust?" And his genius has been asking that question throughout the play. Scene after scene has demonstrated the paragon of animals to be an animal, the world to be so diseased that even its beauty is infected. This speech of homage to man is indeed an example of teasing ambiguity; it can be read without irony or with irony; each reading is equally faithful to the text.

Shakespeare hopes for little from the dust. It is quite certain that he wished to present Hamlet as a bad man, because he twice makes him rejoice at the thought of murdering men who had not made their peace with God. He might have killed Claudius when he came on him at prayer. But he decided this might mean that Claudius would go straight to heaven (III.3.88):

> Up, sword; and know thou a more horrid hent;
> When he is drunk, asleep, or in his rage;
> Or in th'incestuous pleasure of his bed;
> At gaming, swearing or about some act
> That has no relish of salvation in't;
> Then trip him, that his heels may kick at heaven;
> And that his soul may be as damn'd and black
> As hell, whereto it goes.

Later on, when he tells Horatio of his peculiarly cold-blooded murder of Rosenkrantz and Guildenstern, his description of the letter he forged to the King of England shows traces of a like perverse determination to kill the soul as well as the body (V.2.38):

> An earnest conjuration from the king,—
> As England was his faithful tributary;
> As love between them like the palm might flourish;
> As peace should still her wheaten garland wear,
> And stand a comma 'tween their amities;
> And many such-like As-es of great charge,—
> That, on the view and knowing of these contents,
> Without debatement further, more or less,
> He should the bearers put to sudden death,
> Not shriving-time allow'd.

There would be no question at all in the minds of an Elizabethan audience that a murderer who could cheat his victims of their chance of salvation was a very bad man indeed; and indeed most of us would think with repulsion of such an action, if, through the hazards of war or dictatorship, it came within our experience.

But to this bad man Shakespeare ascribes one virtuous action;

and the nature of that action is determined by his most lasting preoccupation. It is a political action. Hamlet gives his dying breath to thought for the future of his people; his last words choose a ruler for them (V.2.337):

> O, I die, Horatio;
> The potent poison quite o'ercrows my spirit;
> I cannot live to hear the news from England;
> But I do prophesy th' election lights
> On Fortinbras: he has my dying voice.
> So tell him, with the occurents, more and less,
> Which have solicited—the rest is silenced.

Hamlet was never more the Renaissance man—who was a statesman, a true Macchiavellian, a prince careful for the safety of his subjects. Even if one be disillusioned with the race, and suspect paragons and the beauty of the world, this is still admirable. These fragile creatures, so little changed from dust that they constantly revert to it, show bravery in their intention that their species shall survive as if it were marble. Yet, all the same, how horrid is the sphere in which they show their excellence. The court was saved by its political conscience; yet it was damned by it too.

Bibliography

The volume of Shakespearean scholarship and criticism is enormous. Each of the plays now has attached to it its own private mountain of critical and scholarly opinion and conjecture, amid which the bibliography of works dealing with *Hamlet* towers like a very Everest. The present list can do little more than suggest the range of studies which the play has occasioned, and direct the reader to some of the more significant sources of information concerning *Hamlet*, Shakespeare, and the background of the Elizabethan period. That the list should not seem even more arbitrary than it inevitably must, it is limited to works published during the past forty years. For the earlier criticism of the play, the student is referred to the Variorum edition of *Hamlet*, edited by H. H. Furness (Philadelphia, 1877), which provides a generous selection of commentary on the play through the third quarter of the nineteenth century. For the years between the Variorum and the mid-1930's, a full account of publications dealing with the play is given in A. A. Raven's *A Hamlet Bibliography and Reference Guide, 1877–1935* (Chicago, 1935). Useful accounts of recent criticism of the play are given by Clifford Leech, "Studies in *Hamlet*", (*Shakespeare Survey*, 1956), and G. K. Hunter, "*Hamlet* Criticism," (*Critical Quarterly*, 1959). Paul S. Conklin, *A History of Hamlet Criticism, 1601–1862* (New York, 1947), gives a valuable survey of the years covered. C. C. H. Williamson's edition of *Readings on the Character of Hamlet* (London, 1950) is a useful anthology of opinion about the Prince through the ages.

Abbreviations

SS	Shakespeare Survey
PMLA	Publications of the Modern Language Association
SQ	Shakespeare Quarterly
ELH	Journal of English Literary History
JHI	Journal of the History of Ideas
RES	Review of English Studies
SP	Studies in Philology
SB	Studies in Bibliography

I. Elizabethan Background.

Shakespeare's England (Oxford, 1916) is a vast store of information concerning the life of the times: social customs, pastimes, trades and professions, education, and the like. J. Dover Wilson's *Life in Shakespeare's England* (Cambridge, 1911) is a useful guide, as is *A Companion to Shake-*

speare Studies, edited by Harley Granville-Barker and G. B. Harrison (Cambridge, 1934). The intellectual frame of reference of the Renaissance is concisely outlined by E. M. W. Tillyard in *The Elizabethan World Picture* (London, 1943).

II. *The Elizabethan Theater.*

All studies of this begin with the four volumes of E. K. Chambers' *The Elizabethan Stage* (Oxford, 1923). T. W. Baldwin, *The Organization and Personnel of the Shakespearean Company* (Princeton, 1926) is another pioneer study of lasting importance. More recent investigations include J. C. Adams, *The Globe Playhouse: Its Design and Equipment* (Cambridge, Mass., 1942); C. Walter Hodges, *The Globe Restored: A Study of the Elizabethan Theatre* (London, 1953); A. M. Nagler, *Shakespeare's Stage* (New Haven, 1958); Leslie Hotson's controversial *Shakespeare's Wooden O* (London, 1959); Richard Hosley, "The Discovery-Space in Shakespeare's Globe" (*SS*, 1959), and "Was there a Music Room in Shakespeare's Globe?" (*SS*, 1960).

III. *Shakespearean Biography.*

The essential documents are fully set forth in the two volumes of E. K. Chambers' *William Shakespeare: A Study of Facts and Problems* (Oxford, 1930). Thomas Marc Parrott's *William Shakespeare: A Handbook* (Oxford, 1934) contains much useful information, as does G. E. Bentley's more recent *Shakespeare, A Biographical Handbook* (New Haven, 1961). Among the numerous accounts of the man and his work are: Peter Alexander, *Shakespeare's Life and Art* (London, 1939); Mark Van Doren, *Shakespeare* (New York, 1939); Hazelton Spencer, *The Art and Life of William Shakespeare* (New York, 1940); Hardin Craig, *An Interpretation of Shakespeare* (New York, 1948); Harold C. Goddard, *The Meaning of Shakespeare* (Chicago, 1951); J. M. Murray, *Shakespeare* (London, 1954, rev. ed.); M. M. Reese, *Shakespeare's World and his Work* (London, 1953).

IV. *Shakespearean Tragedy.*

Hamlet of course looms large in all accounts of the tragedies. The play receives extended treatment in each of the following: Lily B. Campbell, *Shakespeare's Tragic Heroes: Slaves of Passion* (Cambridge, 1930); H. B. Charlton, *Shakespearean Tragedy* (Cambridge, 1948); G. Wilson Knight, *The Wheel of Fire* (London, 1948, rev. ed.), and *The Imperial Theme* (London, 1931); Theodore Spencer, *Shakespeare and the Nature of Man* (New York, 1942); E. E. Stoll, *Art and Artifice in Shakespeare: A Study in Dramatic Contrast and Illusion* (Cambridge, 1933); G. B. Harrison, *Shakespeare's Tragedies* (London, 1951); Harold S. Wilson, *On the Design of Shakespearean Tragedy* (Toronto, 1957); Brents Stirling, *Unity in Shakespearean Tragedy: The Interplay of Theme and Character* (New York, 1957); Paul N. Siegel, *Shakespearean Tragedy and the Elizabethan Compromise* (New York, 1957); John Vyvyan, *The Shakespearean Ethic* (London, 1959); John Lawlor, *The Tragic Sense in Shakespeare* (London, 1960); John Holloway, *The Story of the Night: Studies in Shakespeare's Major Tragedies* (London, 1961); Irving Ribner, *Patterns in Shakespearean Tragedy* (London, 1960); A. P. Rossiter, *Angel With Horns* (London,

1961); Robert Speaight, *Nature in Shakespearean Tragedy* (London, 1955); H. M. V. Matthews, *Character and Symbol in Shakespeare's Plays* (Cambridge, 1962). D. A. Traversi treats *Hamlet* in the context of the problem plays, in *An Approach to Shakespeare* (London, 1957, rev. ed.), as does E. M. W. Tillyard, *Shakespeare's Problem Plays* (London, 1950).

V. *Book-length Studies of Hamlet.*

These include the following: J. Dover Wilson, *What Happens in Hamlet* (Cambridge, 1935); Harley Granville-Barker, *Prefaces to Shakespeare, Third Series: Hamlet* (London, 1937); E. E. Stoll, *Hamlet: An Historical and Comparative Study* (Minneapolis, 1919); J. M. Robertson, *The Problem of "Hamlet"* (London, 1919) and *"Hamlet" Once More* (London, 1923); L. L. Schücking, *The Meaning of Hamlet* (Oxford, 1937); A. J. A. Waldock, *Hamlet: A Study in Critical Method* (Cambridge, 1931); J. W. Draper, *The Hamlet of Shakespeare's Audience* (Durham, N.C., 1938); Richard Flatter, *Hamlet's Father* (London, 1949); Bertram Joseph, *Conscience and the King: A Study of Hamlet* (London, 1953); Roy Walker, *The Time is Out of Joint: A Study of Hamlet* (London, 1948); G. R. Elliott, *Scourge and Minister: A Study of Hamlet as a Tragedy of Revengefulness and Justice* (Durham, N.C., 1951); Peter Alexander, *Hamlet, Father and Son* (Oxford, 1955); Harry Levin, *The Question of Hamlet* (Oxford, 1959); L. C. Knights, *An Approach to Hamlet* (London, 1960).

VI. *Periodical Literature.*

The character of the Prince is considered by Harold R. Walley, "Shakespeare's Conception of Hamlet" (*PMLA*, 1933); W. W. Lawrence, "Hamlet and Fortinbras" (*PMLA*, 1946); S. F. Johnson, "The Regeneration of Hamlet" (*SQ*, 1952); F. T. Bowers, "Hamlet as Minister and Scourge" (*PMLA*, 1955), and "The Death of Hamlet," in *Studies in the English Renaissance Drama* (New York, 1959); Robert R. Reed, Jr., "Hamlet, the Pseudo-Procrastinator" (*SQ*, 1958); Thomas Greene, "The Postures of Hamlet" (*SQ*, 1960). The thought of the play is analyzed by James Feibleman, "The Theory of *Hamlet*" (*JHI*, 1946); Moody E. Prior, "The Thought of *Hamlet* and the Modern Temper" (*ELH*, 1948); J. Swart, "I know not 'seems': A Study of *Hamlet*" (*Rev. of English Literature*, 1961); Raymond H. Reno, "Hamlet's Quintessence of Dust" (*SQ*, 1961). The play's structure is examined by J. M. Nosworthy, "The Structural Experiment in *Hamlet*" (*RES*, 1946); Pearl Hogrefe, "Artistic Unity in *Hamlet*" (*SP*, 1949); O. B. Hardison, Jr., "The Dramatic Triad in *Hamlet*" (*SP*, 1960).

VII. *Shakespeare's Language.*

Studies of the imagery of Shakespeare's plays were launched by Caroline Spurgeon, *Shakespeare's Imagery and What it Tells Us* (Cambridge, 1935), and have been widely carried forward, as in Donald A. Stauffer's *Shakespeare's World of Images: The Development of his Moral Ideas* (New York, 1949); and in W. H. Clemen's *The Development of Shakespeare's Imagery* (London, 1951). There is an illuminating chapter on the language of *Hamlet* in B. Ifor Evans's *The Language of Shakespeare's Plays* (London, 1952). Shorter studies of the language and imagery of this play are

R. A. Foakes, "*Hamlet* and the Court of Elsinore" (*SS*, 1956); R. D. Altick, "*Hamlet* and the Odor of Mortality" (*SQ*, 1954); Arthur Johnston, "The Player's Speech in *Hamlet*" (*SQ*, 1962).

VIII. Sources.

These are discussed by Kemp Malone, *The Literary History of Hamlet: I. The Early Tradition* (Heidelberg, 1923); by Israel Gollancz in the introduction to his *The Sources of Hamlet* (Oxford, 1926); by Kenneth Muir, *Shakespeare's Sources* (London, 1957).

IX. Date.

Evidence for dating the play is adduced by E. K. Chambers, *Shakespearean Gleanings* (Oxford, 1944), and more recently, by E. A. J. Honigmann (*SS*, 1956).

X. Textual Studies.

The fullest account of Q1 is G. I. Duthie's *The 'Bad' Quarto of Hamlet* (Cambridge, 1941). J. Dover Wilson's *The Manuscript of Shakespeare's Hamlet* (Cambridge, 1934) is important for having established the authority of Q2, but details of Wilson's reconstruction of the textual problem have been much modified, and later work should be taken into account, *e.g.*, Fredson Bowers, "The Printing of *Hamlet*, Q2" (*SB*, 1955) and "The Textual Relation of Q2 to Q1 *Hamlet* (*SB*, 1956); Alice Walker, *Textual Problems of the First Folio* (Cambridge, 1953), and "Collateral Substantive Texts, with special reference to *Hamlet*," (*SB*, 1955); J. R. Brown, "The Compositors of *Hamlet* Q2 and *The Merchant of Venice*" (*SB*, 1955); Harold Jenkins, "The Relation between the Second Quarto and the Folio Text of *Hamlet*" (*SB*, 1955). All three texts and their relationship are discussed by W. W. Greg, *The Shakespeare First Folio* (Oxford, 1955). Charlton Hinman's "The Prentice Hand in the Tragedies of the Shakespeare First Folio" (*SB*, 1957) is an important preliminary to his massive account of *The Printing and Proof-reading of the Shakespeare First Folio* (Oxford, 1962).

XI. Other Studies.

There are a number of illuminating accounts of *Hamlet* in works not specifically concerned with Shakespeare. Hiram Haydn, in a chapter of *The Counter-Renaissance* (New York, 1950), deals with it and Shakespeare's other plays in relation to late-Renaissance scepticism; D. J. James devotes a long chapter to it in his study of Shakespeare and Bacon, *The Dream of Learning: An Essay on "The Advancement of Learning," "Hamlet," and "King Lear"* (Oxford, 1951). Fredson Bowers discusses it in relation to the code of revenge and examines it in the context of other Elizabethan revenge plays, in his *Elizabethan Revenge Tragedy* (Princeton, 1940). Lawrence Babb comments on it in relation to contemporary theories of melancholy, in *The Elizabethan Malady: A Study of Melancholia in English Literature from 1580 to 1642* (Michigan State College, 1951). H. D. F. Kitto considers it in relation to the religious tragedy of the Greeks, in *Form and Meaning in Drama* (London, 1956); and Francis Ferguson discusses it in relation to the aesthetics of the theater in *The Idea of a Theatre* (Princeton, 1949).

NORTON CRITICAL EDITIONS

George Herbert and the Seventeenth-Century Religious Poets   selected and edited
     by Mario A. Di Cesare
HOMER   *The Odyssey*   translated and edited by Albert Cook
IBSEN   *The Wild Duck*   translated and edited by Dounia B. Christiani
JAMES   *The Ambassadors*   edited by S. P. Rosenbaum
JAMES   *The American*   edited by James A. Tuttleton
JAMES   *The Portrait of a Lady*   edited by Robert D. Bamberg
JAMES   *The Turn of the Screw*   edited by Robert Kimbrough
JAMES   *The Wings of the Dove*   edited by J. Donald Crowley and Richard A.
     Hocks
Ben Jonson and the Cavalier Poets   selected and edited by Hugh Maclean
MACHIAVELLI   *The Prince*   translated and edited by Robert M. Adams
MALTHUS   *An Essay on the Principle of Population*   edited by Philip Appleman
MELVILLE   *The Confidence-Man*   edited by Hershel Parker
MELVILLE   *Moby-Dick*   edited by Harrison Hayford and Hershel Parker
MEREDITH   *The Egoist*   edited by Robert M. Adams
MILL   *On Liberty*   edited by David Spitz
MILTON   *Paradise Lost*   edited by Scott Elledge
MORE   *Utopia*   translated and edited by Robert M. Adams
NEWMAN   *Apologia Pro Vita Sua*   edited by David J. DeLaura
NORRIS   *McTeague*   edited by Donald Pizer
Adrienne Rich's Poetry   selected and edited by Barbara Charlesworth Gelpi and
     Albert Gelpi
The Writings of St. Paul   edited by Wayne A. Meeks
SHAKESPEARE   *Hamlet*   edited by Cyrus Hoy
SHAKESPEARE   *Henry IV, Part I*   edited by James J. Sanderson
     Second Edition
Bernard Shaw's Plays   selected and edited by Warren Sylvester Smith
Shelley's Poetry and Prose   edited by Donald H. Reiman and Sharon B. Powers
SOPHOCLES   *Oedipus Tyrannus*   translated and edited by Luci Berkowitz and
     Theodore F. Brunner
SPENSER   *Edmund Spenser's Poetry*   selected and edited by Hugh Maclean
STENDHAL   *Red and Black*   translated and edited by Robert M. Adams
SWIFT   *Gulliver's Travels*   edited by Robert A. Greenberg   *Revised Edition*
The Writings of Jonathan Swift   edited by Robert A. Greenberg and
     William B. Piper
TENNYSON   *In Memoriam*   edited by Robert Ross
Tennyson's Poetry   selected and edited by Robert W. Hill, Jr.
THOREAU   *Walden and Civil Disobedience*   edited by Owen Thomas
TOLSTOY   *Anna Karenina* (the Maude translation)   edited by George Gibian
TOLSTOY   *War and Peace* (the Maude translation)   edited by George Gibian
TURGENEV   *Fathers and Sons*   edited with a substantially new translation by
     Ralph E. Matlaw
VOLTAIRE   *Candide*   translated and edited by Robert M. Adams
WHITMAN   *Leaves of Grass*   edited by Sculley Bradley and Harold W. Blodgett
WOLLSTONECRAFT   *A Vindication of the Rights of Woman*   edited by
     Carol H. Poston
Middle English Lyrics   selected and edited by Maxwell S. Luria and
     Richard L. Hoffman
Modern Drama   edited by Anthony Caputi
Restoration and Eighteenth-Century Comedy   edited by Scott McMillin